Randall Jarrell

THE

COMPLETE

POEMS

Randall Jarrell

THE

COMPLETE

POEMS

FABER AND FABER
3 Queen Square
London

First published in England in 1971
by Faber and Faber Limited
3 *Queen Square London W C* 1
Printed in Great Britain by
Latimer Trend & Co Ltd Whitstable
All rights reserved

ISBN 0 571 09385 *X*

811
JAR

CONTENTS

The Woman at the Washington Zoo (1960) 213

The Lost World (1965)

New Poems 341

From The Rage for the Lost Penny (1940) 357

From Blood for a Stranger (1942) 359

From *Little Friend, Little Friend* (1945)   395

From *Losses* (1948)   405

From *The Seven-League Crutches* (1951)   417

Uncollected Poems (1934-1965)   419

Unpublished Poems (1935-1965) 461

CONTENTS

Selected Poems

(1955)

To Mary, Alleyne, and Beatrice

INTRODUCTION

In this Selected Poems there are ten poems from my first book, some of them a great deal changed; almost all the other poems come from *Losses*, *The Seven-League Crutches*, or *Little Friend, Little Friend*. I left out "Orestes at Tauris" because, though I like it and some readers like it, it's very long, it's an earlier poem than any of these, and it's back in print in the new edition of *Losses* [see page 406]. I left out several poems that I am still working on. Only two poems, "A War" and "The Survivor Among Graves," are new; they belong with other poems about the war, and not with the poems I have written in the last three or four years.

I have read these poems many times to audiences of different sorts, and all the audiences liked listening to them better, and found them easier, if I said beforehand something about what a ball turret was, or a B-24, or Tatyana Larina—and said it in "plain American that cats and dogs can read." Not that my poems aren't in plain American, but there it's verse, not prose. Prose helps; it helps just by being prose. In the old days, when readers could take or leave prose, poets sometimes gave them a good deal of it: there are hundreds of pages of notes and prefaces and reminiscences in Wordsworth's or Tennyson's *Collected Poems*. But nowadays, unless you're reading Marianne Moore or Empson or *The Waste Land*, you rarely get any prose to go along with the poems.

The war—the Second World War—has been over for a long time; there are names and events people knew they would never forget which, by now, they have forgotten they ever knew. Some of these poems depend upon, or are helped by, the reader's remembering such names and events; other poems are helped by the reader's being reminded of some particular story or happening or expression—something you remember if you have lived in the South, or been in the Air Force, or gone to *Der Rosenkavalier,* or memorized some verse of the Bible. I've put into this introduction some prose sentences about a few of these things. But they are here for the reader only if he wants them—if you like poems without prose, or see after a few sentences that I am telling you very familiar things, just turn past this introduction.

A GIRL IN A LIBRARY is a poem about the New World and the Old: about a girl, a student of Home Economics and Physical Education, who has fallen asleep in the library of a Southern college; about a woman who looks out of one book, Pushkin's *Eugen Onegin,* at this girl asleep among so many; and about the *I* of the poem, a man somewhere between the two. A *blind date* is an unknown someone you accompany to something; if he promises to come for you and doesn't, he has *stood you up.* The Corn King and the Spring Queen went by many names; in the beginning they were the man and woman who, after ruling for a time, were torn to pieces and scattered over the fields in order that the grain might grow.

Some of my readers will say with a smile, "And now aren't you going to tell us who said, 'Against stupidity the gods themselves struggle in vain'? who said, 'Man wouldn't be the best thing in this world if he were not too good for it'? who had said to him, as a boy, 'Don't cry, little peasant'?" No. This would take too much space, and would be a sort of interference with the reader—and I don't want to do any more, in this introduction, than put in an occasional piece of information that may be useful to some readers.

THE KNIGHT, DEATH, AND THE DEVIL is a description of Dürer's engraving, and the reader might enjoy comparing the details of the poem with those of the picture.

In *Der Rosenkavalier* the Marschallin, looking into her mirror, says that yesterday everybody called her *little Resi,* and tomorrow everybody will be calling her *the old woman, the old Marschallin*. I used her words as an epigraph for THE FACE.

LADY BATES is a little Negro girl whose Christian name is *Lady*. Mock oranges are also called Osage oranges—they look like giant green navel oranges, and are impressive to children. *Trifling* means *worthless, good-for-nothing, no-account*, and is often used affectionately. In the South convicts used sometimes to be farmed out as servants.

When Heine met Goethe he told him that he was working on "my *Faust*," and Goethe grew very cold. This CONVERSATION WITH THE DEVIL isn't anybody's *Faust*, but it does have many allusions to the Devil's past, and a good many to our own past and present. Fortunately, one can understand the poem without recognizing any of the allusions. Let me mention three, though: Will Rogers' "I never saw the man I didn't like"; the old lady who had found so much comfort in repeating "that blessed word, Mesopotamia"; and the little boy in Hardy who wrote, "We was too many."

SEELE IM RAUM is the title of one of Rilke's poems; "Soul in Space" sounded so glib that I couldn't use it instead. An eland is the largest sort of African antelope—the males are as big as a horse, and you often see people gazing at them, at the zoo, in uneasy wonder.

THE NIGHT BEFORE THE NIGHT BEFORE CHRISTMAS takes place in the year 1934; the girl is fourteen. The part about the "cotton-wool that is falling from the ears of God" is a Scandinavian joke that has become a family joke in the little family of the girl and her brother. *The Iron Heel* is a book by Jack London about the workers' fight against the Fascist state of the future. *The Coming Struggle for Power* is a book, once well known, by John Strachey. The girl's father is a Lion, a Moose, just as he might be an Elk or Rotarian or Kiwanian. "In Praise of Learning" is a song, very firm and haunting, with words by Bert Brecht and music by Hanns Eisler; in those days it ran through many heads besides the girl's. Both Engels and Marx are real and present figures to the girl, who has got as far, in *Capital*, as the chapter on the working day, and is reading it that night. She has read *A Tale of Two Cities* at school, and Sidney Carton's "It is a far, far better thing I do . . ." is there in her mind along with Martha and Mary, her squirrel, her brother, and all the other people less fortunate than she.

THE BLACK SWAN is said, long ago, by a girl whose sister is buried under the white stones of the green churchyard.

There is a quilt-pattern called The Tree of Life. The little boy, sick in bed, has a dream in which *good me* and *bad me* (along with the uncontrollable unexplainable *the Other*) take the place of Hänsel and Gretel.

In IN THE WARD: THE SACRED WOOD, the wounded man has cut trees from paper, and made for himself a sacred wood; with these, the bedclothes, the nurse, the doctor, he works his own way through the Garden of Eden, the dove and its olive-leaf, the years in the wilderness, the burning bush, the wars of God and the rebel angels, the birth and death and resurrection of Christ.

I put into A GAME AT SALZBURG a little game that Germans and Austrians play with very young children. The child says to the grown-up, *Here I am,* and the grown-up answers, *There you are;* the children use the same little rising tune, and the grown-ups the same resolving, conclusive one. It seemed to me that if there could be a conversation between the world and God, this would be it.

AN ENGLISH GARDEN IN AUSTRIA is a poem about neo-classicism changing into romanticism, the eighteenth century changing into the nineteenth. Someone going home from an Austrian performance of *Der Rosenkavalier* thinks the poem—thinks it when he comes across an English garden, the first outpost of romanticism there on the Continent. He thinks of Madame de Maintenon's *Athalie* replaced overnight by Nature, with all its ruins and prospects; thinks of Baron Ochs von Lerchenau meeting Rousseau and oldfashionedly mistaking him for Metastasio; and then thinks of the greatest singer of Metastasio's operas, the castrato Farinelli—of Farinelli's life in Spain and in the Italy of the Arcadian Academy, that Academy which lasted long enough to have Goethe for a member. The man, looking at the false ruin inside the garden, the real ruins outside it, thinks of the days when Voltaire ruled Europe, and Frederick the Great could call *Götz von Berlichingen* "a play worthy of the savages of Canada"; thinks of some of the things that led up to, or accompanied, the French Revolution; and thinks at length of that Napoleon Bonaparte who seems to him a precursor of our own time, of the petty bourgeois water-colorist Hitler, of the spoil-sport from a Georgian seminary, Stalin. The present speaks to him in Marx's "Others have understood the world; we change it"; in the pragmatists' "Truth is what works"; in Lincoln Steffens' statement about Russia, "I have seen the Future and it works." Some voices from the opera he has just seen reply, in wondering and helpless opposition, and end with the Marschallin's *Today or tomorrow comes the day*—her *And how shall we bear it? Lightly, lightly.* For a moment the city and its ruins seem to the man the city of the earth, dead, and troubled by a ghostly air.

I can hear the reader's despairing, "Oh, *no!*" so clearly that I hate to tell him that a certain amount of A Rhapsody on Irish Themes is a sort of parody of the *Odyssey*. In the original it's not an adding-machine but an oar that no one must be able to recognize; and I am able to call Ireland *you enclave of Brünn and of Borreby man* only because of reading (and, better still, looking at the pictures in) Carleton Coon's *The Races of Europe.*

The hero of Sears Roebuck, clad, housed, and supplied with a pronouncing Bible by the great mail-order firm, is frightened by other portions of its catalogue, and sees before him the fire of judgment.

The hero of Money, an old man surviving into a different age, says the poem during the '20's, when businessmen used to say that they worked not for money but for Service. *Miss Tarbell* is Ida Tarbell, the famous muckraker; *Ward* is Ward McAllister, equally famous as a "social arbiter." The city of Providence is the capital of Rhode Island. The old man's *But giving does as well* means that when you have bought everything there is to buy, you have only begun: you can still establish foundations, make bequests with conditions, and say *Go* and *Come* in many tax-exempt ways—money, in this "aetherealized" form, is as powerful as ever.

Galileo, Newton, and Bruno are the great emancipators addressed in the first stanza of THE EMANCIPATORS.

LA BELLE AU BOIS DORMANT is a poem about a murdered woman; her body has been put in a trunk, and the trunk checked in a railway station.

EIGHTH AIR FORCE is a poem about the air force which bombed the Continent from England. The man who lies counting missions has one to go before being sent home. The phrases from the Gospels compare such criminals and scapegoats as these with that earlier criminal and scapegoat about whom the Gospels were written.

A ball turret was a plexiglass sphere set into the belly of a B-17 or B-24, and inhabited by two .50 caliber machine-guns and one man, a short small man. When this gunner tracked with his machine-guns a fighter attacking his bomber from below, he revolved with the turret; hunched upside-down in his little sphere, he looked like the foetus in the womb. The fighters which attacked him were armed with cannon firing explosive shells. The hose was a steam hose.

At one time in the Second Air Force—the bomber training command —one member of every bomber crew was ordered to learn to play the ocarina "in order to improve the morale of the crews overseas." It was strange to walk along a dark road and look up at the big desert stars and hear from the distant barracks a gunner playing his ocarina. The hero of TRANSIENT BARRACKS, after some years abroad as a gunner, is a gunnery instructor now. A *G.I. can* is what you and I would call a garbage can; a *'24* is a B-24, a Liberator, a bomber very like a truck. In a *day-room* soldiers spend their evenings shooting pool, or listening to the radio, or writing home. When you shaved in barracks you usually had the choice of a broken glass mirror in which you could recognize part of yourself, or a mirror of unbroken metal in which you could see a face. The *C.Q.* is the soldier in Charge of Quarters. Before a man left a field every department of the field had to sign a clearance saying that he had kept nothing of theirs—but as you see, everyone went away with something.

SIEGFRIED is a poem about a gunner in one of the B-29's which bombed Japan. *To enter so many knots in a window, so many feet:* to enter speed and altitude in a gunsight or bombsight.

In A PILOT FROM THE CARRIER, *genius* is another form of the word *jinnee.*

The title, PILOTS, MAN YOUR PLANES, is the command repeated over the communication system of the carrier; the sound which accompanies it is like the sound of a *giant's jew's-harp. The steel watch-like fish:* torpedoes were called *fish. But on the tubes the raiders oscillate:* on the tubes of the radar sets. *A mile in every nine or thirteen seconds:* nine if they were the fighters, thirteen if they were the torpedo-planes. *Great light buckles . . . raft's hot-water-bottle weight:* the pilot's parachute and rubber life-raft are strapped to him, and dangle at his back. *Locked at last into the bubble, Hope:* the cockpit of the plane has a molded tear-drop canopy. *His gear falls:* his plane's retracted landing-gear falls when he flies into the fire from his own carrier.

THE DEAD WINGMAN: a fighter pilot, on a carrier off Japan, keeps searching in his sleep for his shot-down wingman.

STALAG LUFT: a (German) Prison Camp for Air Force Enlisted Men. One of the American prisoners is speaking.

JEWS AT HAIFA: in the first year and a half after the war ended, many of the Jewish survivors who had left Europe for Palestine were sent from Haifa to concentration camps on the island of Cyprus.

The men in PRISONERS are American prisoners of Americans. They wear a white *P* on their dark blue fatigue clothes. Before and during the first years of the war, this *P* was, instead, a white ball like the bull's-eye of a target: it was there for the M.P. to shoot at if the prisoner tried to escape.

The men in O MY NAME IT IS SAM HALL are three American prisoners and one American M.P., at a B-29 training base in southern Arizona. The guard's song begins

O my name it is Sam Hall, it is Sam Hall.
O my name it is Sam Hall, it is Sam Hall.
O my name it is Sam Hall
And I hate you one and all—
Yes, I hate you one and all,
God damn your eyes.

A CAMP IN THE PRUSSIAN FOREST: an American soldier is speaking after the capture of one of the German death camps. Jews, under the Nazis, were made to wear a yellow star. The Star of David is set over Jewish graves as the Cross is set over Christian graves.

Out of the desert of southern Arizona—a desert spotted with training fields for bombers and fighters—isolated mountain ranges rise nine or ten thousand feet, like islands from a sea of sand. LEAVE is said by a man who is spending a furlough on one of these.

In A FRONT, a front is closing in over a bomber base; the bombers, guided in by signals from the five towers of the radio range, are landing. Only one lands before the base is closed; the rest fly south to fields that are still open. One plane's radio has gone bad—it still transmits, but doesn't receive—and this plane tries to land and crashes.

In SECOND AIR FORCE the woman visiting her son remembers what she has read on the front page of her newspaper the week before, a conversation between a bomber, in flames over Germany, and one of the fighters protecting it: "Then I heard the bomber call me in: 'Little Friend, Little Friend, I got two engines on fire. Can you see me, Little Friend?' I said, 'I'm crossing right over you. Let's go home.'"

In THE RISING SUN, the word *fault* is used in its geological sense. *A five-colored cloud:* an emperor once ordered a year's celebration because a five-colored cloud had been observed by a provincial official. *From its six-cornered roof upon the world:* the roof of the Japanese world, like the roof of a Japanese house, has six corners. *Heads roll/ From the gutted, kneeling sons by rule:* in hara-kiri the kneeling man slashes his abdomen, and his head is cut off by his attendant. *The warrior/ Who bowed in blue, a child of four:* schoolboys were given blue uniforms at that age. *The child's grey ashes . . . the shrine beside the rocks . . . a lacquered box . . . and take the last dry puff of smoke:* the soldier's ashes were shipped home and placed in a temple by his mother or wife, who lit a cigarette for him and took a last puff of smoke in his memory. Motion pictures of this ceremony were shown to our army as part of a documentary film on Japan.

New Georgia: this is an island in the South Pacific. Americans captured it; the speaker is one of them, a Negro.

The Subway from New Britain to the Bronx: this poem's "sparrow" lived among the orchids of subway advertisements and died among the orchids of the rain-forests of the island of New Britain. He came there from the Bronx, where as a child he wandered through the largest zoo in the world, mocking the animals behind its bars.

A Ward in the States: these soldiers are malaria patients home from the South Pacific, in Army hospitals.

The Dead in Melanesia: *Melanesia* means *the black islands*. The *trades* are the trade winds. In parts of Melanesia the most important sacred object is the nautilus-like spiral which a boar's tusk forms when the tusk in the jaw opposite is knocked out. The *ronin* are the most famous of Japanese heroes: they were like the "masterless men" of the sagas, and I once saw the word defined as "landless men, masterless men, men like the waves of the sea."

The little boy who speaks The Truth has had his father, his sister, and his dog killed in one of the early fire-raids on London, and has been taken to the country, to a sort of mental institution for children.

SELECTED POEMS

I

I

LIVES

A Girl in a Library

An object among dreams, you sit here with your shoes off
And curl your legs up under you; your eyes
Close for a moment, your face moves toward sleep . . .
You are very human.
                       But my mind, gone out in tenderness,
Shrinks from its object with a thoughtful sigh.
This is a waist the spirit breaks its arm on.
The gods themselves, against you, struggle in vain.
This broad low strong-boned brow; these heavy eyes;
These calves, grown muscular with certainties;
This nose, three medium-sized pink strawberries
—But I exaggerate. In a little you will leave:
I'll hear, half squeal, half shriek, your laugh of greeting—
Then, *decrescendo,* bars of that strange speech
In which each sound sets out to seek each other,
Murders its own father, marries its own mother,
And ends as one grand transcendental vowel.

(Yet for all I know, the Egyptian Helen spoke so.)
As I look, the world contracts around you:
I see Brünnhilde had brown braids and glasses
She used for studying; Salome straight brown bangs,

A calf's brown eyes, and sturdy light-brown limbs
Dusted with cinnamon, an apple-dumpling's . . .
Many a beast has gnawn a leg off and got free,
Many a dolphin curved up from Necessity—
The trap has closed about you, and you sleep.
If someone questioned you, *What doest thou here?*
You'd knit your brows like an orangoutang
(But not so sadly; not so thoughtfully)
And answer with a pure heart, guilelessly:
I'm studying. . . .
                        If only you were not!
Assignments,
            recipes,
                    the *Official Rulebook*
Of Basketball—ah, let them go; you needn't mind.
The soul has no assignments, neither cooks
Nor referees: it wastes its time.
                                It wastes its time.
Here in this enclave there are centuries
For you to waste: the short and narrow stream
Of Life meanders into a thousand valleys
Of all that was, or might have been, or is to be.
The books, just leafed through, whisper endlessly . . .
Yet it is hard. One sees in your blurred eyes
The "uneasy half-soul" Kipling saw in dogs'.
One sees it, in the glass, in one's own eyes.
In rooms alone, in galleries, in libraries,
In tears, in searchings of the heart, in staggering joys
We memorize once more our old creation,
Humanity: with what yawns the unwilling
Flesh puts on its spirit, O my sister!

So many dreams! And not one troubles
Your sleep of life? no self stares shadowily
From these worn hexahedrons, beckoning
With false smiles, tears? . . .

Meanwhile Tatyana
Larina (gray eyes nickel with the moonlight
That falls through the willows onto Lensky's tomb;
Now young and shy, now old and cold and sure)
Asks, smiling: "But what is she dreaming of, fat thing?"
I answer: She's not fat. She isn't dreaming.
She purrs or laps or runs, all in her sleep;
Believes, awake, that she is beautiful;
She never dreams.
Those sunrise-colored clouds
Around man's head—that inconceivable enchantment
From which, at sunset, we come back to life
To find our graves dug, families dead, selves dying:
Of all this, Tanya, she is innocent.
For nineteen years she's faced reality:
They look alike already.
They say, man wouldn't be
The best thing in this world—and isn't he?—
If he were not too good for it. But she
—She's good enough for it.
And yet sometimes
Her sturdy form, in its pink strapless formal,
Is as if bathed in moonlight—modulated
Into a form of joy, a Lydian mode;
This Wooden Mean's a kind, furred animal
That speaks, in the Wild of things, delighting riddles
To the soul that listens, trusting . . .
Poor senseless Life:
When, in the last light sleep of dawn, the messenger
Comes with his message, you will not awake.
He'll give his feathery whistle, shake you hard,
You'll look with wide eyes at the dewy yard
And dream, with calm slow factuality:
"Today's Commencement. My bachelor's degree
In Home Ec., my doctorate of philosophy
In Phys. Ed.
[Tanya, they won't even *scan*]

Are waiting for me. . . ."
                                        Oh, Tatyana,
The Angel comes: better to squawk like a chicken
Than to say with truth, "But I'm a *good* girl,"
And Meet his Challenge with a last firm strange
Uncomprehending smile; and—then, then!—see
The blind date that has stood you up: your life.
(For all this, if it isn't, perhaps, life,
Has yet, at least, a language of its own
Different from the books'; worse than the books'.)
And yet, the ways we miss our lives are life.
Yet . . . yet . . .
                        to have one's life add up to *yet!*

You sigh a shuddering sigh. Tatyana murmurs,
"Don't cry, little peasant"; leaves us with a swift
"Good-bye, good-bye . . . Ah, don't think ill of me . . ."
Your eyes open: you sit here thoughtlessly.

I love you—and yet—and yet—I love you.

Don't cry, little peasant. Sit and dream.
One comes, a finger's width beneath your skin,
To the braided maidens singing as they spin;
There sound the shepherd's pipe, the watchman's rattle
Across the short dark distance of the years.
I am a thought of yours: and yet, you do not think . . .
The firelight of a long, blind, dreaming story
Lingers upon your lips; and I have seen
Firm, fixed forever in your closing eyes,
The Corn King beckoning to his Spring Queen.

A Country Life

A bird that I don't know,
Hunched on his light-pole like a scarecrow,
Looks sideways out into the wheat
The wind waves under the waves of heat.
The field is yellow as egg-bread dough
Except where (just as though they'd let
It live for looks) a locust billows
In leaf-green and shade-violet,
A standing mercy.
The bird calls twice, *"Red* clay, *red* clay";
Or else he's saying, "Directly, directly."
If someone came by I could ask,
Around here all of them must know—
And why they live so and die so—
Or why, for once, the lagging heron
Flaps from the little creek's parched cresses
Across the harsh-grassed, gullied meadow
To the black, rowed evergreens below.

They know and they don't know.
To ask, a man must be a stranger—
And asking, much more answering, is dangerous;
Asked about it, who would not repent
Of all he ever did and never meant,
And think a life and its distresses,
Its random, clutched-for, homefelt blisses,
The circumstances of an accident?
The farthest farmer in a field,
A gaunt plant grown, for seed, by farmers,

Has felt a longing, lorn urbanity
Jailed in his breast; and, just as I,
Has grunted, in his old perplexity,
A standing plea.

From the tar of the blazing square
The eyes shift, in their taciturn
And unavowing, unavailing sorrow.
Yet the intonation of a name confesses
Some secrets that they never meant
To let out to a soul; and what words would not dim
The bowed and weathered heads above the denim
Or the once-too-often-washed wash dresses?

They are subdued to their own element.
One day
The red, clay face
Is lowered to the naked clay;
After some words, the body is forsaken. . . .
The shadows lengthen, and a dreaming hope
Breathes, from the vague mound, *Life;*
From the grove under the spire
Stars shine, and a wandering light
Is kindled for the mourner, man.
The angel kneeling with the wreath
Sees, in the moonlight, graves.

The Knight, Death, and the Devil

Cowhorn-crowned, shockheaded, cornshuck-bearded,
Death is a scarecrow—his death's-head a teetotum
That tilts up toward man confidentially
But trimmed with adders; ringlet-maned, rope-bridled,
The mare he rides crops herbs beside a skull.
He holds up, warning, the crossed cones of time:
Here, narrowing into now, the Past and Future
Are quicksand.
            A hoofed pikeman trots behind.
His pike's claw-hammer mocks—in duplicate, inverted—
The pocked, ribbed, soaring crescent of his horn.
A scapegoat aged into a steer; boar-snouted;
His great limp ears stuck sidelong out in air;
A dewlap bunched at his breast; a ram's-horn wound
Beneath each ear; a spur licked up and out
From the hide of his forehead; bat-winged, but in bone;
His eye a ring inside a ring inside a ring
That leers up, joyless, vile, in meek obscenity—
This is the devil. Flesh to flesh, he bleats
The herd back to the pit of being.

In fluted mail; upon his lance the bush
Of that old fox; a sheep-dog bounding at his stirrup,
In its eyes the cast of faithfulness (our help,
Our foolish help); his dun war-horse pacing
Beneath in strength, in ceremonious magnificence;
His castle—some man's castle—set on every crag:
So, companioned so, the knight moves through this world.
The fiend moos in amity, Death mouths, reminding:

He listens in assurance, has no glance
To spare for them, but looks past steadily
At—at—
                a man's look completes itself.

The death of his own flesh, set up outside him;
The flesh of his own soul, set up outside him—
Death and the devil, what are these to him?
His being accuses him—and yet his face is firm
In resolution, in absolute persistence;
The folds of smiling do for steadiness;
The face is its own fate—*a man does what he must*—
And the body underneath it says: *I am.*

The Face

Die alte Frau, die alte Marschallin!

Not good any more, not beautiful—
Not even young.
This isn't mine.
Where is the old one, the old ones?
Those were mine.

It's so: I have pictures,
Not such old ones; people behaved
Differently then . . . When they meet me they say:
You haven't changed.
I want to say: You haven't looked.

This is what happens to everyone.
At first you get bigger, you know more,
Then something goes wrong.
You are, and you say: I am—
And you were . . . I've been too long.

I know, there's no saying no,
But just the same you say it. No.
I'll point to myself and say: I'm not like this.
I'm the same as always inside.
—And even that's not so.

I thought: If nothing happens . . .
And nothing happened.

Here I am.
                But it's not *right*.
If just living can do this,
Living is more dangerous than anything:

It is terrible to be alive.

Lady Bates

The lightning of a summer
Storm wakes, in her clay cave
At the end of the weeds, past the mock-orange tree—
Where she would come barefooted, curled-up-footed
Over the green, grained, rotting fruit
To eat blackberries, a scratched handful—
The little Lady Bates.
You have played too long today.
Open your eyes, Lady.
                        Is it a dream
Like the ones your mother used to talk away
When you were little and thought dreams were real?
Here dreams are real.
There are no more dreams, no more real—
There is no more night, there is no more day.

When the Lord God and the Holy Ghost and the Child Jesus
Heard about you, Lady,
They smiled all over their faces
And sang like a quartet: "Lady Bates,
Is it you, the little Lady Bates
Our minister, one Sunday evening,
Held down in the river till she choked
In a white dress like an angel's, red
With the clay of that red river? Lady,
Where are the two we sent to fetch your soul:
One coal-black, one high-yellow angel?
Where is night, where is day?
Where are you, Lady Bates?"

They looked for you east, they looked for you west,
And they lost you here in the cuckoo's nest
Eating the sweet white heart of the grass. . . .
You died before you had even had your hair straightened
Or waited on anybody's table but your own.
You stood there helping your step-mother
Boil clothes in the kettle in the yard,
And heard the girls go by, at play,
Calling to you in their soft mocking voices:
"Lady-Bug, Lady-Bug, fly away home."

You are home.
There is a bed of your own
Here where a few stones
Stick up in the tall grass dried to hay—
And one willow, at the end of summer,
Rustles, too dry to weep for you,
And the screech-owl sheers away
And calls, *Who, who*—you are afraid
And he is afraid: who else could see
A black ghost in the dark?
A black, barefooted, pigtailed, trifling ghost
With eyes like white clay marbles,
Who haunts no one—who lies still
In the darkness, waiting
While the lightning-bugs go on and off?
The darning-needles that sew bad girls' mouths shut
Have sewn up your eyes.
If you could open your eyes
You would see nothing.
                         Poor black trash,
The wind has blown you away forever
By mistake; and they sent the wind to the chain-gang
And it worked in the governor's kitchen, a trusty for life;
And it was all written in the Book of Life;
Day and Night met in the twilight by your tomb
And shot craps for you; and Day said, pointing to your soul,

"This *bad* young colored lady,"
And Night said, "Poor little nigger girl."

But Death, after the habit of command,
Said to you, slowly closing his hand:
"You're a big girl now, not even afraid
Of the dark when you awake—
When the day you sleep through
Is over, and you awake,
And the stars rise in the early evening
An inch or two over the grass of your grave—
Try to open your eyes;
Try to reach to one, to the nearest,
Reach, move your hand a little, try to move—
You can't move, can you?
You can't move. . . .
You're fast asleep, you're fast asleep."

When I Was Home Last Christmas . . .

When I was home last Christmas
I called on your family,
Your aunts and your mother, your sister;
They were kind as ever to me.

They told me how well I was looking
And clearly admired my wife;
I drank tea, made conversation,
And played with my bread, or knife.

Your aunts seemed greyer; your mother's
Lame unexpecting smile
Wandered from doily to doily;
Your dead face still

Cast me, with parted lips,
Its tight-rope-walker's look. . . .
But who is there now to notice
If I look or do not look

At a photograph at your mother's?
There is no one left to care
For all we said, and did, and thought—
The world we were.

A Conversation with the Devil

Indulgent, or candid, or uncommon reader
—I've some: a wife, a nun, a ghost or two—
If I write for anyone, I wrote for you;
So whisper, when I die, *We was too few;*
Write over me (if you can write; I hardly knew)
That I—that I—but anything will do,
I'm satisfied. . . . And yet—

                    and yet, you *were* too few:
Should I perhaps have written for your brothers,
Those artful, common, unindulgent others?

Mortal men, man! mortal men! So says my heart
Or else my belly—some poor empty part.
It warms in me, a dog beside a stove,
And whines, or growls, with a black lolling smile:
I never met the man I didn't love.
Life's hard for them . . . these mortals . . . Lie, man, lie!
Come, give it up—this whining poetry;
To any man be anything. If nothing works,
Why then, Have Faith.

                 That blessed word, Democracy!

But this is strange of you: to tempt me now!
It brings back all the past: those earliest offers
—How can I forget?—EACH POEM GUARANTEED
A LIE OR PERMANENTLY IRRELEVANT.
WE FURNISH POEMS *AND* READERS. What a slogan!
(I had only to give credit to "my daemon";
Say, confidentially, "dictated by the devil.")
I can still see my picture in that schoolroom.

And next—who has it now?—*The World's Enormity,*
That novel of the Wandering Jewess, Lilith,
Who went to bed with six millennia.
(It came complete with sales, scenario,
And testimonials of grateful users:
Not like a book at all. . . . Beats life. . . .)

                                 Beats life.
How ill we knew each other then! how mockingly
I nodded, "Almost thou persuadest me,"
And made my offer:
                      "If ever I don't say
To the hour of life that I can wish for: *Stay,*
Thou art so fair! why, you may have my—
Shadow."
             Our real terms were different
And signed and sealed for good, neither in blood
Nor ink but in my life: *Neither to live*
Nor ask for life—that wasn't a bad bargain
For a poor devil of a poet, was it?
One makes a solitude and calls it peace.
So you phrased it; yet—yet—one is paid:
To see things as they are, to make them what they might be—
Old Father of Truths, old Spirit that Accepts—
That's something. . . . If, afterwards, we broke our bargain—

He interrupts: *But what nobility!*
I once saw a tenor at the Opéra Comique
Who played the Fisher—of Pearls or else of Souls.
He wore a leopard-skin, lay down, and died;
And sang ten minutes lying on his side
And died again; and then, applauded,
Gave six bows, leaning on his elbow,
And at the seventh started on his encore.
He was, I think, a poet.
                  Renounce, renounce,
You sing in your pure clear grave ardent tones

And then give up—whatever you're afraid to take,
Which is everything; and after that take credit
For dreaming something else to take its place.
Isn't what is already enough for you?
Must you always be making *something?*
Must each fool cook a lie up all his own?
You beings, won't even being disgust you
With causing something else to be? Make, make—
You squeak like mice; and yet it's all hypocrisy—
How often each of you, in his own heart,
Has wiped the world out, and thought afterwards:
No need to question, now: "If others are, am I?"
Still, I confess that I and my good Neighbor
Have always rather envied you existence.
Your simple conceits!—but both of us enjoy them:
"Dear God, make me Innocent or Wise,"
Each card in the card-catalogue keeps praying;
And dies, and the divine Librarian
Rebinds him—

              rebinds?that's odd; but then, He's odd
And as a rule—

             I'm lying: there's no rule at all.
The world divides into—believe me—facts.

I see the devil can quote Wittgenstein.
He's blacker than he's painted.

                 Old ink-blot,
What are you, after all? A parody.
You can be satisfied? then how can I?
If you accept, is not that to deny?
A Dog in a tub, who was the Morning Star!
To have come down in the universe so far
As here, and now, and *this*—and all to buy
One bored, stoop-shouldered, sagging-cheeked particular
Lest the eternal bonfire fail—

           ah Lucifer!

But at *blacker* an embarrassed smile
Wavers across his muzzle, he breaks in:
It's odd that you've never guessed: I'm through.
To tempt, sometimes, a bored anachronism
Like you into—but why should I say what?
To stretch out by the Fire and improvise:
This pleases me, now there's no need for me.
Even you must see I'm obsolescent.
A specialist in personal relations,
I valued each of you at his own worth.
You had your faults; but you were bad at heart.
I disliked each life, I assure you, for its own sake.
—But to deal indifferently in life and death;
To sell, wholesale, piecemeal, annihilation;
To—I will not go into particulars—
This beats me.

        To men, now, I should give advice?
I'm vain, as you know; but not ridiculous.
Here in my inglenook, shy, idle, I conclude:
I never understood them: as the consequence
They end without me. . . .

           "Scratch a doctor
And find a patient," I always used to say.
Now that I've time, I've analyzed myself
And find that I am growing, or have grown—
Was always, perhaps, indifferent.
It takes a man to love or hate a man
Wholeheartedly. And how wholeheartedly
You act out All *that is deserves to perish!*
As if to take me at my word—an idle mot
That no one took less seriously than I.
It was so, of course; and yet—and yet—

I find that I've grown used to you. Hell gives us habits
To take the place of happiness, alas!
When I look forward, it is with a pang
That I think of saying, "My occupation's gone."

But twelve's striking: time to be in bed.

I think: He's a changed—all this has shaken him.
He was always delicate: a spirit of society,
A way to come to terms—
                  now, no more terms!

Those pleasant evenings of denunciation!
How gratefully, after five acts' rejection,
A last firm shake and quaver and statistic,
He'd end, *falsetto:* "But let's be realistic"—
Had he, perhaps, exaggerated? He had exaggerated . . .
How quietly, a little later, he'd conclude:
"I accept it all."
              And now to be unable
To accept, to have exaggerated—
                  to do anything:
It's hard for him. How often he has said,
"I like you for always doing as you please"—
He couldn't. Free will appealed so much to him;
He thought, I think: *If they've the choice* . . .

He was right. And now, to have no choice!

Nollekens

(In England during the last part of the eighteenth century there lived a very small, very childish man—a bad speller and a worse miser—who was the most famous portrait sculptor of his day. He had a dog called Cerberus, a cat called Jenny Dawdle, servants called Bronze and Mary Fairy, and a wife named Mary Welch. All that my poem says that he did, he did; I read about it in NOLLEKENS AND HIS TIMES, the book "the little Smith" wrote after Nollekens had died.)

Old Nollekens? No, Little Nollekens:
The Sculptor-Man. "Stand here and you will see
Nine streets commence," he told the little Smith,
Who counted them; "my mother showed them me."
He pricked the King's nose with the calipers.

He stood on King Street in his blue striped hose
And an old bag-wig—the true Garrick-cut—
And stated, in the voice of Samuel Johnson:
"Well, Mrs. Rapsworth, you have just done right.
I wore a pudding as a little boy;
My mother's children all wore puddings."
But Johnson said to him, once: "Bow-wow-wow!"

Dog-Jennings, Shakespeare Steevens, the Athenian
Stuart—these, these too, recalled with joy
The unique power of a Mr. Rich
Who scratched his ear with one foot, like a dog.

Randall Jarrell / The Complete Poems

It took as much wit as the *are-bolloon*.

The milk-maids danced on May-day, and were paid;
The butchers' snow-house was signed: *Nollekens;*
He stole the nutmegs from the R. A.'s punch—
And once gave Cerberus but half his paunch
And told him, "You have had a roll today."
But Mary Fairy scolded Nollekens,
And old Bronze put her arm around his neck
And asked him how he did. Said Nollekens,
"What! now you want some money—I've got none.
Can you dance?" "Dance, Sir! why, to be sure I can.
Give me the cat." While he watched Jenny Dawdle,
His tabby, dancing round the room with Bronze,
The tears of pleasure trickled down his cheeks
Upon his bib.
       And yet one day he fell
Into a passion with this favorite cat
For biting the old feather of a pen
He kept to oil the hinges of the gate.
(He showed it to her, and explained to her
The mischief she had done.) So, catching rats,
He stuffed the rat-trap with a pound of cheese
To catch them all at once; so, from the Tower
He went to model George, and cried: "They've got
Such lions there! The biggest did roar so;
My heart, he did roar so." The Sculptor roared.

In winter, when the birds fell from the branches,
In winter, when his servant fed the beggars,
His wife called, "Betty! Betty! Give them this.
Here is a bone with little or no meat upon it."
One, looking at the other steadfastly,
Repeated: "Bill, we are to have a bone
With little or no meat upon it."
              So.

He left two hundred thousand pounds—and two
Old shoes, the less worn of his last two pairs;
One night-cap, two shirts, and three pairs of stockings;
And the coat in which he married Mary Welch.

Was "Mrs. White delivered of a sun"?
Who measured the dead Pitt? Ah, Nollekens,
To smuggle lace in busts! To leave poor Bronze
But twenty pounds! And yet, whoever dies?

"Ring a bell, ring a bell, my pretty little maid?—
Why, that I will." And I see straining for it
The crescent, tiptoe Nollekens. . . . "My heart,
To sit there in the dark, to save a candle—"
I grieve; but he says, looking steadfastly,
"If you laugh, I'll make a fool of ye."
And I nod, and think acquiescingly:
"Why, it is Nollekens the Sculptor."

Seele im Raum

It sat between my husband and my children.
A place was set for it—a plate of greens.
It had been there: I had seen it
But not somehow—but this was like a dream—
Not seen it so that I knew I saw it.
It was as if I could not know I saw it
Because I had never once in all my life
Not seen it. It was an eland.
An eland! *That* is why the children
Would ask my husband, for a joke, at Christmas:
"Father, is it Donner?" He would say, "No, Blitzen."
It had been there always. Now we put silver
At its place at meals, fed it the same food
We ourselves ate, and said nothing. Many times
When it breathed heavily (when it had tried
A long useless time to speak) and reached to me
So that I touched it—of a different size
And order of being, like the live hard side
Of a horse's neck when you pat the horse—
And looked with its great melting tearless eyes
Fringed with a few coarse wire-like lashes
Into my eyes, and whispered to me
So that my eyes turned backward in their sockets
And they said nothing—

> many times
I have known, when they said nothing,
That it did not exist. If they had heard
They *could* not have been silent. And yet they heard;
Heard many times what I have spoken

When it could no longer speak, but only breathe—
When I could no longer speak, but only breathe.

And, after some years, the others came
And took it from me—it was ill, they told me—
And cured it, they wrote me: my whole city
Sent me cards like lilac-branches, mourning
As I had mourned—
               and I was standing
By a grave in flowers, by dyed rolls of turf,
And a canvas marquee the last brown of earth.

It is over.
It is over so long that I begin to think
That it did not exist, that I have never—
And my son says, one morning, from the paper:
"An eland. Look, an eland!"
                    —It was so.

Today, in a German dictionary, I saw *elend*
And the heart in my breast turned over, it was—

It was a word one translates *wretched*.

It is as if someone remembered saying:
"This is an antimacassar that I grew from seed,"
And this were true.
              And, truly,
One could not wish for anything more strange—
For anything more. And yet it wasn't *interesting* . . .
—It was worse than impossible, it was a joke.

And yet when it was, I *was*—
Even to think that I once thought
That I could see it is to feel the sweat
Like needles at my hair-roots, I am blind

—It was not even a joke, not even a joke.

Yet how can I believe it? Or believe that I
Owned it, a husband, children? Is my voice the voice
Of that skin of being—of what owns, is owned
In honor or dishonor, that is borne and bears—
Or of that raw thing, the being inside it
That has neither a wife, a husband, nor a child
But goes at last as naked from this world
As it was born into it—

And the eland comes and grazes on its grave.

                       This is senseless?
Shall I make sense or shall I tell the truth?
Choose either—I cannot do both.

I tell myself that. And yet it is not so,
And what I say afterwards will not be so:
To be at all is to be wrong.
                    Being is being old
And saying, almost comfortably, across a table
From—
        from what I don't know—
                    in a voice
Rich with a kind of longing satisfaction:
"To own an eland! That's what I call life!"

The Night before the Night
before Christmas

(1934)

In the Arden Apartments
Only a community center and an apartment
From the new lots and the old forest
Of Hillsboro Manor
Lived a girl and her father,
Her aunt, and her one brother.
Nights, warm in her bed,
The girl would still dream of the mother
Who, two years dead,
Looks more like her sister than her mother
—So they had said—
And lays, slowly, a dark shining head
On the dark, stooped shoulder
Of the girl's new teacher.
Is there any question?
The girl has forgotten to answer
And watches him open the door of the cab
That is bringing an Invitation to the Dance:
Till Mother disappears in fur,
The girl trails toward the house
And stares at her bitten nails, her bare red knees—
And presses her chapped, cold hands together
In a middy blouse.

The night before the night before Christmas
Her brother looked out over the snow

That had fallen all day, and saw her
At last, two floors below,
And knocked at the window—drawn-over, frosted-over—
Till she waved and made an O
With her mouth—she was calling.
As she climbed the stairs the snow
Stopped falling, she saw from the landing
Past the big old houses, the small new houses,
And the wood's scrambled boughs
The sun in the hills. . . .
                         Home, home.
She throws her books on the sofa,
And the boy, from his bed,
Calls to her: "Mother, what is snow?"
She answers: "It is the cotton-wool, my Son,
That is falling from the ears of God."
The boys says: "Ho ho ho!
But tell me, Mother,
Why does He keep it in His ears?"
She answers:
"My Son, that He may not hear
How hideously men use His name."

The boy calls, "No, *mis*use, *mis*use!"
She says, "It's just the same."
But she says to herself as she turns on the light in her room:
"How hideously men use His name. . . ."

And she and her father eat dinner with her aunt
And she carries a tray to her brother;
She can hear carols from the radio
In the living-room, as she looks for the dominoes.
After that she offers to read her brother
Another chapter from *The Iron Heel*.
"No, read me from *Stalky*."
She starts to, but says, "When I was your age
I read it all the time." He answers, "It's not real."

She cries, "Oh *isn't* it! Why, in Germany—"
But she stops and finally says, "Well . . ."
And reads about Regulus leaving, full of courage,
For that nigger Manchester, Carthage.
She reads it, *that Negro Manchester,*
But it's just the same, he doesn't understand.
She laughs, and says to her brother: .
"Engels lived in Manchester."
The boy says: "Who was Engels?"
She says: "Don't you even remember *that?*"

In her room that night she looks at herself in the mirror
And thinks: "Do I really look like *that?*"
She stares at her hair;
It's really a beautiful golden—anyway, yellow:
She brushes it with affection
And combs her bang back over so it slants.
How white her teeth are.
A turned-up nose . . .
No, it's no use.
She thinks: What do I *really* look like?
I don't know.

Not really.
       Really.

Some dolls and a letter sweater
And a beige fur bear,
A Pink and a Golden and a Blue
Fairy Book, all, all in a row,
Beam from the light, bright, white-starred blue
Of the walls, the clouding curtains—
Anachronisms
East of the sun and west of the moon.
She wraps in white tissue paper
A shiny *Coming Struggle for Power*

For her best friend—
And ties it, one gold, gritty end
Of the string in her mouth, and one in her left hand;
Her right forefinger presses down the knot. . . .
She wraps some improving and delightful
Things she has got for her brother
And one medium-sized present for her aunt
And the gloves she has knitted, the tie she has picked
For her father—poor Lion,
Poor Moose.
She'd give him something that means something
But it's no use:
People are so *dumb*.
She thinks with regretful indignation:
"Why, he might as well not be alive . . ."
And sees all the mottoes at his office,
Like *Do It Now*
And *To Travel Hopefully*
Is A Better Thing Than To Arrive.

Still, he was sorry when my squirrel . . .
He was sorry as Brother when my squirrel . . .
When the gifts are wrapped she reads.

Outside, the wind is—whatever it is;
Inside, it is its own old
·Terrible comfortable self:
A ghost in a story—it is all a story.
An uneasy, rocking, comfortable tune
Keeps singing itself under the cold words
In her warm head—cold world
In her warm head—
                    in Praise of Learning:
    LEARN it, WOmen in KITCHens . . .
    LEARN it, MEN of SEVenty . . .
She goes on turning
The big small-printed pages—

A kind of world . . .
                        Use-, surplus-, and exchange-
Value (all these, and plain
Value)
Creak slowly by, the wagon groans—
Creak by, like rags, like bottles—
Like rags, like bottles, like old bones . . .
The bones of men. Her breath is quickened
With pitying, indignant pain.
She thinks: *That's* funny . . .
That's funny: a *Cyclopean* machine . . .
It blinks at her with one blind eye.
Who put your eye out?
                        No one.
Watching with parted lips,
A shy sidelong stare,
She makes out, far off, among columns
Of figures, the children laboring:
A figure buried among figures
Looks at her beggingly, a beast in pain.
She puts her hand
Out into the darkness till it touches:
Her flesh freezes, in that instant, to the iron
And pulls away in blood.
The tears of pain,
Of her own passive, guilty, useless pain
Swell in her eyes, she blinks them over and over
    LEARN it, MEN of SEVen
By your mothers, in the mills—
    WHAT you don't LEARN yourSELF you don't KNOW.

She thinks of her brother going down
To the pits with the ponies, too soon for the sun,
And coming back black, too late for the sun—
No school—he wouldn't even know
Who God is, like the one

In the book—
                    not even know
Enough not to believe in God . . .
She thinks, as she has thought,
Her worn old thought,
By now one word:
"But how could this world be
If he's all-powerful, all-good?
No—there's no God."

She reads.

The figures, the values, the one Value
Are clothed with the cloud of her breathing—
The voice echoing over
The dark, stooped shoulder
Ends, hissing a little: "is un*just.*"
The hiss blurs in her head
With the hiss of her slow breath,
The lumps of her feet, her lashes
Stuck fast together, washed shut forever, on the wave
Of . . . that is washing, over and over, on the shore
Of . . . something . . . Something . . .
                    But her head jerks straight,
The song strengthens, its last words strike home:
    YOU must be READy to take POWer!
    YOU must be READy to take POWer!

She is reading a Factory Act, a girl in a room.

And afterwards—the room is getting colder
And she is too tired to hold her head up any longer—
She puts away her book
And gives her hair its counted-off
Strokes, and works in and wipes off
Some cold cream from her jar

Of Rexall's Theatrical Cold Cream; and puts on, yawning
Over and over, her boy's blue silk pajamas,
Her white birthday Angora
Bed-socks. She puts up the window—
Her radiator clanks a minute
As someone in the basement banks
The furnace for the night—
And she puts out the light.

She lies half-in, half-out of moonlight
In the sheer cold of the fresh
Sheets, under the patched star-pattern
Of the quilt; and, curled there, warms a world
Out slowly, a wobbling blind ellipse
That lengthens in half a dozen jumps
Of her numb shrinking feet,
Steadies . . . A train wails, over and over,
At a crossing. "It's like Martha,"
She mumbles. "So's the radiator."
The long, mourning, hollow questions
Of Martha Locomotive-Engineer
(You can't get more than a snore
From Martha Janitor, asleep by now
On his brass bed in the basement)
Vex Mary, in her bed-socks, listening guiltily
To the hollow answers of her Lord.
The poor, the poor . . .
                     Her wandering mind
Comes to what was a joy,
What is a sorrow—
A cave opening into the dark
Earth, down to the dead:
What, played with day after day,
Stroked, called to, fed
In the small, wild, straggling park—
Told of, night after night, to the boy
Who listened, longing, among the games

Strewn on his rumpled bed—

                          was gone, one winter day.
She thought: "Tomorrow
He will be where he always is"; and tomorrow
She thought: "He will be here again, tomorrow.
He is asleep with all the other squirrels
There in the hollow of his favorite tree.
He is living on all the nuts he hid
In his cave in the hollow tree."

On warm days, all that winter,
All the warm days of the spring,
She saw the others—never hers;
She thought, trying not to think, "Why, *anything*
Could have happened to him"; she thought, as the living
Think of their life, "Oh, it's not *right!*"
The squirrels are chattering
From leaf to leaf, as her squirrel chattered.
The Poor, the Poor . . .
They have eaten, rapidly,
From her hand, as though to say:
"But you won't hurt me, will you? *Will you?*"

They have nothing to lose but their lives.
She looks home into
The lancing eyes
In the rat-like face, the sucking
Fish-hooks of the little paws: a clawed
Rat with an Angora tail. A clawed
Dead rat with an Angora tail.

There is something deep
Under her will, against her will,
That keeps murmuring to her, "It's so";
And she murmurs, almost asleep:
"Un*just*—no, it's not *so*.
If he were educated . . ."

She sees six squirrels in a row
Thinking in chorus, in slow, low,
Hissing, radiator-steam-valve voices:
"Wherefore Art Thou, Romeo?"
The big squirrel says, "No.
No, that is not *just* it.
Try it again."
Their skein-silk lashes
Tremble, and they look sidelong up at her—
And cry, softly, in their sly,
Dumb, scared, malicious pain . . .
And try it again.

A dream, a dream.
She whispers: "I'm awake.
No, I'm not dreaming, I'm awake."
There is no more moonlight.
Out there, there is darkness and light,
The cold of night.
The world is no longer hidden
By the fire of her lit room,
By the day of the light of the sun.
Out there nothing moves except with a faint
Choked straining shiver;
Sounds except with a faint
Choked croaking sigh.
They are all there together.

Up over
The last twig, in the wild still sky,
Far under the last root, in the wild still sky,
There is another galaxy
Of so many hundreds of thousands of stars
So many hundreds of thousands of years
Away; and it is one
Of so many hundreds of thousands
Of galaxies—some like our own.

It is good, it is evil?
The girl gives her long straining sigh—
In the cells of the needles of the branches
Of the evergreens, the sap is ice.
Wherever the girl stares—
Hung out over, hung in under
The abyss that is her home—
There is something, something: the universe
Is a mirror backed with black
Out of which her face shines back
In the midst of hundreds of millions of suns.

They are all there together.

In the fields outside
There is not one step on the snow,
And each bough is bent with the burden
That is greater, almost, than it can bear.
The breaths of a world are webs
Of angelhair,
Of glass spun, life by life,
Into the trees' earned, magic tinsel.
A handful
Of snowflakes falls from a branch to a bush;
A star hovers
At the tip of a frozen spruce.
It disappears.
(At the side of the shepherds Hänsel
Stands hand in hand with Gretel
And sparkles, under a sparkling star,
Like Lot's own wife:
Bushes, bushes.)
When the owl calls nothing answers.
In the owl's lungs, strained through feathers,
A breath is the edge of a knife. . . .
The haze of the girl's slow breaths,
Of her spun-sugar, cotton-candy breath,

Floats up, clouding the printed stars
Of the faint walls: white
As the down of the wing of an angel; white
As the beard of Friedrich Engels. . . .

In the fields there is not one angel.
In all these fields
There is not one thing that knows
It is almost Christmas.
                            Staring, staring
At the gray squirrel dead in the snow,
She and her brother float up from the snow—
The last crumbs of their tears
Are caught by the birds that are falling
To strew their leaves on the snow
That is covering, that has covered
The play-mound under the snow. . . .
The leaves are the snow, the birds are the snow,
The boy and girl in the leaves of their grave
Are the wings of the bird of the snow.
But her wings are mixed in her head with the Way
That streams from their shoulders, stars like snow:
They spread, at last, their great starry wings
And her brother sings, "I am dying."

"No: it's not so, not so—
Not *really,*"
She thinks; but she says, "You are dying."
He says, "I didn't know."

And she cries: "I don't know, I don't know, I don't know!"

They are flying.

They look down over the earth.
There is not one crumb.
The rays of the stars of their wings

Strike the boughs of the wood, and the shadows
Are caught up into the night,
The first faint whisper of the wind:
Home, home, whispers the wind;
There are shadows of stars, a working
Hand in the . . .

There are words on the graves of the snow.
She whispers, "When I was alive,
I read them all the time.
I read them all the time."
And he whispers, sighing:
"When I was alive . . ."

And, moving her licked, chapped, parted lips,
She reads, from the white limbs' vanished leaves:
To End Hopefully
Is A Better Thing—
                    A Far, Far Better Thing—
It is a far, far better thing . . .

She feels, in her hand, her brother's hand.
She is crying.

DREAM-WORK

A Sick Child

The postman comes when I am still in bed.
"Postman, what do you have for me today?"
I say to him. (But really I'm in bed.)
Then he says—what shall I have him say?

"This letter says that you are president
Of—this word here; it's a republic."
Tell them I can't answer right away.
"It's your duty." No, I'd rather just be sick.

Then he tells me there are letters saying everything
That I can think of that I want for them to say.
I say, "Well, thank you very much. Good-bye."
He is ashamed, and turns and walks away.

If I can think of it, it isn't what I want.
I want . . . I want a ship from some near star
To land in the yard, and beings to come out
And think to me: "So this is where you are!

Come." Except that they won't do,
I thought of them. . . . And yet somewhere there must be
Something that's different from everything.
All that I've never thought of—think of me!

The Black Swan

When the swans turned my sister into a swan
  I would go to the lake, at night, from milking:
The sun would look out through the reeds like a swan,
  A swan's red beak; and the beak would open
And inside there was darkness, the stars and the moon.

Out on the lake a girl would laugh.
  "Sister, here is your porridge, sister,"
I would call; and the reeds would whisper,
  "Go to sleep, go to sleep, little swan."
My legs were all hard and webbed, and the silky

Hairs of my wings sank away like stars
  In the ripples that ran in and out of the reeds:
I heard through the lap and hiss of water
  Someone's "Sister . . . sister," far away on the shore,
And then as I opened my beak to answer

I heard my harsh laugh go out to the shore
  And saw—saw at last, swimming up from the green
Low mounds of the lake, the white stone swans:
  The white, named swans . . . "It is all a dream,"
I whispered, and reached from the down of the pallet

To the lap and hiss of the floor.
  And "Sleep, little sister," the swans all sang
From the moon and stars and frogs of the floor.
  But the swan my sister called, "Sleep at last, little sister,"
And stroked all night, with a black wing, my wings.

The Venetian Blind

It is the first day of the world
Man wakes into: the bars of the blind
And their key-signature, a leaf,
Stream darkly to two warmths;
One trembles, becomes his face.
He floats from the sunlight
Into a shadowed place:
There is a chatter, a blur of wings—
But where is the edge of things?
Where does the world begin?
                              His dreams
Have changed into this day, this dream;
He thinks, "But where am I?"
A voice calls patiently:
"Remember."
He thinks, "But where am I?"
His great limbs are curled
Through sunlight, about space.
What is that, *remember?*
He thinks that he is younger
Than anything has ever been.
He thinks that he is the world.

But his soul and his body
Call, as the bird calls, their one word—
And he remembers.

He is lost in himself forever.

And the Angel he makes from the sunlight
Says in mocking tenderness:
"Poor stateless one, wert thou the world?"
His soul and his body
Say, "What hast thou made of us, thy servants?
We are sick. We are dull. We are old."
"Who is this man? We know him not," says the world.

They have spoken as he would have made them speak;
And who else is there to speak?

The bars of the sunlight fall to his face.

And yet something calls, as it has called:
"But where am *I*? But where am *I*?"

A Quilt-Pattern

The blocked-out Tree
Of the boy's Life is gray
On the tangled quilt: the long day
Dies at last, after many tales.
Good me, bad me, the Other
Black out, and the humming stare
Of the woman—the good mother—
Drifts away; the boy falls
Through darkness, the leagues of space
Into the oldest tale of all.

All the graves of the forest
Are opened, the scaling face
Of a woman—the dead mother—
Is square in the steam of a yard
Where the cages are warmed all night for the rabbits,
All small furry things
That are hurt, but that never cry at all—
That are skinned, but that never die at all.
Good me, bad me
Dry their tears, and gather patiently
Through the loops of the chicken-wire of the cages
Blackberries, the small hairy things
They live on, here in the wood of the dream.

Here a thousand stones
Of the trail home shine from their strings
Like just-brushed, just-lost teeth.
All the birds of the forest

Sit brooding, stuffed with crumbs.
But at home, far, far away
The white moon shines from the stones of the chimney,
His white cat eats up his white pigeon.

But the house hums, "We are home." Good me, bad me
Sits wrapped in his coat of rabbit-skin
And looks for some little living thing
To be kind to, for then it will help him—
There is nothing to help; good me
Sits twitching the rabbit's-fur of his ears
And says to himself, "My mother is basting
Bad me in the bath-tub—"
                              the steam rises,
A washcloth is turned like a mop in his mouth.
He stares into the mouth
Of the whole house: there in it is waiting—
No, there is nothing.

He breaks a finger
From the window and lifts it to his—
"Who is nibbling at me?" says the house.
The dream says, "The wind,
The heaven-born wind";
The boy says, "It is a mouse."
He sucks at the finger; and the house of bread
Calls to him in its slow singing voice:
"Feed, feed! Are you fat now?
Hold out your finger."
The boy holds out the bone of the finger.
It moves, but the house says, "No, you don't know.
Eat a little longer."
The taste of the house
Is the taste of his—
                    "I don't know,"
Thinks the boy. "No, I don't *know!*"

His whole dream swells with the steam of the oven
Till it whispers, "You are full now, mouse—
Look, I have warmed the oven, kneaded the dough:
Creep in—ah, ah, it is warm!—
Quick, we can slip the bread in now," says the house.
He whispers, "I do not know
How I am to do it."
                         "Goose, goose," cries the house,
"It is big enough—just look!
See, if I bend a little, so—"

He has moved. . . . He is still now, and holds his breath.
If something is screaming itself to death
There in the oven, it is not the mouse
Nor anything of the mouse's. Bad me, good me
Stare into each other's eyes, and timidly
Smile at each other: it was the Other.

But they are waking, waking; the last stair creaks—
Out there on the other side of the door
The house creaks, "How is my little mouse? Awake?"
It is she.
He says to himself, "I will never wake."
He says to himself, not breathing:
"Go away. Go away. Go away."

And the footsteps go away.

The Island

"While sun and sea—and I, and I—
Were warped through summer on our spar,
I guessed beside the fin, the gull,
And Europe ebbing like a sail
A life indifferent as a star.

"My lids were grating to their close,
My palms were loosening to die,
When—failing through its drift of surf,
Whale-humped, its beaches cracked with salt—
The island gave its absent sigh.

"Years notched my hut, my whiskers soughed
Through summer's witless stare: blue day
Flickered above the nothingness
That rimmed me, the unguessed abyss
Broke on my beaches, and its spray

"Frosted or salted with its curling smile
The printless hachures of the sand . . .
I lay with you, Europe, in a net of snows:
And all my trolls—their noses flattened into Lapps'
Against the thin horn of my windows—wept;

"Vole, kobold, the snowshoe-footed hare
—Crowned with the smoke of steamboats, shagg'd with stars—
Whispered to my white mistress: *He is Mars;*
Till I called, laughing: *Friends! subjects! customers!*
And her face was a woman's, theirs were men's.

"All this I dreamed in my great ragged bed . . .
Or so I dreamed. The dawn's outspeaking smile
Curled through my lashes, felled the Märchen's wood;
The sun stripped my last cumulus of stars,
And the sea graved all the marshes of the swan.

"So, so. The years ticked past like crabs
Or an hour inched out to heaven, like the sea.
One day, by my black hand, my beard
Shone silver; I looked in astonishment
And pinched my lean calves, drawn with many scars,

"With my stiff fingers, till the parrot called
In my grum, quavering voice: *Poor Robinson!*
My herd came bleating, licked my salty cheeks;
I sobbed, and petted with a kind of love
These joys of mine—the old, half-human loves

"That had comforted my absent life . . .
I have dreamed of men, and I am old.
There is no Europe." The man, the goats, the parrot
Wait in their grove for death; and there floods to them
In its last thundering spray, the sea, the sea!

In the Ward: The Sacred Wood

The trees rise from the darkness of the world.
The little trees, the paper grove,
Stand woodenly, a sigh of earth,
Upon the table by this bed of life
Where I have lain so long: until at last
I find a Maker for them, and forget
Who cut them from their cardboard, brushed
A bird on each dark, fretted bough.
But the birds think and are still.
The thunder mutters to them from the hills
My knees make by the rainless Garden.
If the grove trembles with the fan
And makes, at last, its little flapping song
That wanders to me over the white flood
On which I float enchanted—shall I fall?
A bat jerks to me from the ragged limb
And hops across my shudder with its leaf
Of curling paper: have the waters gone?
Is the nurse damned who looked on my nakedness?
The sheets stretch like the wilderness
Up which my fingers wander, the sick tribes,
To a match's flare, a rain or bush of fire
Through which the devil trudges, coal by coal,
With all his goods; and I look absently
And am not tempted.
Death scratches feebly at this husk of life
In which I lie unchanging, Sin despairs
Of my dull works; and I am patient . . .
A third of all the angels, in the wars

Of God against the Angel, took no part
And were to God's will neither enemies
Nor followers, but lay in doubt:
                              but lie in doubt.

There is no trade here for my life.
The lamb naps in the crêche, but will not die.
The halo strapped upon the head
Of the doctor who stares down my throat
And thinks, "Die, then; I shall not die"—
Is this the glitter of the cruze of oil
Upon the locks of that Anointed One
Who gazes, dully, from the leafless tree
Into the fixed eyes of Elohim?
I have made the Father call indifferently
To a body, to the Son of Man:
"It is finished." And beneath the coverlet
My limbs are swaddled in their sleep, and shade
Flows from the cave beyond the olives, falls
Into the garden where no messenger
Comes to gesture, "Go"—to whisper, "He is gone."

The trees rise to me from the world
That made me, I call to the grove
That stretches inch on inch without one God:
"I have unmade you, now; but I must die."

THE WIDE PROSPECT

The Orient Express

One looks from the train
Almost as one looked as a child. In the sunlight
What I see still seems to me plain,
I am safe; but at evening
As the lands darken, a questioning
Precariousness comes over everything.

Once after a day of rain
I lay longing to be cold; and after a while
I was cold again, and hunched shivering
Under the quilt's many colors, gray
With the dull ending of the winter day.
Outside me there were a few shapes
Of chairs and tables, things from a primer;
Outside the window
There were the chairs and tables of the world. . . .
I saw that the world
That had seemed to me the plain
Gray mask of all that was strange
Behind it—of all that *was*—was all.

But it is beyond belief.
One thinks, "Behind everything

An unforced joy, an unwilling
Sadness (a willing sadness, a forced joy)
Moves changelessly"; one looks from the train
And there is something, the same thing
Behind everything: all these little villages,
A passing woman, a field of grain,
The man who says good-bye to his wife—
A path through a wood full of lives, and the train
Passing, after all unchangeable
And not now ever to stop, like a heart—

It is like any other work of art.
It is and never can be changed.
Behind everything there is always
The unknown unwanted life.

A Game at Salzburg

A little ragged girl, our ball-boy;
A partner—ex-Afrika-Korps—
In khaki shorts, P. W. illegible.
(He said: "To have been a prisoner of war
In Colorado iss a *privilege*.")
The evergreens, concessions, carrousels,
And D. P. camp of Franz Joseph Park;
A gray-green river, evergreen-dark hills.
Last, a long way off in the sky,
Snow-mountains.

Over this clouds come, a darkness falls,
Rain falls.
                    On the veranda Romana,
A girl of three,
Sits licking sherbet from a wooden spoon;
I am already through.
She says to me, softly: *Hier bin i'*.
I answer: *Da bist du*.

I bicycle home in my raincoat
Through the ponchos and pigtails of the streets,
Bathe, dress, go down four flights of stairs
Past Maria Theresa's sleigh
To the path to the garden, walk along the lake
And kick up, dreamily, the yellow leaves
Of the lindens; the pigeons are cooing
In the morning-glories of the gardener's house,
A dragonfly comes in from the lake.

The nymphs look down with the faces of Negroes,
Pocked, moled with moss;
The stone horse has sunk in marsh to his shoulders.

But the sun comes out, and the sky
Is for an instant the first rain-washed blue
Of becoming: and my look falls
Through falling leaves, through the statues'
Broken, encircling arms
To the lives of the withered grass,
To the drops the sun drinks up like dew.

In anguish, in expectant acceptance
The world whispers: *Hier bin i'*.

An English Garden in Austria

(seen after DER ROSENKAVALIER*)*

It is as one imagined it: an English garden . . .

Mein Gott!—as all the little girls here say—
To see here the path, the first step of that first path
Our own great parents took! Today, *le Roi Soleil* shines
On his mistress's nuns' orphans' *Athalie;*
Saint-Simon, Leibnitz, and some wandering stars
Murmuring for joy together . . . and in the night
A Ruin, a Prospect, and one blasted tree
Lour on their progress; and next day where are they?

On such a path as this, a "rustic beau
[Or bear; one's doubtful, with this orchestration]
Of thirty-five" pauses to hear a man
Reciting in a big fur hat, with feeling—
And growls politely, "Metastasio?"
They whisper: "Quiet! That's J. J. Rousseau,"
And bear him off to the measures of a *Ländler.*
Helped to his coach, the Baron exits grumbling
About the "luck of all us Lerchenaus."

. . . It was not thus that you sang, Farinelli!
By graver stages, up a sterner way,
You won to those fields the candelabra lit,
Paused there; sang, as no man since has sung—
A present and apparent deity—the pure
Impossible airs of Arcady: and the calm
Horsehair-wigged shepherds, Gods of that Arcadian
Academy, wept inextinguishable tears.

Such power has music; and the repeated spell
Once a day, at evening, opened the dull heart
Of old mad Philip: all his courtiers wept
And the king asked, weeping: "Why have I wept?"
And Farinelli sang on; Ferdinand
Buried his father, ruled—

                              and heard, paused, heard again:
The years went on, men withered, Farinelli sang.

You are silent now: you, Faustina Hasse,
Her husband Johann Adolf, the Abate
Metastasio . . . very silent.
They float past; seem to whisper, to the oat
Of a shepherd wintering very far from Weimar:
"We also have dwelt in Arcady."
                              —So Death.

The shades of your Grotto have encompassed me.
How can I make out, among these ruins, your Ruin?
You went for this pleasing terror to the past
And built it here, an image of the Possible:
Well ruined, Ruin! . . .
                              But I come late.

In those years Europe lived beneath the lightning
Of the smile of that certain, all too certain spirit
Whom Almighty God—

                              whom *le bon Dieu* sent for a rod
To these Philistines; he held out sixty years,
Gentling savage Europe with his Alexandrines,
Submitted, went up to Switzerland, and perished.
One spends one's life with fools, and dies among watches.
But see him in flower, in a Prussian garden.
He walks all summer, yawning, in the shade
Of an avenue of grenadiers; and a Great Person
In a tie-wig walks with this monkey, tags his verses,
And—glancing sideways, with suspicion—speaks of *Götz*

Von Berlichingen mit der eisernen Hand.
Said Frederick: "Here's the hand, but where's the glove?"
Or words to that effect; and next year jailed him
For having gone off with his (Pharaoh's) flute
In a sack of corn upon a baggage-camel.
Or words to that effect . . . Then all the world
Shifts to another gear: Count Almaviva and his valet
Shake hands, cry *Citoyen!* are coffined by a sad
Danton; assisting, Anacharsis Clootz—
To the Masons' Funeral Music of their maker.
And one might have seen, presiding among drummers,
An actress named *Raison* (*née* Diderot).
Meanwhile Susanna and the Countess sigh
For someone not yet on the scene; their man of tears
Retires, is rouged as Destiny: Rousseau
Comes in as Cain, upon a charger . . . Instead of his baton
This corporal carries *Werther* in his knapsack.
He reads it seven times, and finds no fault
Except with Werther: he was too ambitious.
The soldier nods—these buzzing Mamelukes
Have made him drowsy; shadows darken all the East
And over his feeling shoulder, as he sleeps,
Die Weltgeschichte peeps down upon his Sorrows.
(He wakes, smiles sleepily, and tweaks its ear.)
At Jena he shows his gratitude, says: "Here's a man!"
(What were the others? . . .
                Dead men. He'd killed them every one.)
A vulgar demon, but our own: he still prepares us
"Plays worthy of the savages of Canada"—
Up from the floorboards soars the infernal
Everything that is deserves to perish,
And actors, author, audience die applauding.
Then he whispers, winking: "Politics is Destiny!"
And some *Spiessbürger,* some *aquarelliste,*
Some *Spielverderber* from a Georgian seminary
Echo him—higher, higher: *"Es muss sein!"*

"Others have understood the world; we change it."
"Truth is what works." "I have seen the Future and it works."

No Lerchenau was e'er a spoilsport,
A ghost sings; and the ghosts sing wonderingly:
Ist halt vorbei! . . . *Ist halt vorbei!* . . .

Then there is silence; a soft floating sigh.
Heut' oder morgen kommt der Tag,
And how shall we bear it?
                              Lightly, lightly.

The stars go down into the West; a ghostly air
Troubles the dead city of the earth.

. . . It is as one imagined it: an English garden.

A Soul

It is evening. One bat dances
Alone, where there were swallows.
The waterlilies are shadowed
With cattails, the cattails with willows.

The moon sets; after a little
The reeds sigh from the shore.
Then silence. There is a whisper,
"Thou art here once more."

In the castle someone is singing.
"Thou art warm and dry as the sun."
You whisper, and laugh with joy.
"Yes, here is one,

"Here is the other . . . *Legs* . . .
And they move so?"
I stroke the scales of your breast, and answer:
"Yes, as you know."

But you murmur, "How many years
Thou hast wandered there above!
Many times I had thought thee lost
Forever, my poor love.

"How many years, how many years
Thou hast wandered in air, thin air!
Many times I had thought thee lost,
My poor soul, forever."

A Rhapsody on Irish Themes

At six in the morning you scratched at my porthole,
Great-grandmother, and looked into my eyes with the eyes
Of a potato, and held out to me—only a dollar—
A handkerchief manufactured with their own hands
By the Little People; a *Post* wet from no earthly press,
Dreamed over the sinking fire
                              of a pub by a Papal Count.
Look: a kerchief of linen, embroidered cunningly
In the green of Their hearts, in Their own hand:
A SOUVENIR OF OLD IRELAND.

Then you turned into the greatest of the gulls
That brood on the seesaw green
Swells of the nest of the harbor of Cóbh.

All is green, all is small, all is—
It is not; the nuns sailing to Ireland
Disembark, and are dovetailed into the black
Nuns sailing from Ireland: a steady state,
But black. And that patch of the red of blood
On the hillside without any trees, by the topless
Tower, is a Cardinal surely? the steak
This Lady with Cromwell's sword in her suitcase
Wolfs for her lonely supper, with a sigh
Like an empire falling? And the sky is the blue
Of the fat priest's brimmed beret,
Of the figuring and clasps of his new
Accordion (that plays all night, by itself, like the sword
Of a hero, a *Mother Machree*
That'd tear your heart out entirely).

The soft, guileful, incessant speech
Plaits into the smack of the feet
In their dance on the deck, every night in the moonlight;
The smile is, almost, the smile
Of the nuns looking on in delight—
The delight of a schoolgirl at recess, a trouble to no one.
But—blue eyes, gray face—
I was troubled by you.

        The old woman, met in sleep,
Skinned herself of her wrinkles, smiled like a goddess—
Skinned herself of the smile, and said to me softly:
"There's no rest for you, grandson, till you've reached the land
Where, walking the roads with an adding-machine on your shoulder,
You meet no one who knows it."
                  Well, I hold nothing
Against you but what you are. One can almost bear
The truth in that soft shameless speech
That everything is a joke—from your Sublime
To your Ridiculous is one false step—
But one settles at birth on that step of the stair
And dislikes being shown that there's nothing there.
But I believe you: the orchestration
Of this world of man is all top or bottom,
And the rest is—
          anything that you say.
To argue longer would be un-Irish,
Unnatural grandson that I am!
                —Great-grandson.

Old sow, old Circe, *I'm* not your farrow.
Yet ah, to be eaten! There honk beside me the Tame Geese
Of the Seven Hills of the City of Dublin,
And it's Stentor I cough like, what with the smoke of peat—
Man is born to Ireland as the sparks fly upward:
A sleepwalker fallen from the edge of Europe,
A goosegirl great among publicans and censors.

—She speaks, smiling, of someone "who felt at home
In whatever was least like home, and fell in love
With the world for not being America"—

Old Sibyl!
It's your last leaf . . . Still, play it: it is so;
I'm from nowhere, I'm Nobody. But if I'm to be reminded
By any nobody—

Ireland, I've seen your cheeks
The red of dawn: the capillaries are broken.

Long ago, the sun set. These are the Western Isles.

—And, waking, I saw on the Irish Sea
Orion, his girdle a cinch, and himself a hunter,
An Irish hunter . . .

that is to say, a horse.

Great-grandmother, I've dreamed of you till I'm hoarse.
It was all a lie: I take back every word.

. . . If your shin *is* speckled,
Your grin, alas! pious—

still, what a brow-ridge!
You Eden of Paleolithic survivals,
You enclave of Brünn and of Borreby man,
Fold your child home, when—weary of Learning—
He sighs for the Night of the Spirit of Man.

. . . What have I said! Faith, I'm raving entirely:
Your taste is like lotus, you Irish air!
Get the wax out of your ears, you oarsmen,
We sail at six . . . And here's the last lesson
I learned from you, Ireland:

what it is I've forgotten.

Well, what if it's gone? Here're some verses of Goethe's—
An old upright man, a lover of Ireland—

You Senate of Ireland, to straighten the conduct
Of such of your people as need it: *In peace*
Keep tidy
Your little coops.
In war
Get along
With quartered troops.

The Memoirs of Glückel of Hameln

We are all children to the past.
Here where no knowledge is sufficient
Even the wise are satisfied with shards
That add at best into an almanac,
And two treaties and a bust afford
The worst fool an hypothesis
A bee would groan all year to check.
"Historians—bad men!—come black as miners
From History; their tongues are dry with Fact;
And ah! their faces do not shine like mine,"
One judges from the armchair of a brain
Or avoids seldom, and with careful pains.
One touch of insight makes the ages kin,
And nothing helps like ignorance to apply it.

The skull one starts at, a carving
(One swims with a flashlight to the cave)
That bulks in the poor light like a senator
Are—not history, merely data,
The discrete and uninstructed facts.
But if one learns little from them, still
One emerges, sometimes, skeptical
Of a little one has known before.

Poor Glückel, mostly I was bored:
The deals all ended in a gain or anguish
Explained and disregarded with a text;
Money and God were too immediate,
The necessities that governed every act.

One marries, one has children whom one marries;
One's husband dies; one mourns, re-marries.
The reader reads, reads, and at last, grown weary
With hearing the amount of every dowry,
He mumbles, Better to burn than marry . . .
Yet when I think of those progressive years,
Of Newton, Leibnitz, Mandeville, and Pope,
You lend a certain body to the thought;
I am perplexed with your fat tearful ghost.
I hear you in the plague: "See, see, she plays
And eats a buttered roll, as nicely as you please . . ."
One can do nothing with these memories.
They are as stubborn, almost, as our lives'.

One goes along the corridor; and, outside certain years,
One hears, if one listens hard, a small
Vivacious sound, a voice that is not stilled.
It speaks as it used to speak—speaks uselessly
As a voice can speak; and if one should enter,
The room is dark, and the dark is empty.
The voice has a hollow sound, without you. Glückel,
The one thing missing in your book is you;
But how can we miss it, we who never knew you?
But we miss it, somehow; and, somehow, we knew you.
We take your place as our place will be taken.
The butter is oily on the roll, and the child plays
As nicely as you please—as nicely as we please.

To the New World

(*For an emigrant of 1939*)

In that bad year and city of your birth
They traded bread for bank-notes weight for weight,
And nothing but the statues kept the smile
The waltzers wore once: excluding, innocent,
The face of old and comfortable injustice.
And if you wept,
Dropped red into a city where the husbandless
And fatherless were weeping too, who cared
For one more cry or one more child? You grew,

Time put words into your mouth, and you put sugar
Upon your windowsill and waited for a brother—
The stork was greedy, ate, brought nothing in return.
But your life was thinking of you, took you back to Prague,
At school there, timid, boisterous, you spoke
The unaccustomed Czech—
The children laughed at you. For you were learning
New words and a new life, the old
City and its new country too were learning
An old wish: to be just; yes, to be free.

"I saw summer in my time." Summer is ending.
The storms plunge from the tree of winter, death
Moves like an impulse over Europe. Child,
What man is just or free?—but fortunate,
Warm in time's hand, turning and trusting to his face;
And that face changes.
Time is a man for men, and He is willing

For many a new life, for others death. Already
He buys His trench-coat, falls, writes His big book;

Points here, points here: to Jews, to wicked friends—
His words are the moments of a man's life . . .
And now the men march. One morning you awoke
And found Vienna gone, your father said:
"Us next!" And you were next.
Us next!
Cried map and mouth, oppressors and oppressed,
The appeasers as they gave you—but you were gone.
"I had a speech, a city." *What is your name?*
"My name is what my name was." *You have no name.*

So the dream spoke to you: in Zurich, Paris,
In London on a lawn. The unbefriending sea
Cried to you, "Stranger!" Superb, inhospitable,
The towers of the island turned their gaze
Past the girl who looked to the great statue:
So green, so gay . . .
That is how you came. Your face shows white
Against the dark time, your words are indistinct,
One cry among so many, lost in the sound

Of degradation and of agony, the peoples dying.
The net was laid for you, and you are free.
Past the statue there is summer, and the summer smiles
The smile of justice or injustice: blind,
Comfortable, including. Here are the lives
And their old world;
Far off, inside you, a conclusive face
Watches in accusation, in acceptance. It is He.
You escaped from nothing: the westering soul
Finds Europe waiting for it over every sea.

The Märchen

Listening, listening; it is never still.
This is the forest: long ago the lives
Edged armed into its tides (the axes were its stone
Lashed with the skins of dwellers to its boughs);
We felled our islands there, at last, with iron.
The sunlight fell to them, according to our wish,
And we believed, till nightfall, in that wish;
And we believed, till nightfall, in our lives.

The bird is silent; but its cold breast stirs
Raggedly, and the gloom the moonlight bars
Is blurred with the fluff its long death strewed
In the crumpled fern; and far off something falls.
If the firs forget their breath, if the leaf that perishes
Holds, a bud, to spring; sleeps, fallen, under snow—
It is never still. The darkness quakes with blood;
From its pulse the dark eyes of the hunter glow
Green as their forest, fading images
Of the dream in the firelight: shudder of the coals
In their short Hell, vined skeleton
Of the charcoal-burner dozing in the snow.
Hänsel, to map the hard way, cast his bones
Up clouds to Paradise; His sparrows ate
And he plunged home, past peat and measures, to his kin
Furred in the sooty darkness of the cave
Where the old gods nodded. How the devil's beard
Coiled round the dreaming Hänsel, till his limbs
Grew gnarled as a fakir's on the spindling Cross

The missions rowed from Asia: eternal corpse
Of the Scapegoat, gay with His blood's watered beads,
Red wax in the new snow (strange to His warmed stare);
The wooden mother and the choir of saints, His stars;
And God and His barons, always, iron behind.
Gorged Hänsel felt His blood burn thin as air
In a belly swollen with the airy kine;
How many ages boiled Christ's bark for soup!
Giddy with emptiness, a second wife
Scolding the great-eyed children of a ghost,
He sends them, in his tale, not out to death
(Godfather Death, the reaping messenger),
Nor to the devil cringing in the gloom,
Shifting his barred hooves with a crunch like snow—
But to a king: the blind untroubled Might
Renting a destiny to men on terms—
Come, mend me and wed half of me, my son!
Behind, the headsman fondles his gnawn block.
So men have won a kingdom—there are kings;
Are giants, warlocks, the unburied dead
Invulnerable to any power—the Necessity
Men spring from, die under: the unbroken wood.

Noon, the gold sun of hens and aldermen
Inked black as India, on the green ground,
Our patterns, homely, mercenary, magnified—
Bewitching as the water of Friar Bacon's glass.
(*Our* farmer fooled the devil with a turnip,
Our tailor won a queen with seven flies;
Mouser and mousie and a tub of fat
Kept house together—and a louse, a louse
Brewed small beer in an eggshell with a flea.)
But at evening the poor light, far-off, fantastic—
Sun of misers and of mermen, the last foolish gold
Of soldiers wandering through the country with a crutch—
Scattered its leagues of shadows on the plots
Where life, horned sooty lantern patched with eyes,

Hides more than it illumines, dreams the hordes
Of imps and angels, all of its own hue.
In the great world everything is just the same
Or just the opposite, we found (we never went).
The tinkers, peddlers brought their pinch of salt:
In our mouths the mill of the unresting sea
Ground till their very sores were thirsty.
Quaking below like quicksand, there is fire—
The dowser's twig dips not to water but to Hell;
And the Father, uncomfortable overseer,
Shakes from the rain-clouds Heaven's branding bolt.
Beyond, the Alps ring, avalanche on avalanche,
And the lost palmers freeze to bliss, a smile
Baring their poor teeth, blackened as the skulls
Of sanctuaries—splinters of the Cross, the Ark, the Tree
Jut from a saint's set jawbone, to put out
With one bought vision many a purging fire.
As the circles spread, the stone hopes like a child.
The weak look to the helpless for their aid—
The beasts who, ruled by their god, Death,
Bury the son with their enchanted thanks
For the act outside their possibility:
The victim spared, the labors sweated through, for love
Neither for mate nor litter, but for—anything.
When had it mattered whom we helped? It always paid.
When the dead man's heart broke they found written there
(He could not write): *The wish has made it so.*
Or so he wished. The platter appliquéd
With meals for parents, scraps for children, gristle
For Towser, a poor dog; the walnut jetting wine;
The broom that, fretting for a master, swept a world;
The spear that, weeping for a master, killed a child;
And gold to bury, from the deepest mines—
These neither to wisdom nor to virtue, but to Grace,
The son remembered in the will of God—
These were wishes. The glass in which I saw
Somewhere else, someone else: the field upon which sprawled

Dead, and the ruler of the dead, my twin—
Were wishes? Hänsel, by the eternal sea,
Said to the flounder for his first wish, *Let me wish
And let my wish be granted;* it was granted.
Granted, granted. . . . Poor Hänsel, once too powerless
To shelter your own children from the cold
Or quiet their bellies with the thinnest gruel,
It was not power that you lacked, but wishes.
Had you not learned—have we not learned, from tales
Neither of beasts nor kingdoms nor their Lord,
But of our own hearts, the realm of death—
Neither to rule nor die? to change, to change!

Hohensalzburg: Fantastic Variations on
a Theme of Romantic Character

I should always have known; those who sang from the river,
Those who moved to me, trembling, from the wood
Were the others: when I crushed on a finger, with a finger,
A petal of the blossom of the lime, I understood
(As I tasted, under the taste of the flower, the dark
Taste of the leaf, the flesh that has never flowered)
All the words of the wood but a final word:
Pure, yearning, unappeasable—
A word that went on forever, like the roar
The peoples of the bees made in the limes.

When they called from the rushes I heard you answer:
I am a dweller of the Earth.

The old woman who sat beside her wheel
In her cottage under the hill, and gave you tea
When the mist crept up around her, evenings,
And you came to her, slowly, out of the mist
Where you had run, all evening, by the shore
Naked, searching for your dress upon the sand—
She would say to you, each evening: "What you do will do,
But not forever . . .
                    What you want is a husband and children."
And you would answer: *They will do,*
But not forever.
                    The old woman,
The stone maid sunk in the waters of the Earth
Who murmured, "You too are fair—
Not so fair as I, but fair as I was fair—"

These said to you, softly: "You are only a child.
What would you be, if you could have your wish?
You are fair, child, as a child is fair.
How would you look, if you could have your wish?"
You answered:
                    I would be invisible.

When I woke it was still night.
I saw, as I always saw,
A castle rising above limes—
A castle that has never been taken.
I felt in the map-pocket of the skirt
Of my leather coat, but mice had eaten the bar
Of chocolate, and left me foil like tinsel.
There was moonlight.
At the path out into the wood, a deer
Stood with stars in the branches of its antlers:
An iron deer.
Then there was nothing but night.
I felt at my hand
For an instant, the wing of a swallow—
Your hand opened across my hand.

I reached to you, but you whispered: *Only look.*
I whispered: "I see only moonlight."

I am here behind the moonlight.

You are there.
I thought at first
That you were only a ghost,
A ghost asleep in a castle that is asleep.
But these German ghosts—harsh clumsy things—
Haunt no one, but only change
Men into things, things into things.
Many a chandelier
Clouded with china roses, many a swan

Floating beside its shepherd, among cresses,
Many a star
Set in the antlers of an iron deer
Was once a sleeper wandering through the wood.
Some walked through the pits of the glade to a ghost
And were changed: a ghost wants blood;
And it will do—
                              but not forever.
But I shall be with you here forever:
Past the dust of thorns, past the sleepers wound
Like worms in the terrible chains of their breath,
I shall lie in your arms forever.
If you sleep I shall sleep, if you wake I shall wake,
If you die I shall also die.

You said: *I am then not dead?*
You are only sleeping . . .
When I come to you, sprawled there asleep
At the center of all the webs, at the final
Point of the world: one drop of your blood,
I shall bend to you, slowly—
                              You are asleep.
The leaves breathe with your breath. The last, least stir
Of the air that stumbles through a fur of leaves
Says the sound of your name, over and over, over and over;
But someday—
Years off, many and many years—
I shall come to you there asleep,
I shall take you and . . .
                              Tell me.
No, no, I shall never.
                              Tell me.
You must not know.
                              Tell me.
I—I shall kiss your throat.

My throat?

There, it is only a dream.
I shall not so—I shall never so.

I saw, in your eyes beside my eyes,
A gaze pure, yearning, unappeasable:
Your lips trembled, set
For an instant in the slightest smile
I ever saw;
Your cold flesh, faint with starlight,
Wetted a little with the dew,
Had, to my tongue, the bloom of fruit—
Of the flower: the lime-tree-flower.
And under the taste of the flower
There was the taste of—

I felt in the middle of the circle
Of your mouth against my flesh
Something hard, scraping gently, over and over
Against the skin of my throat.
I woke and fell asleep and woke:
Your face above me
Glowed faintly now—something light, a life
Pulsed there. When I saw that it was my blood,
I used my last strength and, slowly,
Slowly, opened my eyes
And pushed my arms out, that the moonlight pierced and held—
I said: "I want you"; and the words were so heavy
That they hung like darkness over the world,
And you said to me, softly: *You must not so.*
I am only a girl.
Before I was a ghost I was only a girl.

I said to you, "Before I was a ghost
I was only a—
                    a ghost wants blood:
When they find me, here except for my blood,
They will search for you all night—harsh clumsy things

In their tunics and leather shorts and pigtails.
All the badges along the bands of their hats will shine. . . .
When all but one has said to you, *Gute Nacht,*
And you have answered, are almost free
To call to me there in the bonds of the moonlight,
The last will mutter cunningly, *Grüss Gott.*
Then as all my blood
Flows from your limbs into your heart—
When, at the name of God,
You can say nothing, O dweller of the Earth—
You will cry out bitterly, and they will seize you
And bind you and boil you to death—the dead also die—
There at the fountain of the square
Just under the castle, by the iron deer;
Make of you a black-pudding, deck it with schillings and thaler,
And serve it, all *herrlich,* to the Man of the castle
With a sign stuck on it:
                    To eat is *verboten.*"

Or so it went once: I have forgotten. . . .

What shall I call you, O Being of the Earth?
What I wish you to call me I shall never hear.

We shall change; we shall change; but at last, their stars,
We shall rest in the branches of the antlers
Of the iron deer.
                    But not forever:
Many a star
Has fallen, many a ghost
Has met, at the path to the wood, a ghost
That has changed at last, in love, to a ghost—
We should always have known. In this wood, on this Earth
Graves open, the dead are wandering:
In the end we wake from everything.

Except one word—

In the end one wakes from everything.
                    Except one word
Goes on, always, under the years,
A word we have never understood—
And our life, our death, and what came past our life
Are lost within that steady sound:
Pure, yearning, unappeasable,
The one spell turns above us like the stars.

And yet surely, at the last, all these are one,
We also are forever one:
A dweller of the Earth, invisible.

ONCE UPON A TIME

Moving

Some of the sky is grey and some of it is white.
The leaves have lost their heads
And are dancing round the tree in circles, dead;
The cat is in it.
A smeared, banged, tow-headed
Girl in a flowered, flour-sack print
Sniffles and holds up her last bite
Of bread and butter and brown sugar to the wind.

Butter the cat's paws
And bread the wind. We are moving.
I shall never again sing
Good morning, Dear Teacher, to my own dear teacher.
Never again
Will Augusta be the capital of Maine.
The dew has rusted the catch of the strap of my satchel
And the sun has fallen from the place where it was chained
With a blue construction-paper chain. . . .
Someone else must draw the bow
And the blunderbuss, the great gobbler
Upside-down under the stone arrow
In the black, bell-brimmed hat—

And the cattycornered bat.
The witch on the blackboard
Says: "Put the Plough into the Wagon
Before it turns into a Bear and sleeps all winter
In your play-house under the catalpa."
Never again will Orion
Fall on my speller through the star
Taped on the broken window by my cot.
My knee is ridged like corn
And the scab peels off it.

We are going to live in a new pumpkin
Under a gold star.

There is not much else.
The wind blows somewhere else.
The brass bed bobs to the van.
The broody hen
Squawks upside-down—her eggs are boiled;
The cat is dragged from the limb.
The little girl
Looks over the shoulders of the moving-men
At her own street;
And, yard by lot, it changes.
Never again.
But she feels her tea-set with her elbow
And inches closer to her mother;
Then she shuts her eyes, and sits there, and squashed red
Circles and leaves like colored chalk
Come on in her dark head
And are darkened, and float farther
And farther and farther from the stretched-out hands
That float out from her in her broody trance:
She hears her own heart and her cat's heart beating.

She holds the cat so close to her he pants.

The Sleeping Beauty: Variation of
the Prince

After the thorns I came to the first page.
He lay there gray in his fur of dust:
As I bent to open an eye, I sneezed.
But the ball looked by me, blue
As the sky it stared into . . .
And the sentry's cuirass is red with rust.

Children play inside: the dirty hand
Of the little mother, an inch from the child
That has worn out, burst, and blown away,
Uncurling to it—does not uncurl.
The bloom on the nap of their world
Is set with thousands of dawns of dew.

But at last, at the center of all the webs
Of the realm established in your blood,
I find you; and—look!—the drop of blood
Is there still, under the dust of your finger:
I force it, slowly, down from your finger
And it falls and rolls away, as it should.

And I bend to touch (just under the dust
That was roses once) the steady lips
Parted between a breath and a breath
In love, for the kiss of the hunter, Death.
Then I stretch myself beside you, lay
Between us, there in the dust, His sword.

When the world ends—it will never end—
The dust at last will fall from your eyes

In judgment, and I shall whisper:
"For hundreds of thousands of years I have slept
Beside you, here in the last long world
That you had found; that I have kept."

When they come for us—no one will ever come—
I shall stir from my long light sleep,
I shall whisper, "Wait, wait! . . . She is asleep."
I shall whisper, gazing, up to the gaze of the hunter,
Death, and close with the tips of the dust of my hand
The lids of the steady—
                              Look, He is fast asleep!

The Prince

After the door shuts, and the footsteps die,
I call out, "Mother?" No one answers.
I chafe my numb feet with my quaking hands
And hunch beneath the covers, in my curled
Red ball of darkness; but the floor creaks, someone stirs
In the other darkness—and the hairs all rise
Along my neck, I whisper: "It is he!"

I hear him breathing slowly, as he bends
Above me; and I pull my eyes
Back into me, and shrink up like the rabbit
They gave me when he—Then he waits, I wait.
I hear his fingers rasping, like five paws,
Up through the dirt, until I cannot breathe
But inch my cold hand out to his cold hand:

Nothing, nothing! I throw off the furs
And sit up shaking; but the starlight bars
A vague window, in the vacant dark
The sentry calls out something, like a song.
I start to weep because—because there are no **ghosts**;
A man dies like a rabbit, for a use.
What will they pay me, when I die, to die?

The Carnegie Library, Juvenile Division

The soot drifted from the engines to the marble
The readers climbed to: stone, and the sooty casts
(Dark absent properties confused with crates
And rest-rooms in the darkness of a basement,
And constant in their senseless line, like dates:
A past that puzzles no one, or a child)
All overlooking—as the child too overlooked—
The hills and stone and steeples of the town
Grey in the pure red of the dying sun.

Here under the waves' roof, where the seals are men;
In the rhymes' twilight, where the old cup ticks
Its gnawing lesson; where the beasts loom in the green
Firred darkness of the märchen: country the child thought life
And wished for and crept to out of his own life—
Must you still isle such, raiders from a world
That you so long ago lost heart to represent?
The child tugs the strap tight round four books
To leave the cavern. And the cut-out ornaments
In colors harsh and general as names,
The dolls' scarred furniture, too small
For anything but pity, like the child—
Surely you recognize in these the hole
That widens from the middle of a field
To that one country where the poor see gold?
The woodman dances home, rich, rich; but a shade glides
Into the bright strange sunlight of the world
He owned once; the thaler blur out like a tear,

He knocks like a stranger and a stranger speaks,
And he sees, brass on the knocker, the gnome's joyless smile.

The books too read to ashes—for one owns
Nothing, and finds that there is no exchange
For all the uses lined here, free as air,
Fleeting as air: the sad repeated spell
Of that deep string, half music and half pain—
How many have believed you worth a soul!
How many here will purchase with a world
These worlds still smoldering for the perpetual
Children who haunt this fire-sale of the centuries.
Wandering among so many lives, they too will bear
The life from which they cannot yet escape;
And learn to doubt, with our sad useless smile,
That single universe the living share—
The practice with which even the books are charred.

We learned from you so much about so many things
But never what we were; and yet you made us that.
We found in you the knowledge for a life
But not the will to use it in our lives
That were always, somehow, so different from the books'.
We learn from you to understand, but not to change.

The Blind Sheep

The Sheep is blind; a passing Owl,
A surgeon of some local skill,
Has undertaken, for a fee,
The cure. A stump, his surgery,
Is licked clean by a Cat; his tools—
A tooth, a thorn, some battered nails—
He ranges by a shred of sponge
And he is ready to begin.
Pushed forward through the gaping crowd,
"Wait," bleats the Sheep; "is all prepared?"
The Owl lists forceps, scalpel, lancet—
The old Sheep interrupts his answer;
"These lesser things may all be well;
But tell me, friend—how goes the world?"
The Owl says blankly: "You will find it
Goes as it went ere you were blinded."
"What?" cries the Sheep. "Then take your fee
But cure some other fool, not me:
To witness that enormity
I would not give a blade of grass.
I am a Sheep, and not an Ass."

The Skaters

I stood among my sheep
As silent as my staff.
Up the sea's massy floor
I saw the skaters pass.

Long as the wind, as light
I flowed upon their track
Until at evening's edge
I marked their breathless flock.

I moved among them then
Like light along its lands,
Lust wreathed their lips, and speed
Stiffened their tissue limbs.

North through the months of night
We skirred along the floes;
The million glances flecked
Upon my flickering gaze

Bent to me in the stars
Of one obsessing face—
The urgent and engrossed,
The fast and flattering glass.

How long we pled our love!
How thorough our embrace!
By post and igloo, we prolonged
The Way and splendors of our kiss

Until at man's last mark
"Here we must pause," I cried,
"To block from the eternal ice
Our shelter from this endless night."

But the iron's dazzling ring, the roar
Of the starred ice black below
Whirl our dazed and headlong strides
Through the whirling night into

The abyss where my deaf limbs forget
The cold mouth's dumb assent—
The skaters like swallows flicker
Around us in the long descent.

Jonah

As I lie here in the sun
And gaze out, a day's journey, over Nineveh,
The sailors in the dark hold cry to me:
"What meanest thou, O sleeper? Arise and call upon
Thy God; pray with us, that we perish not."

All thy billows and thy waves passed over me.
The waters compassed me, the weeds were wrapped about my head;
The earth with her bars was about me forever.
A naked worm, a man no longer,
I writhed beneath the dead:

But thou art merciful.
When my soul was dead within me I remembered thee,
From the depths I cried to thee. For thou art merciful:
Thou hast brought my life up from corruption,
O Lord my God. . . . When the king said, "Who can tell

But God may yet repent, and turn away
From his fierce anger, that we perish not?"
My heart fell; for I knew thy grace of old—
In my own country, Lord, did I not say
That thou art merciful?

Now take, Lord, I beseech thee,
My life from me; it is better that I die . . .
But I hear, "Doest thou well, then, to be angry?"
And I say nothing, and look bitterly
Across the city; a young gourd grows over me

And shades me—and I slumber, clean of grief.
I was glad of the gourd. But God prepared
A worm that gnawed the gourd; but God prepared
The east wind, the sun beat upon my head
Till I cried, "Let me die!" And God said, "Doest thou well

To be angry for the gourd?"
And I said in my anger, "I do well
To be angry, even unto death." But the Lord God
Said to me, "Thou hast had pity on the gourd"—
And I wept, to hear its dead leaves rattle—

"Which came up in a night, and perished in a night.
And should I not spare Nineveh, that city
Wherein are more than six-score thousand persons
Who cannot tell their left hand from their right;
And also much cattle?"

Song: Not There

I went to the cupboard, I opened the door,
I cried to my people, *O it's not there!*
"How long did you think it would last?" said the cook,
Said the butler, "Does anyone care?"
But where is it, where is it? O it's not there,
Not there to be saved, not there to be saved,
If I'm saved it will not be there.

I ran to a plate, to a pig, to a dish,
An old china pig, a plate, to a pear,
Said, *To find it, O, I will look anywhere,*
Said, *Anywhere, Anywhere* . . . "Look anywhere,"
Said the plate as it laughed, "yes, look anywhere;
There's as good as here, there's as good as there—
For where shall you look to be saved?"

I said to my people, the plate, to the cupboard,
The pig on its platter, the pear, the pear:
O where is my salvation?
                            "O it's not anywhere.
You break in my head like a dish," said the plate,
"A pig," said the pig, "a pear," said the pear—
Not there to be saved, go not there to be saved,
If you're saved it will not be there.

Children Selecting Books in a Library

With beasts and gods, above, the wall is bright.
The child's head, bent to the book-colored shelves,
Is slow and sidelong and food-gathering,
Moving in blind grace . . . Yet from the mural, Care,
The grey-eyed one, fishing the morning mist,
Seizes the baby hero by the hair

And whispers, in the tongue of gods and children,
Words of a doom as ecumenical as dawn
But blanched, like dawn, with dew. The children's cries
Are to men the cries of crickets, dense with warmth
—But dip a finger into Fafnir, taste it,
And all their words are plain as chance and pain.

Their tales are full of sorcerers and ogres
Because their lives are: the capricious infinite
That, like parents, no one has yet escaped
Except by luck or magic; and since strength
And wit are useless, be kind or stupid, wait
Some power's gratitude, the tide of things.

Read meanwhile . . . hunt among the shelves, as dogs do, grasses,
And find one cure for Everychild's diseases
Beginning: *Once upon a time there was*
A wolf that fed, a mouse that warned, a bear that rode
A boy. Us men, alas! wolves, mice, bears bore.
And yet wolves, mice, bears, children, gods and men

In slow perambulation up and down the shelves
Of the universe are seeking . . . who knows except themselves?

What some escape to, some escape: if we find Swann's
Way better than our own, and trudge on at the back
Of the north wind to—to—somewhere east
Of the sun, west of the moon, it is because we live

By trading another's sorrow for our own; another's
Impossibilities, still unbelieved in, for our own . . .
"I am myself still"? For a little while, forget:
The world's selves cure that short disease, myself,
And we see bending to us, dewy-eyed, the great
CHANGE, dear to all things not to themselves endeared.

THE WORLD IS EVERYTHING
THAT IS THE CASE

Sears Roebuck

"A passing cyclist winks; well, let her, let her!
If even my baked, cream blinds are alloy,
Slatted to bare me to these lambs of Satan—
My cotton nainsook union suit, my shoes
Elk-tanned, with woodsman's heels and safety toes,
Will sheathe me through the wilds of this bad world.
I write once more for a pronouncing Bible.

"But thumbing these leaves, I light upon a plasterer's hawk,
A wilderness of Women's Intimate Apparel.
A girl slides to me in ribbed flannel panties. . . .
Ah, gauds of earth! My heart catches in my throat:
Beware! the rockets poised above the world!
How even my oilskins, in the evil hour,
Blaze up around me! Ah, the fire, the fire!"

—So John Doe, Don Juan—ah, poor Honest John,
Mailing your endless orders west from Patmos!

A Utopian Journey

"In a minute the doctor will find out what is wrong
And cure me," the patients think as they wait.
They are as patient as their name, and look childishly
And religiously at the circumstances of their hope,
The nurse, the diplomas, the old magazines.

And their childishness is natural; here in this office
The natural perplexities of their existence,
The demands they can neither satisfy nor understand,
Are reduced to the child's, "I hurt," the bare
Intention of any beast: to go on being.

And they go in to the doctor at last
And go out to the hospitals, sanitoria, or graves
He prescribes—look into the masked unnoticing
Faces of their saviors, smell the sick
Sweet smell of nothing, leave, send back their checks;

But what was it? What am I?
The convalescent stitched up with black thread,
His pains withering, his uneasy head
Quieted with enemas and orange-juice, the inconclusive
Evasive silence—remembers, silently, a sweet,

Evasive, and conclusive speech . . . Goes back to his living,
Day and Night ask, *Child, have you learned anything?*
He answers, *Nothing*—walled in these live ends,
In these blind blossoming alleys of the maze
That lead, through a thousand leaves, to the beginning

Or that lead at last into—dark, leaved—a door.

Hope

The spirit killeth, but
the letter giveth life.

The week is dealt out like a hand
That children pick up card by card.
One keeps getting the same hand.
One keeps getting the same card.

But twice a day—except on Saturday—
But every day—except on Sunday—
The wheel stops, there is a crack in Time:
With a hiss of soles, a rattle of tin,
My own gray Daemon pauses on the stair,
My own bald Fortune lifts me by the hair.

> *Woe's me! woe's me! In Folly's mailbox*
> *Still laughs the postcard, Hope:*
> *Your uncle in Australia*
> *Has died and you are Pope.*
> *For many a soul has entertained*
> *A Mailman unawares—*
> *And as you cry, Impossible,*
> *A step is on the stairs.*

One keeps getting the same dream
Delayed, marked *Postage Due,*
The bill that one has paid
Delayed, marked *Payment Due—*

Twice a day, in a rotting mailbox,
The white grubs are new:
And Faith, once more, is mine
Faithfully, but Charity
Writes hopefully about a new
Asylum—but Hope is as good as new.

Woe's me! woe's me! In Folly's mailbox
Still laughs the postcard, Hope:
Your uncle in Australia
Has died and you are Pope.
For many a soul has entertained
A Mailman unawares—
And as you cry, Impossible,
A step is on the stairs.

90 North

At home, in my flannel gown, like a bear to its floe,
I clambered to bed; up the globe's impossible sides
I sailed all night—till at last, with my black beard,
My furs and my dogs, I stood at the northern pole.

There in the childish night my companions lay frozen,
The stiff furs knocked at my starveling throat,
And I gave my great sigh: the flakes came huddling,
Were they really my end? In the darkness I turned to my rest.

—Here, the flag snaps in the glare and silence
Of the unbroken ice. I stand here,
The dogs bark, my beard is black, and I stare
At the North Pole . . .
                              And now what? Why, go back.

Turn as I please, my step is to the south.
The world—my world spins on this final point
Of cold and wretchedness: all lines, all winds
End in this whirlpool I at last discover.

And it is meaningless. In the child's bed
After the night's voyage, in that warm world
Where people work and suffer for the end
That crowns the pain—in that Cloud-Cuckoo-Land

I reached my North and it had meaning.
Here at the actual pole of my existence,
Where all that I have done is meaningless,
Where I die or live by accident alone—

Where, living or dying, I am still alone;
Here where North, the night, the berg of death
Crowd me out of the ignorant darkness,
I see at last that all the knowledge

I wrung from the darkness—that the darkness flung me—
Is worthless as ignorance: nothing comes from nothing,
The darkness from the darkness. Pain comes from the darkness
And we call it wisdom. It is pain.

The Snow-Leopard

His pads furring the scarp's rime,
Weightless in greys and ecru, gliding
Invisibly, incuriously
As the crystals of the cirri wandering
A mile below his absent eyes,
The leopard gazes at the caravan.
The yaks groaning with tea, the burlaps
Lapping and lapping each stunned universe
That gasps like a kettle for its thinning life
Are pools in the interminable abyss
That ranges up through ice, through air, to night.
Raiders of the unminding element,
The last cold capillaries of their kind,
They move so slowly they are motionless
To any eye less stubborn than a man's. . . .
From the implacable jumble of the blocks
The grains dance icily, a scouring plume,
Into the breath, sustaining, unsustainable,
They trade to that last stillness for their death.
They sense with misunderstanding horror, with desire,
Behind the world their blood sets up in mist
The brute and geometrical necessity:
The leopard waving with a grating purr
His six-foot tail; the leopard, who looks sleepily—
Cold, fugitive, secure—at all that he knows,
At all that he is: the heart of heartlessness.

The Boyg, Peer Gynt, the One Only One

"Well, I have had a happy life," said Hazlitt;
Swift's eye was as big as an egg.
What did the Moor say? I forget.
The servant who killed Greville cried.
They all died well: that is, they died.

How can one learn all this from Works?
It wasn't Gulliver the keeper beat;
The informer was impressed with Marx,
Not *Capital*. On the picnics
Those Sundays, no one mentioned politics.

They lived, they died. "I am what I am,"
Someone heard Swift stammer: he was crazy.
Beethoven, dying, learned to multiply.
What does it mean? Why, nothing.
Nothing? . . . How well we all die!

Money

I sit here eating milk-toast in my lap-robe—
They've got my nightshirt starchier than I told 'em . . . Huh! . . .
I'll tell 'em. . . .
                    Why, I wouldn't have given
A wooden nickel to a wooden Indian, when I began.
I never gave a soul a cent that I could help
That I remember: now I sit here hatching checks
For any mortal cause that writes in asking,
And look or don't look—I've been used to 'em too long—
At seven Corots and the Gobelins
And my first Rembrandt I outbid Clay Frick for:
A dirty Rembrandt bought with dirty money—
But nowadays we've all been to the cleaners'.
(Harriet'd call Miss Tarbell Old Tarbaby—
It none of it will stick, she'd say when I got mad;
And she was right. She always was.)
I used to say I'd made my start in railroads
—"Stocks, that is," I'd think and never say—
And made my finish in philanthropy:
To think that all along it'uz Service!
I could have kicked myself right in the face
To think I didn't think of that myself. . . .
"There isn't one of you that couldn't have done what I did—"
That was *my* line; and I'd think: "if you'd been me."
SEES U.S. LAND OF OPPORTUNITY,
A second-page two-column headline,
Was all I got, most years.

                    They never knew a thing!

Why, when I think of what I've done, I can't believe it!

. . . A Presbyterian'd say it's Providence.
In my time I've bought the whole Rhode Island Legislature
For—I disremember how much; what for too. . . .
Harriet'd have Nellie Melba in
To entertain our friends—it never entertained *me* none—
And I'd think: "Birdie, I could buy you
The way you'd buy a piece of Melba toast."
I had my troubles—nothing money wouldn't cure.
A percentage of the world resented me
There on my money bags in my silk hat.
(To hear Ward I'd still straw stuck in my fur.)
But in the end the money reconciled 'em all.
Don't someone call it the Great Reconciler?
When my boys dynamited thirteen trestles
On the New York Central, I went against my custom then
And told the papers: "Money's a *responsibility*."

I'd talk down money if I hadn't any. As it was,
The whole office force could hear me through two doors.
E. J. said they said: "Listen to the Old Man go!"

Why, it was money
That got me shut of my poor trusting wife,
And bought my girl from her, and got me Harriet—
What else would Harriet've married *me* for? . . . She's gone now
And they're gone too, but it's not gone. . . .
You can take it with you anywhere *I*'m going.

. . . While I was looking up my second son-in-law
In Dun and Bradstreet, the social secretary
Came on him in the *Almanach de Gotha*.
It was like I figured, though: he didn't take.

You couldn't tell my grandson from a Frenchman.

And Senators! . . .

     I never saw the man I couldn't buy.

When my Ma died I boarded with a farmer
In the next county; I used to think of her,
And I looked round me, as I could,
And I saw what it added up to: money.
Now I'm dying—I can't call this living—
I haven't any cause to change my mind.
They say that money isn't everything: it isn't;
Money don't help you none when you are sighing
For something else in this wide world to buy. . . .
The first time I couldn't think of anything
I didn't have, it shook me.

     But giving does as well.

The Emancipators

When you ground the lenses and the moons swam free
From that great wanderer; when the apple shone
Like a sea-shell through your prism, voyager;
When, dancing in pure flame, the Roman mercy,
Your doctrines blew like ashes from your bones;

Did you think, for an instant, past the numerals
Jellied in Latin like bacteria in broth,
Snatched for by holy Europe like a sign?
Past sombre tables inched out with the lives
Forgotten or clapped for by the wigged Societies?

You guessed this? The earth's face altering with iron,
The smoke ranged like a wall against the day?
—The equations metamorphose into use: the free
Drag their slight bones from tenements to vote
To die with their children in your factories.

Man is born in chains, and everywhere we see him dead.
On your earth they sell nothing but our lives.
You knew that what you died for was our deaths?
You learned, those years, that what men wish is Trade?
It was you who understood; it is we who change.

Variations

I

"I lived with Mr. Punch, they said my name was Judy,
I beat him with my rolling-pin, he hit me with his cane.
I ran off with a soldier, he followed in a carriage,
And he drew a big revolver and he shot me through the brain.
But that was his duty, he only did his duty—"

Said Judy, said the Judy, said poor Judy to the string.

"O hear her, just hear her!" the string said softly.
And the string and Judy, they said no more.
Yes, string or Judy, it said no more.
But they hanged Mr. Punch with a six-inch rope,
And "Clap," said the manager; "the play is over."

II

"I lay like a swan upon the down of Heaven.
When the clouds came the rain grew
Into the rice of my palaces, the great wits
Were the zithers of my garden, I stood among sedge
And held to the peoples the gold staff of God."

Said Grace, said Good, O said the son of God.

The wives and wise, the summer's willows
Nodded and were fed by the wind; when the snow fell

And the wind's steps were pink in the pure winter,
Who spared his charcoal for the son of God,
The vain wind failing at the pass to Hell?

III

"I lived in a room full of bears and porridge,
My mother was dead and my nurse was horrid.
I sat all day on a white china chamber
And I lay all night in my trundle bed.
And she wasn't, she wasn't, O not a bit dead!"

The boy said, the girl said—and Nurse she said:

"I'll stew your ears all day, little hare,
Just as God ate your mother, for you are bad,
Are bad, are bad—" and the nurse is the night
To wake to, to die in: and the day I live,
The world and its life are her dream.

IV

"I was born in a hut, my wit is heavy.
My sister died, they killed my father.
There is no time I was not hungry.
They used me, I am dying.
I stand here among graves."

The white, the yellow, the black man said.

And the world said: Child, you will not be missed.
You are cheaper than a wrench, your back is a road;
Your death is a table in a book.
You had our wit, our heart was sealed to you:
Man is the judgment of the world.

Le Poète Contumace

(*Tristan Corbière*)

On the coast of ARMORICA. A monastery.
The winds complained, inside: *Another windmill;*
    All the donkeys of the county
Came to grate their teeth off in the seedy ivy
Of a wall so holey that no living man
        Had ever come in through the doorway.

Alone—but still on its own feet, full of poise,
Corrugated as the jaw of an old woman,
Its roof knocked onto the corner of its ear,
Gaping like a ninny, the tower stood there

As vain as ever: it had its memories. . . .
It wasn't anything but a nest of black sheep,
Lovers from the bush, a rat down on his luck,
Stray dogs, benighted hobos—smugglers and customs-inspectors.

One year, the tenant of this low tower
Was a wild poet with a ball in his wing
Fallen among owls: the venerable owls
Who, from some height, considered him.—He respected their holes—
He, the only paying owl, as his lease stated:
Twenty-five écus a year: door to be replaced.

As for the people of the place, he didn't see them:
Only, passing by, they looked from below,
    Turning their noses up at his window;
The priest guessed that he was a leper;

And the mayor answered: "What can *I* do?
    He's more likely an Englishman . . . some such creature."

The women learned—no doubt from the buzzards—
That he *lived in concubinage with the Muses!* . . .
In short, a heretic . . . Some Parisian
From Paris or some such place?—Alas, nobody knew a thing.
He was invisible; and as *his Wenches*
Didn't advertise themselves, nobody said a word.

As for him, he was simply an idler, tall, thin, pale;
An amateur hermit, chased in by a squall. . . .
The far green fields—the feverish ones—he'd loved too well.
Given up by process-servers, by physicians,
He had lit here, fed up, looking for a spot
To die by himself or to live by default. . . .

    Making, from something almost like an artist,
    Something almost like a philosopher;
    Rain or shine, always complaining;
    Off any human track.

There remained to him a hammock, a hurdy-gurdy,
A spaniel who slept under the name of Fido.
No less faithful, sad and sweet as she,
Was another companion: he called it Ennui.

Dying in his sleep, he lived in dreams.
His dreams were the tide that rose on the shore,
    The tide that fell.
Sometimes, vaguely, he took up waiting. . . .
Waiting for what . . . the tide to rise—the tide to fall—
    Someone . . . Who knows?

He knows! . . . Floating in the wind of his watch-tower,
Has he forgotten how quick are the dead?
He? Which *he?* the stray ghost? the dilapidated
Body searching for its own ill-buried spirit?

Surely, She isn't far—She for whom you bellow,
O Stag of St. Hubert! Ah, sad flameless forehead. . . .
Poor old sport, have they dug you up without a permit?
Play dead if you can . . . For She has wept for you!

—But could he, He? Wasn't he a poet . . .
Immortal as any other? . . . And inside his poor head,
His moved-out-of head, he still could feel them,
The hexameters marching their cater-cornered rounds.

For want of knowing how to live, he kept alive—
For want of knowing how to die, he wrote:

"Dear, this is someone dead for so many ages
In that poet's heart of yours, he's already a myth.
I rhyme, therefore I am . . . but don't be afraid, it's *blank*
—The shell of an oyster torn from its bed!
I've pinched myself all over: it's me. Last mistake
En route to Heaven—for my niche is high as that!—
I asked myself, all ready to take wing:
Heads or tails . . . —And here I am, still asking. . . .

"It was to you I said, *Good-bye to life.*
How you wept! I watched you crying for me
Till it made me want to stay and help you cry.
But it's over now: I'm just a doting ghost,
Some bones and (I was going to say *flesh*). There's no mistake.
It's me all right, here I am—but like an erasure.

"We were connoisseurs of all the curiosities:
Notice this *objet d'art.*—I'm sick of it.—
In my distastes especially, I had good taste.
You know, I have let go of Life with gloves.
The Other one wouldn't touch with tweezers. . . .
I'm looking for *something different* for this—window-dummy.

"Come back to me: Your eyes in these eyes here! Your lips
Upon these lips! . . . Feel how hot my face is—here: that's You,

It's You I'm sick with . . . Remember?—those nights that could
  have burned
The rainbow out of heaven—

                          what's become of it? It's charcoal.
And that star? . . . It's no use looking for the star
    You tried to see upon my brow.
    A spider has set its web
    At the same spot—on the ceiling.

"I am a stranger.—Perhaps it's better so.
Isn't it? . . . No, come back and notice me a little.
You always doubted, Thomas: I want to see your faith,
I want to see you touch the wound and whisper:—You!—

"Come finish me off again—it's quite amusing:
You'll see my harvests from your bedroom . . . it's December;
My great fir-forests, the golden flowers of broom,
My heather of Armorica . . . piled on the andirons.
Come gorge yourself on fresh air. Here there's a breeze
So crisp! . . . the ends of my roof curl.
The sun's so mild . . . it freezes all the time.
The spring . . . —Spring, isn't it your twenty years?
It's you I'm waiting for: look, already a swallow
. . . Nailed to my turret, a rusty swallow.
Soon we can go gathering mushrooms. . . .
On my staircase, gilded . . . by a candle-end.
On the greening wall a dried-up periwinkle
Exists. . . . Then we'll take the waters, lie there drying
On the sand-dunes with the other driftwood.
The sea coos its *Lullaby for Castaways;*
A barcarole at dusk . . . for the wild ducks.

"Like *Paul* and *Virginia*—virginal, if you wish—
We'll graze on the grass of our lost paradise. . . .
Or *Robinson* with *Friday*—why, it's easy:
The rain has made an island of my kingdom.

"But if, near me, you're afraid of being lonely,
We've friends, plain honest ones—a poacher;
Not to count that blue cloak that habitually
Paces its rounds and holds a customs-inspector. . . .
No more process-servers! I've got moonlight,
I've got friends—all poor broke lovesick fools.

—"And our nights! *Whispering I know not what of wild and sweet,*
Nights for a Romeo!—Day will never break.—
Aurora awak'ning, burst from the bonds of sleep,
Dropping her white sheet . . . stops up my chimney.
Look, my nightingales! . . . nightingales of the tornado,
Gay as larks, wailing like screech-owls!
My weathercock, way up there, rubs the rust off his yodel,
And you can hear my Aeolian door lamenting
As did Saint Anthony in his temptation . . .
Come, pretty limb of Sata—of seduction!

"Hoy! the rats in the garret are dancing farandoles!
The roof's slates rattle down like castanets!
The witches in my belfry—
                                        No, I've not one witch!

"Ah, but wouldn't I retail my skin to Satan
If he'd only tempt me with a little ghost—
You. I see you everywhere, but white as a seer
I worship you . . . And that's pitiful: to worship what one loves!
Appear, a dagger in thy heart!—That's it,
You know, like *Inés de La Sierra.* . . .
A knock . . . Someone's there! . . .
                                        Alas! it's a rat.

"I daydream . . . and it's always you. On everything
Your memory perches, like a mocking spirit:
My loneliness . . . —*You!*—My owls with golden eyes:
—*You!*—My crazy weathercock: oh, *You!*—Any more?—
—*You!* my shutters flinging their arms out to the storm. . . .

A far-off voice: Your song!—this is ecstasy!
The squalls that beat at Your lost name—this is crazy . . .
Crazy, but it's You! My heart, wide open
 As my own disordered shutters,
 Beats in senseless circles, to the breath
 Of the most fantastic gusts.

"Wait . . . a ready shadow, for an instant, came
To trace your profile on the naked wall,
And I turned my head—to hope or to remember—
Sister Anne, Sister Anne, do you see no one coming?

"No one . . . I see—I see, in my cold chamber,
My bed padded with its push-cart satin
And my dog asleep on it—poor beast—
And I laugh . . . because it makes me a little sick.

"I've used, to summon you, my hurdy-gurdy and my lyre;
My heart's cracked jokes—the imbecile—to fool itself. . . .
Come weep, if my lines have made you laugh;
 Come laugh, if they have made you weep. . . .

"It will be comical. . . . Come play at poverty.
Back to Nature: *Come live with me and be my love.* . . .
It's raining in my hearth, it's raining in my heart:
In my late heart.
    Come! my candle's out, I've no more fire."

* * *

His lamp went out. He opened the window.
The sun was rising. He looked at his letter,
Laughed and tore it up . . . The little white pieces
Seemed, through the fog, a flight of gulls.

THE GRAVES IN THE
FOREST

La Belle au Bois Dormant

She lies, her head beneath her knees,
In their old trunk; and no one comes—
No porter, even, with a check
Or forceps for her hard delivery.
The trains pant outside; and she coils breathlessly
Inside his wish and is not waked.

She is sleeping but, alas! not beautiful.
Travelers doze around; are borne away;
And the thorns clamber up her stony veins.
She is irreparable; and yet a state
Asks for her absently, and citizens
Drown for an instant in her papery eyes.

Yet where is the hunter black enough to storm
Her opening limbs, or shudder like a fish
Into the severed maelstrom of her skull?
The blood fondles her outrageous mouth;
The lives flourish in her life, to alienate
Their provinces from her outranging smile.

What wish, what keen pain has enchanted her
To this cold period, the end of pain,
Wishes, enchantment: this suspending sleep?
She waits here to be waked—as he has waited
For her to wake, for her to wake—
Her lips set in their slack conclusive smile.

A Story

Even from the train the hill looked empty.
When I unpacked I heard my mother say:
"Remember to change your stockings every day—
Socks, I mean." I went on walking past their
Buildings gloomy with no lights or boys
Into the country where the roads were lost.

But when I woke I thought: The roads aren't lost.
That night the buildings were no longer empty
But packed and blazing with unpacking boys.
Up by the trestle I heard someone say:
"Then they haven't heard of it." I strained to hear their
Quiet funny voices, but it turned to day.

What do the students talk about all day?
Today the dean said: "There's a new boy lost."
He said it to the matron, I could hear their
Footsteps in the corridor, but it was empty.
I must tell them what I heard those people say.
When I get up I'll tell the other boys.

I liked home better, I don't like these boys.
When I wake up I think: "It's dark today."
When I go out these people hardly say
A word to me, I wrote home I had lost
My fountain pen, my mail-box is still empty
Because they've all forgotten me, they love their

New friends better—if I don't get their
Letters ever I don't care, I like these boys

Better than them, I'll write them. "We've still one room empty,"
The matron told the man who came today.
How *could* she lie like that? When the roads leave here they're lost,
The signs in the country can't think of what to say.

Someone must know. The people here all say
'I don't," I dream I ask them, and I see their
Thoughts don't either, all of them are lost.
Don't signs, don't roads know any more than boys?
When I feel better, they'll wake up one day
And find *my* bed's the one that's empty.

Loss

Bird of the spray, the tree of bones:
The tendrils shower you with dew, the smells
Of petals patter to the holes of bone—
The yellow nostrils feathered with a bar
That stripes, like blood, your ragged wings;
But the harsh, stopped sounds, the iron of your life,
Rust in the rains of autumn; and the drifts
Entomb, at last, the small nest where a skull
Flimsier than an egg, a drumstick like a straw
Lie like the crushed works of a watch: your child. . . .
When the roofs rise to you, and last year's limb
Holds a cone to your bill, and you hang hammering,
Does the down pulse still, an aching ball,
In your sleek, beaked, uncertain skull?

The Breath of Night

The moon rises. The red cubs rolling
In the ferns by the rotten oak
Stare over a marsh and a meadow
To the farm's white wisp of smoke.

A spark burns, high in heaven.
Deer thread the blossoming rows
Of the old orchard, rabbits
Hop by the well-curb. The cock crows

From the tree by the widow's walk;
Two stars, in the trees to the west,
Are snared, and an owl's soft cry
Runs like a breath through the forest.

Here too, though death is hushed, though joy
Obscures, like night, their wars,
The beings of this world are swept
By the Strife that moves the stars.

Afterwards

(*Four adaptations from Corbière's* RONDELS POUR APRÈS)

I

Sleep: here's your bed . . . You'll not come, any more, to ours.
The hungry sleep, and are fed?—Your tongue is all grass.
Sleep: oh, they love you, now—the loved one is always
The Other. Dream: the last fields are all flowers.

Sleep: they'll call you star-snatcher, bareback-rider
Of the rays! . . . though it will be dark there, very dark.
And the angel of attics, at dusk—lean spider,
Hope—comes to spin, for your vacant brow, its webs.

Veiled silencer! . . . But for you a kiss is waiting
Under the veil . . . where, no one knows; close your eyes to see.
Laugh: here under the pall, the first prize is waiting.

—They'll break your nose with a smart blow of the censer,
A fine bouquet! for the big, blooming, tallowy mug
Of a well-to-do sexton with his candle-snuffer.

II

It's getting dark, little thief of starlight!
There're no nights any longer, there're no days.
Sleep . . . till they come for you, child, some morning—
Those who said: *Never!* Those who said: *Always!*

Do you hear their steps? They are not heavy:
Oh, the light feet!—Love has wings . . .
It's getting dark, little thief of starlight!

Don't you hear them asking? . . . You're not listening.
Sleep: it's light, your load of everlastings.
They're not coming at all, your friends the bears,
To throw bricks at your bottle of fireflies.
It's getting dark, little thief of starlight!

III

Good morning! . . . Go to sleep: your candle-end
Is there where they put it; then they left you.
You're not afraid of being alone, though—
Poor little thing, are you? It's light as day.

You scared of that old maid and her ruler!
Go on! . . . Why, who's got the nerve to wake you?
Good evening! . . . Go to sleep: your candle-end . . .

Is out.—There's not even a janitor:
Only, the north wind, the south wind, will come to weigh
In their great scales, a thread of gossamer.
—*They* drive you out in the cold, those flatfeet!
Good night! . . . Go to sleep: your candle-end . . .

IV

Run away, little comet's-hair-comber!
The wild grass, in the wind, will be your hair;
From your broken eye there will gush out the
Will-o'-the-wisps, prisoners in your weak head.

The grave-flowers they call Love-in-Idleness
Will seed there, to swell your earthy laugh . . .

And Solitary's flowers, forget-me-nots.

Go, little poet: your coffin's a plaything
For the undertaker's-men, a sound-box
For your penitentiary's last siren . . .
They think you're dead—they're so dumb, these grown-ups—
Run away, little comet's-hair-comber!

The Place of Death

"The wreath is plaited wicker: the green varnish
Still traps, in its tarred pits, a race of gnats;
The flowers in the fruit-jar fail—and vanish,
Drying a stem for judgment. The outlandish
Angel fixing a grey granite Bible
With his red granite eyeballs; the red squirrel that squats
In the black walnut with a wormy nut,
Gnawing mechanically: these, the red
And white and blue woodpecker hammering
This light-pole, are enough to wake the dead—"
The living student walking with Spinoza
In his thin freckled hand, has sometimes felt,
Sinking upon a mound; the grassy airs,
The wood and meadow of their comprehension,
Have murmured to him, from the yellowing page,
That all determination is negation—
He has felt the boundaries of being fade,
These long-outmoded, mounded, dewy modes
Lapse to the seeding and inhuman Substance
Whose infinite, unchanging, and eternal thought
Is here extended in a thousand graves.
These shining bodies—vagrant as a flaw
Of the breath that, in the made, dead flower, mourns—
Involved in their essences the little existence
That survives their thought of it; in part denied
But real, and hence perfect, they hunch here,
A realm within a realm, the last contrary
Being of all used, persisting things—
Till the avenging angel sheathe his sword,

Forget that he is guardian, and dream
(His pocked head pillowed on the book of Life)
The flower and the fruit-jar Victory,
And these graves serving an eternal God
That happiness itself, and final liberty
Which (from the delta of the Alp-born Rhine)
The dead Spinoza named necessity. . . .
But the squirrel flames within the flaming wood
That soars above the poor mounds and their sigh:
"The pity that made us was not womanish";
But the gay bird hammers at the dying tree
Whose wires bring to the peoples light and death;
But the mourners gather for the dying gnat—
The dancers sparkling in their mating cloud—
And the sounds of the lens-grinder cease:
The mourners and the mourned are one. Once more
The great wind dances from the ends of Time
To breathe upon these leaves the student drops,
Napping an hour on this grassy grave.
But the angel whispers from the leafy tomb,
He is not here—see, see, he is not here;
But the leaves blow home to that inhuman kind
Who play their lives out in the place of death
And—dying, dying—from the unmourned grave
Cry to him: "Only man is miserable."

SELECTED POEMS

II

BOMBERS

Eighth Air Force

If, in an odd angle of the hutment,
A puppy laps the water from a can
Of flowers, and the drunk sergeant shaving
Whistles *O Paradiso!*—shall I say that man
Is not as men have said: a wolf to man?

The other murderers troop in yawning;
Three of them play Pitch, one sleeps, and one
Lies counting missions, lies there sweating
Till even his heart beats: One; One; One.
O murderers! . . . Still, this is how it's done:

This is a war. . . . But since these play, before they die,
Like puppies with their puppy; since, a man,
I did as these have done, but did not die—
I will content the people as I can
And give up these to them: Behold the man!

I have suffered, in a dream, because of him,
Many things; for this last saviour, man,
I have lied as I lie now. But what is lying?
Men wash their hands, in blood, as best they can:
I find no fault in this just man.

The Death of the Ball Turret Gunner

From my mother's sleep I fell into the State,
And I hunched in its belly till my wet fur froze.
Six miles from earth, loosed from its dream of life,
I woke to black flak and the nightmare fighters.
When I died they washed me out of the turret with a hose.

Losses

It was not dying: everybody died.
It was not dying: we had died before
In the routine crashes—and our fields
Called up the papers, wrote home to our folks,
And the rates rose, all because of us.
We died on the wrong page of the almanac,
Scattered on mountains fifty miles away;
Diving on haystacks, fighting with a friend,
We blazed up on the lines we never saw.
We died like aunts or pets or foreigners.
(When we left high school nothing else had died
For us to figure we had died like.)

In our new planes, with our new crews, we bombed
The ranges by the desert or the shore,
Fired at towed targets, waited for our scores—
And turned into replacements and woke up
One morning, over England, operational.
It wasn't different: but if we died
It was not an accident but a mistake
(But an easy one for anyone to make).
We read our mail and counted up our missions—
In bombers named for girls, we burned
The cities we had learned about in school—
Till our lives wore out; our bodies lay among
The people we had killed and never seen.
When we lasted long enough they gave us medals;
When we died they said, "Our casualties were low."

They said, "Here are the maps"; we burned the cities.

It was not dying—no, not ever dying;
But the night I died I dreamed that I was dead,
And the cities said to me: "Why are you dying?
We are satisfied, if you are; but why did I die?"

Transient Barracks

(1944)

Summer. Sunset. Someone is playing
The ocarina in the latrine:
You Are My Sunshine. A man shaving
Sees—past the day-room, past the night K.P.'s
Bent over a G.I. can of beets
In the yard of the mess—the red and green
Lights of a runway full of '24's.
The first night flight goes over with a roar
And disappears, a star, among mountains.

The day-room radio, switched on next door,
Says, "The thing about you is, you're *real*."
The man sees his own face, black against lather,
In the steamed, starred mirror: it is real.
And the others—the boy in underwear
Hunting for something in his barracks-bags
With a money-belt around his middle—
The voice from the doorway: "Where's the C.Q.?"
"Who wants to know?" "He's gone to the movies."
"Tell him Red wants him to sign his clearance"—
These are. Are what? Are.
                    "Jesus Christ, what a field!"
A gunner without a pass keeps saying
To a gunner without a pass. The man
Puts down his razor, leans to the window,
And looks out into the pattern of the field,
Of light and of darkness. His throat tightens,
His lips stretch into a blinded smile.

He thinks, *The times I've dreamed that I was back* . . .
The hairs on the back of his neck stand up straight.

He only yawns, and finishes shaving.
When the gunner asks him, "When you leaving?"
He says: "I just got in. This is my field."
And thinks: *I'm back for good. The States, the States!*
He puts out his hand to touch it—
And the thing about it is, it's *real*.

Siegfried

In the turret's great glass dome, the apparition, death,
Framed in the glass of the gunsight, a fighter's blinking wing,
Flares softly, a vacant fire. If the flak's inked blurs—
Distributed, statistical—the bombs' lost patterning
Are death, they are death under glass, a chance
For someone yesterday, someone tomorrow; and the fire
That streams from the fighter which is there, not there,
Does not warm you, has not burned them, though they die.
Under the leather and fur and wire, in the gunner's skull,
It is a dream: and he, the watcher, guiltily
Watches the him, the actor, who is innocent.
It happens as it does because it does.
It is unnecessary to understand; if you are still
In this year of our warfare, indispensable
In general, and in particular dispensable
As a cartridge, a life—it is only to enter
So many knots in a window, so many feet;
To switch on for an instant the steel that understands.
Do as they said; as they said, there is always a reason—
Though neither for you nor for the fatal
Knower of wind, speed, pressure: the unvalued facts.
(In Nature there is neither right nor left nor wrong.)

So the bombs fell: through clouds to the island,
The dragon of maps; and the island's fighters
Rose from its ruins, through blind smoke, to the flights—
And fluttered smashed from the machinery of death.
Yet inside the infallible invulnerable
Machines, the skin of steel, glass, cartridges,

Duties, responsibilities, and—surely—deaths,
There was only you; the ignorant life
That grew its weariness and loneliness and wishes
Into your whole wish: "Let it be the way it was.
Let me not matter, let nothing I do matter
To anybody, anybody. Let me be what I was."

And you are home, for good now, almost as you wished;
If you matter, it is as little, almost, as you wished.
If it has changed, still, you have had your wish
And are lucky, as you figured luck—are, truly, lucky.
If it is different, if you are different,
It is not from the lives or the cities;
The world's war, just or unjust—the world's peace, war or peace;
But from a separate war: the shell with your name
In the bursting turret, the crystals of your blood
On the splints' wrapped steel, the hours wearing
The quiet body back to its base, its missions done;
And the slow flesh failing, the terrible flesh
Sloughed off at last—and waking, your leg gone,
To the dream, the old, old dream: *it happens,*
It happens as it does, it does, it does—

But not because of you, write the knives of the surgeon,
The gauze of the theatre, the bearded and aging face
In the magic glass; if you wake and understand,
There is always the nurse, the leg, the drug—
If you understand, there is sleep, there is sleep . . .
Reading of victories and sales and nations
Under the changed maps, in the sunlit papers;
Stumbling to the toilet on one clever leg
Of leather, wire, and willow; staring
Past the lawn and the trees to nothing, to the eyes
You looked away from as they looked away: the world outside
You are released to, rehabilitated
—*What will you do now? I don't know*—
It is these. If, standing irresolute

By the whitewashed courthouse, in the leafy street,
You look at the people who look back at you, at home,
And it is different, different—you have understood
Your world at last: you have tasted your own blood.

THE CARRIERS

A Pilot from the Carrier

Strapped at the center of the blazing wheel,
His flesh ice-white against the shattered mask,
He tears at the easy clasp, his sobbing breaths
Misting the fresh blood lightening to flame,
Darkening to smoke; trapped there in pain
And fire and breathlessness, he struggles free
Into the sunlight of the upper sky—
And falls, a quiet bundle in the sky,
The miles to warmth, to air, to waking:
To the great flowering of his life, the hemisphere
That holds his dangling years. In its long slow sway
The world steadies and is almost still. . . .
He is alone; and hangs in knowledge
Slight, separate, estranged: a lonely eye
Reading a child's first scrawl, the carrier's wake—
The travelling milk-like circle of a miss
Beside the plant-like genius of the smoke
That shades, on the little deck, the little blaze
Toy-like as the glitter of the wing-guns,
Shining as the fragile sun-marked plane
That grows to him, rubbed silver tipped with flame.

Pilots, Man Your Planes

Dawn; and the jew's-harp's sawing seesaw song
Plucks at the starlight where the planes are folded
At the lee of their blank, wind-whipped, hunting road—
A road in air, the road to nowhere
Turreted and bucketed with guns, long undermined
With the thousand necessary deaths that breathe
Like fire beside a thousand men, who sleep
Hunched in the punk of Death: slow, dreaming sparks
Who burrow through the block-long, light-split gloom
Of their great hangar underground and oversea
Into the great tanks, dark forever; past the steam
Of turbines, laundries—under rockets,
Bakeries, war-heads, the steel watch-like fish,
To the hull's last plates and atmosphere:
The sea sways with the dazed, blind, groping sway
Of the raw soul drugged with sleep, the chancy life
Troubling with dreams its wars, its own earned sea
That stretches year on year, death after death,
And hemisphere on blind black hemisphere
Into the stubborn corners of its earth.

Here in the poor, bleak, guessing haze of dawn
The giant's jew's-harp screeches its two notes
Over and over, over and over; from the roar
Of the fighters waved into the blazing clouds
The lookout lifts his scrubbed tetanic stare
Into the East of light, the empty day.
But on the tubes the raiders oscillate
A mile in every nine or thirteen seconds

To the target's first premonitory bursts;
To the boy with a ball of coffee in his stomach,
Snapping the great light buckles on his groin,
Shifting his raft's hot-water-bottle weight
As he breasts the currents of the bellowing deck
And, locked at last into the bubble, Hope,
Is borne along the foaming windy road
To the air where he alone is still
Above the world's cold, absent, searching roll.

The carrier meshed in its white whirling wake,
The gray ship sparkling from the blue-black sea,
The little carrier—erupts in flak,
One hammering, hysterical, tremendous fire.
Flickering through flashes, the stained rolling clouds,
The air jarred like water tilted in a bowl,
The red wriggling tracers—colonies
Whose instant life annexes the whole sky—
Hunt out the one end they have being for,
Are metamorphosed into one pure smear
Of flame, and die
In the maniacal convulsive spin
Of the raider with a wing snapped off, the plane
Trailing its flaming kite's-tail to the wave.
A miss's near, near bloom, a hill of foam,
Is bulged skyward, crashes back; crest after crest
Patterns the ships' cat's-cradle wakes, the racing
Swells that hiss outward from a plane's quenched flame:
There is traced in the thousand meetings of the grave
Of matter and of matter, man and man,
The print of the running feet upon the waves. . . .
The Jill threads her long, blind, unbearable
Way into fire (the waves lick past her, her whole sky
Is tracer and the dirt of flak, the fire
Flung from the muzzles riddling sea and sky),
Comes on, comes on, comes on; and the fighter flames to her
Through his own flak, the hammering guns

Stitch one long line along his wing, his gear
Falls, his dive staggers as his tracer strikes,
And he breaks off and somersaults into the sea.
Under the canopy's dark strangling green,
The darkening canopy, he struggles free
To float into the choking white, to breathe—
His huge leg floating and immovable,
His goggles blackened with his own bright blood—
On the yellow raft, to see his carrier
Still firing, but itself a fire, its planes
Flung up like matches from the stern's white burst.
Now rockets arch above the deck's great blaze,
Shells break from it, trail after trail; its steel
Melts in steam into the sea, its tanks explode
In one last overwhelming sound; and silently
The ship, a flame, sinks home into the sea.
The pilot holds his striped head patiently
Up out of the dancing smother of the sea
And weeps with hatred, longing, agony—
The sea rises and settles; and the ship is gone.

The planes fly off looking for a carrier,
Destroyers curve in their long hunting arcs
Through the dead of the carrier: the dazed, vomiting,
Oil-blackened and fire-blistered, saved or dying men
Cling with cramped shaking fingers to the lines
Lowered from their old life: the pilot,
Drugged in a blanket, straining up to gulp
From the mug that scrapes like chalk against his mouth,
Knows, knows at last; he yawns the chattering yawn
Of effort and anguish, of hurt hating helplessness—
Yawns sobbingly, his head falls back, he sleeps.

The Dead Wingman

Seen on the sea, no sign; no sign, no sign
In the black firs and terraces of hills
Ragged in mist. The cone narrows, snow
Glares from the bleak walls of a crater. No.
Again the houses jerk like paper, turn,
And the surf streams by: a port of toys
Is starred with its fires and faces; but no sign.

In the level light, over the fiery shores,
The plane circles stubbornly: the eyes distending
With hatred and misery and longing, stare
Over the blackening ocean for a corpse.
The fires are guttering; the dials fall,
A long dry shudder climbs along his spine,
His fingers tremble; but his hard unchanging stare
Moves unacceptingly: *I have a friend.*

The fires are grey; no star, no sign
Winks from the breathing darkness of the carrier
Where the pilot circles for his wingman; where,
Gliding above the cities' shells, a stubborn eye
Among the embers of the nations, achingly
Tracing the circles of that worn, unchanging *No*—
The lives' long war, lost war—the pilot sleeps.

Burning the Letters

(The wife of a pilot killed in the Pacific is speaking several years after his death. She was once a Christian, a Protestant.)

Here in my head, the home that is left for you,
You have not changed; the flames rise from the sea
And the sea changes: the carrier, torn in two,
Sinks to its planes—the corpses of the carrier
Are strewn like ashes on the star-reflecting sea;
Are gathered, sewn with weights, are sunk.
The gatherers disperse.

      Here to my hands
From the sea's dark, incalculable calm,
The unchanging circle of the universe,
The letters float: the set yellowing face
Looks home to me, a child's at last,
From the cut-out paper; and the licked
Lips part in their last questioning smile.
The poor labored answers, still unanswering;
The faded questions—questioning so much,
I thought then—questioning so little;
Grew younger, younger, as my eyes grew old,
As that dreamed-out and wept-for wife,
Your last unchanging country, changed
Out of your own rejecting life—a part
Of accusation and of loss, a child's eternally—
Into my troubled separate being.

A child has her own faith, a child's.
In its savage figures—worn down, now, to death—
Men's one life issues, neither out of earth
Nor from the sea, the last dissolving sea,
But out of death: by man came death
And his Life wells from death, the death of Man.
The hunting flesh, the broken blood
Glimmer within the tombs of earth, the food
Of the lives that burrow under the hunting wings
Of the light, of the darkness: dancing, dancing,
The flames grasp flesh with their last searching grace—
Grasp as the lives have grasped: the hunted
Pull down the hunter for his unused life
Parted into the blood, the dark, veined bread
Later than all law. The child shudders, aging:
The peering savior, stooping to her clutch,
His talons cramped with his own bartered flesh,
Pales, flickers, and flares out. In the darkness—darker
With the haunting after-images of light—
The dying God, the eaten Life
Are the nightmare I awaken from to night.

(The flames dance over life. The mourning slaves
In their dark secrecy, come burying
The slave bound in another's flesh, the slave
Freed once, forever, by another's flesh:
The Light flames, flushing the passive face
With its eternal life.)
                        The lives are fed
Into the darkness of their victory;
The ships sink, forgotten; and the sea
Blazes to darkness: the unsearchable
Death of the lives lies dark upon the life
That, bought by death, the loved and tortured lives,
Stares westward, passive, to the blackening sea.
In the tables of the dead, in the unopened almanac,
The head, charred, featureless—the unknown mean—

Is thrust from the waters like a flame, is torn
From its last being with the bestial cry
Of its pure agony. O death of all my life,
Because of you, because of you, I have not died,
By your death I have lived.
                              The sea is empty.
As I am empty, stirring the charred and answered
Questions about your home, your wife, your cat
That stayed at home with me—that died at home
Gray with the years that gleam above you there
In the great green grave where you are young
And unaccepting still. Bound in your death,
I choose between myself and you, between your life
And my own life: it is finished.
                                   Here in my head
There is room for your black body in its shroud,
The dog tags welded to your breastbone, and the flame
That winds above your death and my own life
And the world of my life. The letters and the face
That stir still, sometimes, with your fiery breath—
Take them, O grave! Great grave of all my years,
The unliving universe in which all life is lost,
Make yours the memory of that accepting
And accepted life whose fragments I cast here.

PRISONERS

Stalag Luft

In the yard, by the house of boxes,
I lay in the ditch with my bow;
And the train's long mourning whistle
Wailed from the valley below
Till the sound of my rabbit gnawing
Was the grasses' tickling shadow,
And I lay dazed in my halo
Of sunlight, a napping echo.

I saw through rainbow lashes
The barred and melting gaze
Of my far-raiding captors.
(The dappled mustangs graze
By the quills of the milky leggings.)
After some feverish days
They smile, and the numbing laces
Are cut from my wrists with praise.

When I woke the rabbit was gnawing
His great, slow, ragged bites
From the wood of the wired-in hutches,
And dusk had greyed the white

Leghorns hunched on the roosts of their run.
The train mourned below
For the captives—a thinning echo. . . .
It all comes back to me now.

Jews at Haifa

The freighter, gay with rust,
Coasts to a bare wharf of the harbor.
From the funnel's shade (the arbor
Of gourds from which the prophet, without trust,
Watched his old enemies,
The beings of this earth) I scrutinize

The hundreds at the rail
Lapped in the blue blaze of this sea
Who stare till their looks fail
At the earth that they are promised; silently
See the sand-bagged machine-guns,
The red-kneed soldiers blinking in the sun.

A machine-gun away
Are men with our faces: we are torn
With the live blaze of day—
Till we feel shifting, wrenched apart, the worn
Named stones of our last knowledge:
That all men wish our death. Here on the edge

Of the graves of Europe
We believe: truly, we are not dead;
It seems to us that hope
Is possible—that even mercy is permitted
To men on this earth,
To Jews on this earth. . . . But at Cyprus, the red earth,

The huts, the trembling wire
That wreathes us, are to us familiar

As death. All night, the fires
Float their sparks up to the yellow stars;
From the steel, stilted tower
The light sweeps over us. We whisper: "Ours."

Ours; and the stones slide home.
There is no hope; "in all this world
There is no other wisdom
Than ours: we have understood the world,"
We think; but hope, in dread
Search for one doubt, and whisper: "Truly, we are not dead."

Prisoners

Within the wires of the post, unloading the cans of garbage,
The three in soiled blue denim (the white *P* on their backs
Sending its chilly *North* six yards to the turning blackened
Sights of the cradled rifle, to the eyes of the yawning guard)
Go on all day being punished, go on all month, all year
Loading, unloading; give their child's, beast's sigh—of despair,
Of endurance and of existence; look unexpectingly
At the big guard, dark in his khaki, at the dust of the blazing plain,
At the running or crawling soldiers in their soiled and shapeless green.

The prisoners, the guards, the soldiers—they are all, in their way,
   being trained.
From these moments, repeated forever, our own new world will be
   made.

O My Name It Is Sam Hall

Three prisoners—the biggest black—
   And their one guard stand
By the new bridge over the drainage ditch:
   They listen once more to the band

Whose marches crackle each day at this hour
   From the speakers of the post.
The planes drone over; the clouds of summer
   Blow by and are lost

In the air that they and the crews have conquered—
   But the prisoners still stand
Listening a little after the marches.
   Then they trudge through the sand

To the straggling grass, and the castor bushes,
   And the whitewashed rocks
That stand to them for an army and Order
   (Though their sticks and sacks

And burned slack faces and ambling walk—
   The guard's gleaming yawn—
Are as different as if the four were fighting
   A war of their own).

They graze a while for scraps; one is whistling.
   When the guard begins
Sam Hall in his slow mountain voice
   They all stop and grin.

A Camp in the Prussian Forest

I walk beside the prisoners to the road.
Load on puffed load,
Their corpses, stacked like sodden wood,
Lie barred or galled with blood

By the charred warehouse. No one comes today
In the old way
To knock the fillings from their teeth;
The dark, coned, common wreath

Is plaited for their grave—a kind of grief.
The living leaf
Clings to the planted profitable
Pine if it is able;

The boughs sigh, mile on green, calm, breathing mile,
From this dead file
The planners ruled for them. . . . One year
They sent a million here:

Here men were drunk like water, burnt like wood.
The fat of good
And evil, the breast's star of hope
Were rendered into soap.

I paint the star I sawed from yellow pine—
And plant the sign
In soil that does not yet refuse
Its usual Jews

Their first asylum. But the white, dwarfed star—
This dead white star—
Hides nothing, pays for nothing; smoke
Fouls it, a yellow joke,

The needles of the wreath are chalked with ash,
A filmy trash
Litters the black woods with the death
Of men; and one last breath

Curls from the monstrous chimney. . . . I laugh aloud
Again and again;
The star laughs from its rotting shroud
Of flesh. O star of men!

CAMPS AND FIELDS

A Lullaby

For wars his life and half a world away
The soldier sells his family and days.
He learns to fight for freedom and the State;
He sleeps with seven men within six feet.

He picks up matches and he cleans out plates;
Is lied to like a child, cursed like a beast.
They crop his head, his dog tags ring like sheep
As his stiff limbs shift wearily to sleep.

Recalled in dreams or letters, else forgot,
His life is smothered like a grave, with dirt;
And his dull torment mottles like a fly's
The lying amber of the histories.

Mail Call

The letters always just evade the hand.
One skates like a stone into a beam, falls like a bird.
Surely the past from which the letters rise
Is waiting in the future, past the graves?
The soldiers are all haunted by their lives.

Their claims upon their kind are paid in paper
That establishes a presence, like a smell.
In letters and in dreams they see the world.
They are waiting: and the years contract
To an empty hand, to one unuttered sound—

The soldier simply wishes for his name.

Absent with Official Leave

The lights are beginning to go out in the barracks.
They persist or return, as the wakeful hollow,
But only for a moment; then the windows blacken
For all the hours of the soldier's life.

It is life into which he composes his body.
He covers his ears with his pillow, and begins to drift
(Like the plumes the barracks trail into the sky)
Past the laughs, the quarrels, and the breath of others

To the ignorant countries where civilians die
Inefficiently, in their spare time, for nothing . . .
The curved roads hopping through the aimless green
Dismay him, and the cottages where people cry

For themselves and, sometimes, for the absent soldier—
Who inches through hedges where the hunters sprawl
For birds, for birds; who turns in ecstasy
Before the slow small fires the women light

His charmed limbs, all endearing from the tub.
He dozes, and the washed locks trail like flax
Down the dark face; the unaccusing eyes
That even the dream's eyes are averted from

See the wind puff down the chimney, warm the hands
White with the blossoms it pretends are snow . . .
He moans like a bear in his enchanted sleep,
And the grave mysterious beings of his years—

The causes who mourn above his agony like trees—
Are moved for their child, and bend across his limbs
The one face opening for his life, the eyes
That look without shame even into his.

And the man awakes, and sees around his life
The night that is never silent, broken with the sighs
And patient breathing of the dark companions
With whom he labors, sleeps, and dies.

A Front

Fog over the base: the beams ranging
From the five towers pull home from the night
The crews cold in fur, the bombers banging
Like lost trucks down the levels of the ice.
A glow drifts in like mist (how many tons of it?),
Bounces to a roll, turns suddenly to steel
And tires and turrets, huge in the trembling light.
The next is high, and pulls up with a wail,
Comes round again—no use. And no use for the rest
In drifting circles out along the range;
Holding no longer, changed to a kinder course,
The flights drone southward through the steady rain.
The base is closed. . . . But one voice keeps on calling,
The lowering pattern of the engines grows;
The roar gropes downward in its shaky orbit
For the lives the season quenches. Here below
They beg, order, are not heard; and hear the darker
Voice rising: *Can't you hear me? Over. Over—*
All the air quivers, and the east sky glows.

The Sick Nought

Do the wife and baby travelling to see
Your grey pajamas and sick worried face
Remind you of something, soldier? I remember
You convalescing washing plates, or mopping
The endless corridors your shoes had scuffed;
And in the crowded room you rubbed your cheek
Against your wife's thin elbow like a pony.
But you are something there are millions of.
How can I care about you much, or pick you out
From all the others other people loved
And sent away to die for them? You are a ticket
Someone bought and lost on, a stray animal:
You have lost even the right to be condemned.
I see you looking helplessly around, in histories,
Bewildered with your terrible companions, Pain
And Death and Empire: what have you understood, to die?
Were you worth, soldiers, all that people said
To be spent so willingly? Surely your one theory, to live,
Is nonsense to the practice of the centuries.
What is demanded in the trade of states
But lives, your lives?—the one commodity.

Leave

One winds through firs—their weeds are ferns
Four brown feet high—to aspens three feet wide.
Woodpeckers hammer at the pine-cones, upside-down—
The burros wander through the forest with their bells,
And the deer trample the last stalky meadow.
But the plants evolve into a rock, the precipice
Habitual, in Chinese ink, to such a scene;
Persisting in a cleft, one streaming fir
Must shelter at its root a fat philosopher
Reducing to his silence this grey upper world.

But he is missing (dead perhaps, perhaps a prisoner).
Cold, airy, silent, the half-sunken floes
Stream south from the mountain-top: the seven ranges.
Below are the fields, the dim fields—and the fighter
Turning to them with its thin spectral whine;
Below the moss tracks, rock to rock, the fall of water—
The mote dances in a Nature full of squirrels.

The Range in the Desert

Where the lizard ran to its little prey
And a man on a horse rode by in a day
They set their hangars: a continent
Taught its conscripts its unloved intent
In the scrawled fire, the singing lead—
Protocols of the quick and dead.
The wounded gunner, his missions done,
Fired absently in the range's sun;
And, chained with cartridges, the clerk
Sat sweating at his war-time work.
The cold flights bombed—again, again—
The craters of the lunar plain. . . .

All this was priceless: men were paid
For these rehearsals of the raids
That used up cities at a rate
That left the coals without a State
To call another's; till the worse
Ceded at last, without remorse,
Their conquests to their conquerors.
The equations were without two powers.

Profits and death grow marginal:
Only the mourning and the mourned recall
The wars we lose, the wars we win;
And the world is—what it has been.

The lizard's tongue licks angrily
The shattered membranes of the fly.

Second Air Force

Far off, above the plain the summer dries,
The great loops of the hangars sway like hills.
Buses and weariness and loss, the nodding soldiers
Are wire, the bare frame building, and a pass
To what was hers; her head hides his square patch
And she thinks heavily: My son is grown.
She sees a world: sand roads, tar-paper barracks,
The bubbling asphalt of the runways, sage,
The dunes rising to the interminable ranges,
The dim flights moving over clouds like clouds.
The armorers in their patched faded green,
Sweat-stiffened, banded with brass cartridges,
Walk to the line; their Fortresses, all tail,
Stand wrong and flimsy on their skinny legs,
And the crews climb to them clumsily as bears.
The head withdraws into its hatch (a boy's),
The engines rise to their blind laboring roar,
And the green, made beasts run home to air.
Now in each aspect death is pure.
(At twilight they wink over men like stars
And hour by hour, through the night, some see
The great lights floating in—from Mars, from Mars.)
How emptily the watchers see them gone.

They go, there is silence; the woman and her son
Stand in the forest of the shadows, and the light
Washes them like water. In the long-sunken city
Of evening, the sunlight stills like sleep
The faint wonder of the drowned; in the evening,

In the last dreaming light, so fresh, so old,
The soldiers pass like beasts, unquestioning,
And the watcher for an instant understands
What there is then no need to understand;
But she wakes from her knowledge, and her stare,
A shadow now, moves emptily among
The shadows learning in their shadowy fields
The empty missions.
                              Remembering,
She hears the bomber calling, *Little Friend!*
To the fighter hanging in the hostile sky,
And sees the ragged flame eat, rib by rib,
Along the metal of the wing into her heart:
The lives stream out, blossom, and float steadily
To the flames of the earth, the flames
That burn like stars above the lands of men.

She saves from the twilight that takes everything
A squadron shipping, in its last parade—
Its dogs run by it, barking at the band—
A gunner walking to his barracks, half-asleep,
Starting at something, stumbling (above, invisible,
The crews in the steady winter of the sky
Tremble in their wired fur); and feels for them
The love of life for life. The hopeful cells
Heavy with someone else's death, cold carriers
Of someone else's victory, grope past their lives
Into her own bewilderment: The years meant *this?*

But for them the bombers answer everything.

THE TRADES

The Rising Sun

The card-house over the fault
Was spilt in a dream; your mother's terraces
Of hair fell home to hide
The wooden pillow, the sleek dazzled head
That bobbed there, a five-colored cloud.
Above black pines, the last cloud-girdled peak
Was brushed on the starlight like a cone of rice.
The clear flame wavered in the brazier;
The floor, cold under the quilt,
Pressed its cramped ground into your dream.
The great carp, a kite, swam up to you
Along his line; but you were riding there,
A sun in air, the pure sky gazing down
From its six-cornered roof upon the world.
The kettle gave its hissing laugh, you bowed,
The characters of moonlight were your name
Across the bare, old order of the room,
And you awoke. In your rice-marshed, sea-margined plain
The flakes, like petals, blew from peak to peak;
The petals blew from peak to peak, like snow.

Dwarfed and potted cherry, warped
With the sea-wind, frost with moonlight: child,
The hunting ghosts throng here for love
Where water falls, a steady wish;
The *ronin* stalk by, girded with two swords—
These kill, these kill, and have not died;
You raise, as you have raised, the wooden sword—
The great two-handed sword; and your fat breast
Glows, trembling, in the patched
And patchwork armor of your school. . . .
On this stage even a wall is silk
And quakes according to a will; heads roll
From the gutted, kneeling sons by rule.

So man is pressed into obedience
Till even the eldest, unaccounting wish
Of his bull's heart, is safe by rote
From his tormentors—who are honorable
In their way: which is your way, child.

The brushed ink of clerks, the abacus
That tells another's fortune, life by life;
The rice-ball garnished with a shred of flesh
Or plum, or blossom, and thus named—
Are these the commerce of the warrior
Who bowed in blue, a child of four,
To the fathers and their father, Strife?

But War delivers all things—men from men
Into the hope of death: Deliverer,
Who whirled the child's grey ashes from the West
Into the shrine beside the rocks: O Way
That led the twitching body to the flame,
Bring to this temple of the blind, burnt dead
The mourning who awaken from your dream
Before a lacquered box, and take the last
Dry puff of smoke, in memory
Of this weak ghost.

New Georgia

Sometimes as I woke, the branches beside the stars
Were to me, as I drowsed, the bars of my cell;
The creepers lumped through my blanket, hard as a bed
In the old ward, in the time before the war—

In the days when, supperless, I moaned in sleep
With the stripes of beating, the old, hard, hampering dream
That lay like the chains on my limbs; till I woke
To a world and a year that used me, when I had learned to obey.

By the piece with the notch on the stock, by the knife from the States,
The tags' chain stirs with the wind; and I sleep
Paid, dead, and a soldier. Who fights for his own life
Loses, loses: I have killed for my world, and am free.

The Subway from New Britain
to the Bronx

Under the orchid, blooming as it bloomed
In the first black air: in the incessant
Lightning of the trains, tiled swarming tubes
Under the stone and Reason of the states;

Under the orchid flowering from the hot
Dreams of the car-cards, from the black desires
Coiled like converters in the bowels of trade
To break to sunlight in one blinding flame
Of Reason, under the shaking creepers of the isles;

Under the orchid, rank memorial,
From the armature about which crystallized
A life—its tanks, its customers, its Christ—
The rain-forest's tepid siftings leach
Its one solution: of lust, torment, punishment—
Of a man, a man.

             Here under the orchid
Of florists, Geography, and flesh,
A little water and a little dirt
Are forever urban, temperate: a West
Dead in the staring Orient of earth.

The air-fed orchid, the unquestioning
Trades of the leaf, of longing, of the isles
Sigh for you, sparrow, the same yearning sigh
Their beasts gave once, in summer, to the bars
And peoples of the Bronx, their conquerors.

1945: The Death of the Gods

In peace tomorrow, when your slack hands weigh
Upon the causes; when the ores are rust
And the oil laked under the mandates
Has puffed from the turbines; when the ash of life
Is earth that has forgotten the first human sun
Your wisdom found: O bringers of the fire,
When you have shipped our bones home from the bases
To those who think of us, not as we were
(Defiled, annihilated—the forgotten vessels
Of the wrath that formed us; of the murderous
Dull will that worked out its commandment, death
For the disobedient and for us, obedient)—
When you have seen grief wither, death forgotten,
And dread and love, the witnesses of men,
Swallowed up in victory: you who determine
Men's last obedience, yourselves determined
In the first unjudged obedience of greed
And senseless power: you eternal States
Beneath whose shadows men have found the stars
And graves of men: O warring Deities,
Tomorrow when the rockets rise like stars
And earth is blazing with a thousand suns
That set up there within your realms a realm
Whose laws are ecumenical, whose life
Exacts from men a prior obedience—
Must you learn from your makers how to die?

A Ward in the States

The ward is barred with moonlight,
  The owl hoots from the snowy park.
The wind of the rimed, bare branches
  Slips coldly into the dark

Warmed ward where the muttering soldiers
  Toss, dreaming that they still sigh
For home, for home; that the islands
  Are stretched interminably

Past their lives—past their one wish, murmured
  In the endless, breathless calm
By the grumbling surf, by the branches
  That creak from the splintered palm.

In bed at home, in the moonlight,
  Ah, one lies warm
With fever, the old sweat darkens
  Under the upflung arm

The tangled head; and the parted
  Lips chatter their old sigh,
A breath of mist in the moonlight
  That beams from the wintry sky.

The Wide Prospect

—saw The Wide Prospect, and the Asian fen—

Who could have figured, when the harnesses improved
And men pumped kobolds from the coal's young seams
There to the west, on Asia's backward cape—
The interest on that first raw capital?
The hegemony only the corpses have escaped?

When the earth turns, the serfs are eaten by the sheep;
The ploughland frees itself from men with deeds.
The old Adam sells his hours to an alderman
(Who adds them, in Arabic, in his black books);
Men learn it takes nine men to make a pin.

The star-led merchants steer with powder and with steel
Past dragonish waters, to the fabled world
Whose ignorant peoples tear the heart with stone.
Their lashed lines transport to the galleons' holds
New vegetables, tobacco, and the gold—the gold

That cracked our veins with credit, till the indices
Of old commodities were changed as Christ,
Till serf and lord were hammered into States
The lettered princes mortgaged for their lace
To lenders shrewder than Poor Richard, crude as Fate.

What traffickers, the captains! How the merchants war!
Beneath their blood and gilt swim like a shade
Black friars who survey with impartial eyes
The flames where Fathers or the heathen die,
Who bless alike the corpses and the Trade.

Here the horseman—steel, and backed with wings,
The salt sails rising from the centuries—
Holds laws: the tables flash like steel
Under the hollows of the high head, whitening
The eyes that watch unseeingly, like coins,

The deaths of the peoples. They are entered in his books;
For them he keeps, as God for Adam, work
And death and wisdom. They are money.
Their lives, enchanted to a thousand forms,
Are piled in holds for Europe; and their bones

Work out their ghostly years, despair, and die.
The mills rise from the sea . . . The mother and the son
Stare past the ponies of the pit, to wheels
Beaten from their iron breath, to shuttles
Threading their gnarled and profitable flesh like bones;

Whirled on pulleys to the knife, drayed to the shuttling tramps,
Through post or mission, the long bolts of their lives
Run out, run out: the flesh lasts to those last isles
Where in mine and compound the man-eaters die
Under the cross of their long-eaten Kin.

All die for all. And the planes rise from the years:
The years when, West or West, the cities burn,
And Europe is the colony of colonies—
When men see men once more the food of Man
And their bare lives His last commodity.

The Dead in Melanesia

Beside the crater and the tattered palm
The trades, the old trades, sigh their local psalm:
But their man-god in his outrigger,
The boars' tusks curling like a nautilus,
Fell to the schooners cruising here for niggers.
To the Nature here these deaths are fabulous;

And yet this world works, grain by grain, into the graves
Till the poor *ronin* in their tank-sealed caves
Are troubled by its alien genius
That takes uncomprehendingly the kites, the snow—
Their decomposing traces. And the conquerors
Who hid their single talent in Chicago,

Des Moines, Cheyenne, are buried with it here.
The including land, mistaking their success,
Takes the tall strangers to its heart like failures:
Each missionary, with his base and cross,
Sprawls in the blood of an untaken beachhead;
And the isles confuse him with their own black dead.

CHILDREN AND CIVILIANS

The State

When they killed my mother it made me nervous;
I thought to myself, It was *right:*
Of course she was crazy, and how she ate!
And she died, after all, in her way, for the State.
But I minded: how queer it was to stare
At one of them not sitting there.

When they drafted Sister I said all night,
"It's healthier there in the fields";
And I'd think, "Now I'm helping to win the War,"
When the neighbors came in, as they did, with my meals.
And I was, I was; but I was scared
With only one of them sitting there.

When they took my cat for the Army Corps
Of Conservation and Supply,
I thought of him there in the cold with the mice
And I cried, and I cried, and I wanted to die.
They were there, and I saw them, and that is my life.
Now there's nothing. I'm dead, and I want to die.

Come to the Stone . . .

The child saw the bombers skate like stones across the fields
As he trudged down the ways the summer strewed
With its reluctant foliage; how many giants
Rose and peered down and vanished, by the road
The ants had littered with their crumbs and dead.

"That man is white and red like my clown doll,"
He says to his mother, who has gone away.
"I didn't cry, I didn't cry."
In the sky the planes are angry like the wind.
The people are punishing the people—why?

He answers easily, his foolish eyes
Brightening at that long simile, the world.
The angels sway above his story like balloons.
A child makes everything—except his death—a child's.
Come to the stone and tell me why I died.

The Angels at Hamburg

In caves emptied of their workers, turning
From spent mines to the ruins of factories,
The soul sleeps under the hive of earth.
Freed for an hour from its deadly dreams
Of Good and Evil, from the fiery judge
Who walks like an angel through the guilty state
The world sets up within the laboring breast,
It falls past Heaven into Paradise:
Here man spins his last Eden like a worm.

Here is Knowledge, the bombs tempt fruitlessly.
In the darkness under the fiery missions
That fail, and are renewed by every season,
He is estranged from suffering, and willingly
Floats like a moon above the starving limbs
Oppressed with remembrance, tossed uncertainly
Under the angels' deadly paths—he whispers,
"My punishment is more than I can bear."
He knows neither good, nor evil, nor the angels,
Nor their message: There is no justice, man, but death.
He watches the child and the cat and the soldier dying,
Not loving, not hating their judges, who neither love nor hate;
In his heart Hamburg is no longer a city,
There is no more state.

The judges come to judge man in the night.
How bitterly they look on his desire!
Here at midnight there is no darkness,
At day no light.

The air is smoke and the earth ashes
Where he was fire;
He looks from his grave for life, and judgment
Rides over his city like a star.

Protocols

(Birkenau, Odessa; the children speak alternately.)

We went there on the train. *They had big barges that they towed,*
We stood up, there were so many I was squashed.
There was a smoke-stack, then they made me wash.
It was a factory, I think. *My mother held me up*
And I could see the ship that made the smoke.

When I was tired my mother carried me.
She said, "Don't be afraid." But I was only tired.
Where we went there is no more Odessa.
They had water in a pipe—like rain, but hot;
The water there is deeper than the world

And I was tired and fell in in my sleep
And the water drank me. That is what I think.
And I said to my mother, "Now I'm washed and dried,"
My mother hugged me, and it smelled like hay
And that is how you die. And that is how you die.

The Metamorphoses

Where I spat in the harbor the oranges were bobbing
All salted and sodden, with eyes in their rinds;
The sky was all black where the coffee was burning,
And the rust of the freighters had reddened the tide.

But soon all the chimneys were burning with contracts,
The tankers rode low in the oil-black bay,
The wharves were a maze of the crated bombers,
And they gave me a job and I worked all day.

And the orders are filled; but I float in the harbor,
All tarry and swollen, with gills in my sides,
The sky is all black where the carrier's burning,
And the blood of the transports is red on the tide.

The Truth

When I was four my father went to Scotland.
They *said* he went to Scotland.

When I woke up I think I thought that I was dreaming—
I was so little then that I thought dreams
Are in the room with you, like the cinema.
That's why you don't dream when it's still light—
They pull the shades down when it is, so you can sleep.
I thought that then, but that's not right.
Really it's in your head.

And it was light then—light at *night*.
I heard Stalky bark outside.
But really it was Mother crying—
She coughed so hard she cried.
She kept shaking Sister,
She shook her and shook her.
I thought Sister had had her nightmare.
But he wasn't barking, he had died.
There was dirt all over Sister.
It was all streaks, like mud. I cried.
She didn't, but she was older.
                                        I thought she didn't
Because she was older, I thought Stalky had just gone.
I got *everything* wrong.
I didn't get one single thing right.
It seems to me that I'd have thought
It didn't happen, like a dream,
Except that it was light. At night.

They burnt our house down, they burnt down London.
Next day my mother cried all day, and after that
She said to me when she would come to see me:
"Your father has gone away to Scotland.
He will be back after the war."

The war then was different from the war now.
The war now is *nothing*.

I used to live in London till they burnt it.
What was it like? It was just like here.
No, that's the truth.
My mother would come here, some, but she would cry.
She said to Miss Elise, "He's not himself";
She said, "Don't you love me any more at all?"
I was *my*self.
Finally she wouldn't come at all.
She never said one thing my father said, or Sister.
Sometimes she did,
Sometimes she was the same, but that was when I dreamed it.
I could tell I was dreaming, she was just the same.

That Christmas she bought me a toy dog.

I asked her what was its name, and when she didn't know
I asked her over, and when she didn't know
I said, "You're not my mother, you're not my mother.
She *hasn't* gone to Scotland, she is dead!"
And she said, "Yes, he's dead, he's dead!"
And cried and cried; she *was* my mother,
She put her arms around me and we cried.

SOLDIERS

Port of Embarkation

Freedom, farewell! Or so the soldiers say;
And all the freedoms they spent yesterday
Lure from beyond the graves, a war away.
The cropped skulls resonate the wistful lies
Of dead civilians: truth, reason, justice;
The foolish ages haunt their unaccepting eyes.

From the green gloom of the untroubled seas
Their little bones (the coral of the histories)
Foam into marches, exultation, victories:
Who will believe the blood curled like a moan
From the soaked lips, a century from home—
The slow lives sank from being like a dream?

The Lines

After the centers' naked files, the basic line
Standing outside a building in the cold
Of the late or early darkness, waiting
For meals or mail or salvage, or to wait
To form a line to form a line to form a line;
After the things have learned that they are things,
Used up as things are, pieces of the plain
Flat object-language of a child or states;
 After the lines, through trucks, through transports, to the lines
Where the things die as though they were not things—
But lie as numbers in the crosses' lines;
After the files that ebb into the rows
Of the white beds of the quiet wards, the lines
Where some are salvaged for their state, but some
Remanded, useless, to the centers' files;
After the naked things, told they are men,
Have lined once more for papers, pensions—suddenly
The lines break up, for good; and for a breath,
The longest of their lives, the men are free.

A Field Hospital

He stirs, beginning to awake.
A kind of ache
Of knowing troubles his blind warmth; he moans,
And the high hammering drone
Of the first crossing fighters shakes
His sleep to pieces, rakes
The darkness with its skidding bursts, is done.
All that he has known

Floods in upon him; but he dreads
The crooked thread
Of fire upon the darkness: "The great drake
Flutters to the icy lake—
The shotguns stammer in my head.
I lie in my own bed,"
He whispers, "dreaming"; and he thinks to wake.
The old mistake.

A cot creaks; and he hears the groan
He thinks his own—
And groans, and turns his stitched, blind, bandaged head
Up to the tent-flap, red
With dawn. A voice says, "Yes, this one";
His arm stings; then, alone,
He neither knows, remembers—but instead
Sleeps, comforted.

1914

Now it is no longer the war, but a war: our own has taken its place. The World War is only the First World War; and, truly, these are photographs not of the world, but of the first world. But for twenty years, while the wire and trenches in the mud were everybody's future, how could any of it seem old-fashioned to us?—it was our death. But when we died differently we saw that it was old.

The men who seize Princip wear little vests and sashes, skirts with under-leggings, fezzes; one tugs at his arm in a stand-up collar, peg-top trousers, and a chauffeur's cap; and he himself has hair like a rope wig, a face the camera draws out into the Mad Hatter's. The Archduke, spotted with the blood that does, indeed, look exactly like our own (the trees, too, are human), has moustaches like a Keystone Cop's. No one is laughing.

This, next week, is the war the crowds hear. The crowds in their stiff straw hats, their starched high collars—the women in shirtwaists or muslin, their hats shapeless with fruit and flowers— the crowds stand in black under the summer sun, holding their rolled-up umbrellas: does Job fear God for naught? It is a universe where even the Accuser is troubled, and Time hesitates: Surely these States are eternal? Troops march through the crowds; some in blue swallow-tailed coats, their bayonets high as hop-poles; some in grey. One of these, his pockets bulging, wears a round cap like an old joke; he is smoking a cigar, and breaks ranks to take the bouquet of a middle-aged woman, who holds the flowers out with her left hand and bows her head so that her face is hidden. Next page an old woman walking along a road, leading a white horse—he is pulling off her home, in a wooden cart half again as high as she—bows her head exactly as far. These are the poor, whom we have with us: in their shoulders there is neither grief nor joy, something more passive than acceptance.

The wet sand is torn by feet, the grass blows by the marsh's edge; here, lost in the flat land, seven soldiers are waiting. They lie looking into the horizon, around the machine-gun they have brought here on a cart; to the cart a dog is harnessed—a spotted medium-sized dog, who stares backward and upward into the eyes of man. *Unorganized Innocence: an impossibility,* said Blake; but this was possible; and it vanishes, leaving only this print, beneath the wave that goose-steps into Brussels. Under the spiked enameled helmets, behind moustaches issued with the cheap field-grey, the faces know better than their game; but their officer, wood in his saddle, holds his sabre out like Ney, and stares forward and downward into the camera's lens.

Now the forts of Antwerp, broken into blocks, slide into a moat as bergs break off into the sea; the blocks, metamorphosed into the dead, sprawl naked as grave-mounds in the stalky fields; black crowds, their faces fiery with evening, stumble through the typed bodies nailed in rows outside a postoffice; the innocent armies, marching over the meadows to three haystacks, a mill-dam, and a hedge, dig a trench for their dead and vanish there. Over them the machine-guns hammer, like presses, the speeches into a common tongue: the object-language of the Old Man of Laputa; here is the fetishism of one commodity, all the values translated into a piece of meat. A wire-coiled Uhlan, pressing to his lips a handkerchief dampened with chlorine, looks timidly into the great blaze of the flame-thrower his supply-sergeant hands to him; the sergeant takes away the haystacks, one by one, the hedge, the mill-dam, and puts in their place the craters of the moon. The winter comes now, flake by flake; the snowflakes or soldiers (it is impossible to distinguish—under the microscope each one is individual) are numbered by accountants, who trace with their fingers, in black trenches filled with the dancing snow, the unlikely figures of the dead. The fingers, wooden with cold, work slowly and at last are still; the last figures, whitening, whitening, vanish into their shining ground . . .

But before, somewhere else, there is a soldier. He is half-sitting, half-lying against what seems a hillside; but at the bottom, under the grass and weeds and dirt, there are sandbags. He is dressed all in grey—even his boots are grey, and merge imperceptibly into his trousers, just as his coat and hat merge imperceptibly into his face—grey with wrinkles and spots and ragged holes: he has become grey as a snowman is white. He has pushed his grey hand between his grey knees (drawn up a little) as if it were cold; but his dark brown hand is folded under his head, as if he were leaning on it patiently or thoughtfully. Part of his face is dark brown, and the rest has trickles of dark brown like contours on its grey; his nose is the white bill of a goose.

He has been dead for months—that is to say for minutes, for a century; if because of his death his armies have conquered the world, and have brought to its peoples food, justice, and art, it has been a good bargain for all of them but him. Underneath his picture there is written, about his life, his death, or his war: *Es war ein Traum.*

It is the dream from which no one wakes.

Gunner

Did they send me away from my cat and my wife
To a doctor who poked me and counted my teeth,
To a line on a plain, to a stove in a tent?
Did I nod in the flies of the schools?

And the fighters rolled into the tracer like rabbits,
The blood froze over my splints like a scab—
Did I snore, all still and grey in the turret,
Till the palms rose out of the sea with my death?

And the world ends here, in the sand of a grave,
All my wars over? . . . It was easy as that!
Has my wife a pension of so many mice?
Did the medals go home to my cat?

Good-bye, Wendover; Good-bye, Mountain Home

(*Wendover, Mountain Home, Lowrie, Kearns, Laredo:
Second Air Force fields. Men going to Overseas Replacement Depots like Kearns were called ORD's.*)

Wives on day-coaches traveling with a baby
From one room outside Lowrie to a room near Kearns.
Husbands firing into sagebrush near Wendover,
Mesquite outside Laredo: you're on Shipping. Kearns.

    Or if it isn't Kearns, it might as well be Kearns.
    (I asked the first sergeant up at Operations.
    The Wac at Transportation says you're ORD.)
    The orders are cut. I tell you you're on Shipping
    And you might as well get used to it, you ORD's.

Wives on day-coaches crying, talking to sailors,
Going home, going somewhere from a room near Kearns.
Husbands getting shots for cholera, yellow fever,
And shipping in the morning on a train from Kearns.

    Or if it wasn't Kearns, it might as well be Kearns.
    (I asked, but they've forgotten. Up at History
    There're no wives, no day-coaches, and no ORD.)
    The book is finished. I tell you you're not in it
    And you might as well get used to it, you ORD's.

The Survivor among Graves

There are fields beyond. The world there obeys
The living Word; names, numbers do for this.
The grave's cross, the grave's grass, the grave's polished granite
THESE DIED THAT WE MIGHT LIVE

                        —that I may live!—

Are customary, but not necessary;
This world needs only the dead.

                    That all-replacing dream
Through which our dark lives led in waiting—
The dream I woke to, that holds you sleepers still—
What is it now, The War? A war now, numbered
As your lives and graves are numbered; that one can lose,
That we have lost.

            Lost too, the overmastering
Demand that delivered us from all demands
Except its metal *Live!*—that left bare life
The sense life made, stripping from all there is
Its old, own sense: till simply to restore
One—to sit reading the papers on a Sunday morning—
Was enough, an end beyond all ends, the dream
Dreams dream of . . . until this, at last restored,
Was an end no longer, and the senselessness
Our lives had reached from came to seem the sense
We had reached to; and we saw that we had lived
For some few years longer than the rest within
The future where, the child says, *we shall live.*

Where shall we live? For your lives are not lived
But, there in mid-air, cease, and do not fall
And are what is not, but that could have been.
And ours are—what they are; and, slowly, end.

Our lives have made their peace with the existence
That has leached from their old essences, in time,
All that is not itself. What we remember
You are: a waiting.
                         Without you, all you dead,
What rag could wipe this scrawled slate clean of life,
What haunted body guess for me the world   .
Of which this earth, this life, are one spoiled seed?

We endure to fulfillment; it is victory
The living lose. And loss? The living lose
All things alike; and, recompensed, in the survival
That brings them, daily, that indifference, death,
Ride in the triumph of the world in chains—
Their world, their triumph.
                         We sleep lightly; waking,
Some still success, succession, weighs us down,
Enchanting our limbs to yours . . . our veins averted
Into another world, our vacant hope
Long since fulfilled, our last necessity
Remembered sometimes (with the accustomed smile
Of cold acceptance) as the luxury our youth
Demanded ignorantly.
                         Your ignorance
Is immortal in your deaths, a spring
Of blood to which the living come, to bend
In dry half-dreaming supplication . . .

The haunters and the haunted, among graves,
Mirror each other sightlessly; in soundless
Supplication, a last unheard
Unison, reach to each other: *Say again,*
Say the voices, *say again*
That life is—what it is not;
That, somewhere, there is—something, something;
That we are waiting; that we are waiting.

A War

There set out, slowly, for a Different World,
At four, on winter mornings, different legs . . .
You can't break eggs without making an omelette
—That's what they tell the eggs.

Terms

One-armed, one-legged, and one-headed,
The pensioner sits in the sun.
He is telling a story to the leaf
Of the new maple in his new yard:
"The Department of the Interior has sent Jack Frost with a spray-gun
To paint you red."
The leaf pulls hard
To get away—it believes the man—
And a blue Chevrolet sedan
Draws up and leaves a check for the man in the mail-box.

"You're as good as dead,"
Says the man, with a mocking smile, to the leaf;
And somebody knocks
At the front door, the man doesn't answer,
But sits back in his white board chair—
Holding a mallet, by a stake with rainbow rings—
And rubs his eyes, and yawns like a dog when the dog
Next door whines and rattles its chain.
He looks at the leaf, as he looks at things,
With mixed feelings—
And says, "I've changed."

The good dreams keep haunting
The ghost with a check in the mail-box, the fox
With four quick brown wooden legs.
With one military brush, in the morning,

He pulls forward, or brushes back, the fair
Hair on the living head,
And brushes his firm white teeth, and the porcelain jacket
On his left front tooth, that is dead.
The leaf is alive, and it is going to be dead;
It is like any other leaf.
You keep flipping the coin and it comes down heads
And nobody has ever seen it come down anything but heads
And the man has stopped looking:

                                    it's heads.

He looks at the leaf—it is green—
And says with a flat black leather gesture:
"Never again."

II

He says: "My arm and leg—
My wooden arm, my wooden leg—
Wrestled with each other all last night
The way you whet a carving-knife
Till they stood crisscross against dawn
Over what seemed to me a tomb.
I felt for the dog tags on the cross.

"I could find one number on the leg
And a different number on the arm.
The grave was empty.

"I thought first, 'I have arisen,'
And looked up past the cross into the dawn
And saw my own head, burning there,
Go out.
        But in the darkness
The leaves fell one by one, like checks,
Into the grave;
And I thought: I am my own grave.

"Then I awoke: I could see the toaster
On its rack over the waffle-iron
And the dew on the wickets; at breakfast the bread
Pops up, all brown, from its—
                                        'It's all a dream,'
I said to myself. 'I am a grave dreaming
That it is a living man.' "

The man, as he has learned to,
Gets up and walks to the door.
As he opens the door
He watches his hand opening the door
And holds out his good hand—
And stares at them both, and laughs;
Then he says softly: "I am a man."

The Woman at the
Washington Zoo

(1960)

To Mary

The Woman at the Washington Zoo

The saris go by me from the embassies.

Cloth from the moon. Cloth from another planet.
They look back at the leopard like the leopard.

And I. . . .
           this print of mine, that has kept its color
Alive through so many cleanings; this dull null
Navy I wear to work, and wear from work, and so
To my bed, so to my grave, with no
Complaints, no comment: neither from my chief,
The Deputy Chief Assistant, nor his chief—
Only I complain. . . . this serviceable
Body that no sunlight dyes, no hand suffuses
But, dome-shadowed, withering among columns,
Wavy beneath fountains—small, far-off, shining
In the eyes of animals, these beings trapped
As I am trapped but not, themselves, the trap,
Aging, but without knowledge of their age,
Kept safe here, knowing not of death, for death—
Oh, bars of my own body, open, open!

The world goes by my cage and never sees me.
And there come not to me, as come to these,
The wild beasts, sparrows pecking the llamas' grain,
Pigeons settling on the bears' bread, buzzards
Tearing the meat the flies have clouded. . . .
                              Vulture,
When you come for the white rat that the foxes left,

Take off the red helmet of your head, the black
Wings that have shadowed me, and step to me as man:
The wild brother at whose feet the white wolves fawn,
To whose hand of power the great lioness
Stalks, purring. . . .
                    You know what I was,
You see what I am: change me, change me!

Cinderella

Her imaginary playmate was a grown-up
In sea-coal satin. The flame-blue glances,
The wings gauzy as the membrane that the ashes
Draw over an old ember—as the mother
In a jug of cider—were a comfort to her.
They sat by the fire and told each other stories.

"What men want. . . ." said the godmother softly—
How she went on it is hard for a man to say.
Their eyes, on their Father, were monumental marble.
Then they smiled like two old women, bussed each other,
Said, "Gossip, gossip"; and, lapped in each other's looks,
Mirror for mirror, drank a cup of tea.

Of cambric tea. But there is a reality
Under the good silk of the good sisters'
Good ball gowns. *She* knew. . . . Hard-breasted, naked-eyed,
She pushed her silk feet into glass, and rose within
A gown of imaginary gauze. The shy prince drank
A toast to her in champagne from her slipper

And breathed, "Bewitching!" Breathed, "I am bewitched!"
—She said to her godmother, "Men!"
And, later, looking down to see her flesh
Look back up from under lace, the ashy gauze
And pulsing marble of a bridal veil,
She wished it all a widow's coal-black weeds.

A sullen wife and a reluctant mother,
She sat all day in silence by the fire.

Better, later, to stare past her sons' sons,
Her daughters' daughters, and tell stories to the fire.
But best, dead, damned, to rock forever
Beside Hell's fireside—to see within the flames

The Heaven to whose gold-gauzed door there comes
A little dark old woman, the God's Mother,
And cries, "Come in, come in! My son's out now,
Out now, will be back soon, may be back never,
Who knows, eh? *We* know what they are—men, men!
But come, come in till then! Come in till then!"

The End of the Rainbow

Far from the clams and fogs and bogs
—The cranberry bogs—of Ipswich,
A sampler cast upon a savage shore,
There dwells in a turquoise, unfrequented store
A painter; a painter of land- and seascapes.

At nine o'clock, past Su-Su
—Asleep on the threshold, a spirited
Dwarf Pekinese, exceptionally loving—
The sun of Southern California streams
Unlovingly, but as though lovingly,
Upon the spare, paint-spotted and age-spotted hand's
Accustomed gesture.
                    Beyond the mahlstick a last wave
Breaks in Cobalt, Vert Emeraude, and Prussian Blue
Upon a Permanent White shore.

Her long hair, finer and redder once
Than the finest of red sable brushes, has been brushed
Till it is silver. The hairdresser, drunk with sunlight,
Has rinsed it a false blue. And blue
Are all the lights the seascapes cast upon it, blue
The lights the false sea casts upon it. Su-Su
—Su-Su is naturally black.

Five sheets of plate-glass, tinted green
And founded on the sand, now house the owner
Of the marsh-o'erlooking, silver-grey, unpainted salt-box
To which, sometimes, she writes a letter

THE WOMAN AT THE WASHINGTON ZOO   [219

—Home is where the dead are—
And goes with it, past CALIFORNIA,
And drops it in a mail-slot marked THE STATES.
The Frog-Prince, Marsh-King
Goggles at her from the bottom of the mail-slot.

There is brandy on his breath.
The cattails quivering above his brute
Imploring eyes, the tadpoles feathering
The rushes of his beard—black beard brought down
In silver to the grave—rustle again
In flaws or eddies of the wet wind: "Say.
Say. Say now. Say again."

                    She turns away
Into the irrigated land
With its blond hills like breasts of hay,
Its tall tan herds of eucalyptus grazing
Above its lawns of ice-plant, of geranium,
Its meadows of eternal asphodel.

The dark ghosts throng by
Shaking their locks at her—their fair, false locks—
Stretching out past her their bare hands, burnt hands.
And she—her face is masked, her hands are gloved
With a mask and gloves of bright brown leather:
The hands of a lady left out in the weather
Of resorts; the face of a fine girl left out in the years.

Voices float up: seals are barking
On the seal-rocks as, once, frogs were croaking
On rushy islands in the marsh of night.

Voices—the voices of others and her voice
Tuned flat like a country fiddle, like a Death
Rubbing his bow with resin at a square-dance—
Voices begin: . . . *A spider a frying-pan, and tonic pop,*

And—fancy!—put tomatoes in their chowder.
Go slow. Go slow. You owe it to yourself.
Watch out for the engine. You owe it to yourself.
Neither a borrower nor a lender be.
Better to be safe than sorry.
Better to be safe than sorry. Say to yourself,
Is it my money they're asking or me?
It must have been the money.
                              The harsh
Voice goes on, blurred with darkness: *Cheat*
Or be cheaten. Let
And live let.

          Great me. Great me. Great me.
Proverbs of the night
With the night's inconsequence, or consequence,
Sufficient unto the night. . . . *Every maid her own*
Merman—and she has left lonely forever,
Lonely forever, the kings of the marsh.
She says to Su-Su, "Come to your Content."
—A name in the family for more
Than seven generations. And Su-Su
—Su-Su is Su-Su IV.

Twelve o'clock: she locks
The door that she has painted, walks away
Straightforwardly, her Su-Su frisking
Before, on the leash that she has braided; eats
At a little table in a sunny courtyard
A date milkshake and an avocadoburger.
Thus evil communications
Corrupt good manners. . . .

                    Little Women, Little Men,
Upon what shores, pink-sanded, beside what cerulean
Seas have you trudged out, nodded over, napped away
Your medium-sized lives!

THE WOMAN AT THE WASHINGTON ZOO   [221

Poor Water Babies

Who, summer evenings, sent to bed by sunlight,
Sat in your nightdress on a rag-rug island
Seeming some Pole, or Northwest Passage, or Hesperides
Of your bedchamber's humped, dark-shining Ocean:
The last sunbeam shone
Upon the marble set there at the center
Of that grey-glassed, black-eaved, white-dormered chamber
Until, not touched by any human hand,
Slowly,
Fast, faster, the red agate rolled
Into the humpbacked floor's scrubbed corner.
From your bed that night, you looked for it
And it was gone—gone, gone forever
Out into darkness, far from the warm flickering
Hemisphere the candle breathed
For you and your *Swiss Family Robinson,* marooned
With one down pillow on an uninhabited
Hair mattress. . . .

Su-Su is looking: it's the last of lunch.
She takes a piece of candy from her purse
—Dog-candy—and says, "Beg, sir!"
                              Su-Su begs.
They walk home in all amity, in firm
And literal association. She repeats: *With dogs
You know where you are;* and Su-Su's oil-brown,
                              oil-blue stare
—The true Su-Su's true-blue stare—
Repeats: *With people you know where you are.*

Her thin feet, pointed neither out nor in
But straight before her, like an Indian's,
And set upon the path, a detour of the path
Of righteousness; her unaccommodating eyes'
Flat blue, matt blue
Or grey, depending on the point of view—

On whether one looks from here or from New England—
All these go unobserved, are unobservable:
She is old enough to be invisible.

Opening the belled door,
She turns once more to her new-framed, new-glassed
Landscape of a tree beside the sea.
It is light-struck.

If you look at a picture the wrong way
You see yourself instead.
                    —The wrong way?
A quarter of an hour and we tire
Of any landscape, said Goethe; eighty years
And he had not tired of Goethe. The landscape had,
And disposed of Goethe in the usual way.

She has looked into the mirror of the marsh
Flawed with the flight of dragonflies, the life of rushes,
And seen—what she had looked for—her own face
Staring up into her; but underneath,
In the depths of the dark water, witnessing
Unmoved, with a seal's angelic
More-than-human less-than-human eyes, a strange
Animal, some wizard ruling other realms,
The King of the Marsh.
                    She says: "He was a—*strange* man."

And the voice of a departed friend, a female
Friend, replies as crystal
Replies to a teaspoon, to a fingernail:
"A *strange* man. . . . But all men are, aren't they?
A man is like a merman." "A merman?"
"Mermen were seals, you know. They called them silkies."
"You mean the Forsaken Merman was a *seal?*"
"What did you think it was, a merman?
And mermaids were manatees." "The things you know!"
"The things you don't know!"

The Great Silkie,
His muzzle wide in love, holds out to her
His maimed flippers, and an uncontrollable
Shudder runs through her flesh, and she says, smiling:
"A goose was walking on my grave.
—And the Frog-Prince?" "Oh, I don't know.
If you ask me the Frog-Prince was a frog."

These days few men, few women, and no frogs
Enter "my little studio-shop," "my little paint-store,"
To buy paint; paintings; small black dogs,
Pieces of Pilgrim Rock; pomander-apples
In rosemary; agates; a marsh-violet pressed
In *Compensation*—red goatskin, India paper,
Inscribed in black ink, "For my loving daughter";
A miniature of Great-Great-Great-
Grandfather Wotkyns, pressed to death in Salem
For a wizard; a replica, life-sized, of a female friend
In crystal—wound, the works say, "Men!";
A framed poem signed *Beddoes:* she has dreams to sell.

She has spent her principal on dreams.
Some portion, though, is left—left to her in
                                    the Commonwealth
Of Massachusetts, in trust to the end of time.
But life, though, is not left in trust?
Life is not lived, in trust?
True, true—but how few live!
The gift for life, the gift of life
Are rarer, surely, than the gift of making
In a life-class, a study from the life
Of some girl naked for an hour, by the hour;
Of making, from an egg, a jug,
An eggplant, at cross-purposes on drapery,
A still-life; of rendering, with a stump,
Art-gum, and four hardnesses of charcoal, life
Whispering to the naked girl, the naked egg, the naked
Painter: "What am I offered for this frog?"

A kiss? The Frog-Prince, kissed,
Is a prince indeed; a king, a husband, and a father;
According to his State, a citizen; according to
                                    his God, a soul;
According to his—*fiancée,* a risk
Uncalculated, incalculable; a load
Whose like she will not look upon again; a responsibility
She is no longer saddled with, praise Heaven!
[Applause.] And, smiling as she used to smile,
She murmurs as she used to murmur: "Men!"

She looks into the mirror and says: "Mirror,
Who is the fairest of us all?"

According to the mirror, it's the mirror.

Great me. Great me. Great me. The voices tune themselves
And keep on tuning: there is no piece, just tuning.
. . . But there are compensations; there is *Compensation.*
She reads it (it, or else the Scriptures
With a *Key* by Mrs. Eddy) when she wakes
In the night as she so often does: the earth
Lies light upon the old, and they are wakeful.

She reads patiently: the bed-lamp lights
Above her sunlit, moonlit, starlit bed
The little slogan under which she sleeps
Or is wakeful: HE WHO HAS HIMSELF FOR FRIEND
IS BEST BEFRIENDED—this in gothic.
One sees, through the bars of the first *H,* a landscape
Manned with men, womaned with women,
                                    dogged with a dog,
And influenced—Content says—by the influence
Of *The Very Rich Hours of the Duke of Burgundy.*
The hours of the earth
—The very rich hours, the very poor hours,
                                    the very long hours—
Go by, and she is wakeful.

THE WOMAN AT THE WASHINGTON ZOO   [225

She wakes, sometimes, when she has met a friend
In the water; he is just standing in the water, bathing.
He has shaved now, and smells of peppermint.
He holds out to her
With hands like hip-boots, like her father's waders,
A corsage of watercress: the white bridal-veil-lace flowers
Are shining with water-drops. In their clear depths
She sees, like so many cupids, water babies:
Little women, little men.
He pulls his feet with a slow sucking sound
From the floor where he is stuck, like a horse in concrete,
And, reaching to her, whispers patiently
—Whispers, or the wind whispers, water whispers: "Say.
Say. Say now. Say again."

                    A slow
Delicious shudder runs along her spine:
She takes off her straw sailor.
Red again, and long enough to sit on,
Her hair floats out to him—and, slowly,
                              she holds out to him
In their white, new-washed gloves, her dry
Brown leather hands, and whispers: "Father,
If you come any closer I'll call Father."

He melts, in dark drops, to a little dark
Pool drying on the floor, to Su-Su. It is Su-Su!
She holds out to the little dark
Grave drying in the grass, her little dry
Bouquet of ice-plant, of geranium,
And reads: *In Loving Memory of Su-Su*
I, II, III, IV.
She says: "That four is a mistake.
One two three is right, but leave out four."

The Prince is dead. . . . The willows waver
Above the cresses of his tomb.
                    —His tomb?

The Frog-Prince is married to a frog, has little frogs,
Says sometimes, after dinner, in his den:
"There was a mortal once. . . ." And his Content
Goes through the suburbs with a begging-bowl
Of teak, a Wedgwood cowbell, ringing, ringing,
Calling: *Untouched! Untouched!*
                                        The doors shut themselves
Not helped by any human hand, mail-boxes
Pull down their flags, the finest feelers
Of the television sets withdraw.
                                        Beside her, Death
Or else Life—spare, white, permanent—
Works out their *pas de deux:* here's Death
Arranging a still-life for his own Content;
Death walking Su-Su; Death presenting
To the trustees of the estate, a varied
Portfolio; Death digging
For gold at the end of the rainbow—strikes water,
Which is thinner than blood; strikes oil,
That water will not mix with—no, nor blood;
Pauses, mops his skull, says: *The wrong end.*

At home in Massachusetts gold, red gold
Gushes above the Frog-Prince, Princess, all the Princelets
Digging with sand-pails, tiny shovels, spoons, a porringer
Planned, ages since, by Paul Revere. They call:
                                        "Come play! Come play!"
Death breaks the ice
On her Hopi jar and washes out the brushes;
Says, as he hands her them: *Life's work. It's work.*
Out here at the wrong end of the rainbow
Say to yourself: What's a rainbow anyway?

She looks into the mirror, through the rainbow
—The little home-made rainbow, there in tears—
And hears the voices the years shatter into
As the sunlight shatters into colors: *Me. Me. Me,*

The voices tune themselves.
She says: "Look at my life. Should I go on with it?
It seems to you I have . . . a real gift?
I shouldn't like to keep on if I only. . . .
It seems to you my life is a success?"

Death answers, *Yes. Well, yes.*

She looks around her:
Many waves are breaking on many shores,
The wind turns over, absently,
The leaves of a hundred thousand trees.
How many colors, squeezed from how many tubes
In patient iteration, have made up the world
She draws closer, like a patchwork quilt,
To warm her, all the warm, long, summer day!
The local colors fade:
She hangs here on the verge of seeing
In black and white,
And turns with an accustomed gesture
To the easel, saying:
"Without my paintings I would be—

                why, whatever *would* I be?"

Safe from all the nightmares
One comes upon awake in the world, she sleeps.
She sleeps in sunlight, surrounded by many dreams
Or dreams of dreams, all good—how can a dream be bad
If it keeps one asleep?

              The unpeopled landscapes
Run down to the seal-less, the merman-less seas,
And she rolls softly, like an agate, down to Su-Su
Asleep upon the doorsill of the seas.
The first Su-Su, the second Su-Su, the third Su-Su
Are dead?

       Long live Su-Su IV!

The little black dog sleeping in the doorway
Of the little turquoise store, can dream
His own old dream: that he is sleeping
In the doorway of the little turquoise store.

In Those Days

In those days—they were long ago—
The snow was cold, the night was black.
I licked from my cracked lips
A snowflake, as I looked back

Through branches, the last uneasy snow.
Your shadow, there in the light, was still.
In a little the light went out.
I went on, stumbling—till at last the hill

Hid the house. And, yawning,
In bed in my room, alone,
I would look out: over the quilted
Rooftops, the clear stars shone.

How poor and miserable we were,
How seldom together!
And yet after so long one thinks:
In those days everything was better.

The Elementary Scene

Looking back in my mind I can see
The white sun like a tin plate
Over the wooden turning of the weeds;
The street jerking—a wet swing—
To end by the wall the children sang.

The thin grass by the girls' door,
Trodden on, straggling, yellow and rotten,
And the gaunt field with its one tied cow—
The dead land waking sadly to my life—
Stir, and curl deeper in the eyes of time.

The rotting pumpkin under the stairs
Bundled with switches and the cold ashes
Still holds for me, in its unwavering eyes,
The stinking shapes of cranes and witches,
Their path slanting down the pumpkin's sky.

Its stars beckon through the frost like cottages
(Homes of the Bear, the Hunter—of that absent star,
The dark where the flushed child struggles into sleep)
Till, leaning a lifetime to the comforter,
I float above the small limbs like their dream:

I, I, the future that mends everything.

Windows

Quarried from snow, the dark walks lead to doors
That are dark and closed. The white- and high-roofed houses
Float in the moonlight of the shining sky
As if they slept, the bedclothes pulled around them.
But in some the lights still burn. The lights of others' houses.

Those who live there move seldom, and are silent.
Their movements are the movements of a woman darning,
A man nodding into the pages of the paper,
And are portions of a rite—have kept a meaning—
That I, that they know nothing of. What I have never heard
He will read me; what I have never seen
She will show me.
                        As dead actors, on a rainy afternoon,
Move in a darkened living-room, for children
Watching the world that was before they were,
The windowed ones within their windowy world
Move past me without doubt and for no reason.

These actors, surely, have known nothing of today,
That time of troubles and of me. Of troubles.
Morose and speechless, voluble with elation,
Changing, unsleeping, an unchanging speech,
These have not lived; look up, indifferent,
At me at my window, from the snowy walk
They move along in peace. . . . If only I were they!
Could act out, in longing, the impossibility
That haunts me like happiness!
Of so many windows, one is always open.

Some morning they will come downstairs and find me.
They will start to speak, and then smile speechlessly,
Shifting the plates, and set another place
At a table shining by a silent fire.
When I have eaten they will say, "You have not slept."

And from the sofa, mounded in my quilt,
My face on *their* pillow, that is always cool,
I will look up speechlessly into a—

It blurs, and there is drawn across my face
As my eyes close, a hand's slow fire-warmed flesh.

It moves so slowly that it does not move.

Aging

I wake, but before I know it it is done,
The day, I sleep. And of days like these the years,
A life is made. I nod, consenting to my life.
. . . But who can live in these quick-passing hours?
I need to find again, to make a life,
A child's Sunday afternoon, the Pleasure Drive
Where everything went by but time; the Study Hour
Spent at a desk, with folded hands, in waiting.

In those I could make. Did I not make in them
Myself? The Grown One whose time shortens,
Breath quickens, heart beats faster, till at last
It catches, skips. . . . Yet those hours that seemed, were endless
Were still not long enough to have remade
My childish heart: the heart that must have, always,
To make anything of anything, not time,
Not time but—
                    but, alas! eternity.

Nestus Gurley

Sometimes waking, sometimes sleeping,
Late in the afternoon, or early
In the morning, I hear on the lawn,
On the walk, on the lawn, the soft quick step,
The sound half song, half breath: a note or two
That with a note or two would be a tune. ·
It is Nestus Gurley.

It is an old
Catch or snatch or tune
In the Dorian mode: the mode of the horses
That stand all night in the fields asleep
Or awake, the mode of the cold
Hunter, Orion, wheeling upside-down,
All space and stars, in cater-cornered Heaven.
When, somewhere under the east,
The great march begins, with birds and silence;
When, in the day's first triumph, dawn
Rides over the houses, Nestus Gurley
Delivers to me my lot.

As the sun sets, I hear my daughter say:
"He has four routes and makes a hundred dollars."
Sometimes he comes with dogs, sometimes with children,
Sometimes with dogs and children.
He collects, today.
I hear my daughter say:
"Today Nestus has got on his derby."
And he says, after a little: "It's two-eighty."

"How could it be two-eighty?"
"Because this month there're five Sundays: it's two-eighty."

He collects, delivers. Before the first, least star
Is lost in the paling east; at evening
While the soft, side-lit, gold-leafed day
Lingers to see the stars, the boy Nestus
Delivers to me the Morning Star, the Evening Star
—Ah no, only the Morning *News,* the Evening *Record*
Of what I have done and what I have not done
Set down and held against me in the Book
Of Death, on paper yellowing
Already, with one morning's sun, one evening's sun.

Sometimes I only dream him. He brings then
News of a different morning, a judgment not of men.
The bombers have turned back over the Pole,
Having met a star. . . . I look at that new year
And, waking, think of our Moravian Star
Not lit yet, and the pure beeswax candle
With its red flame-proofed paper pompom
Not lit yet, and the sweetened
Bun we brought home from the love-feast, still not eaten,
And the song the children sang: *O Morning Star—*

And at this hour, to the dew-hushed drums
Of the morning, Nestus Gurley
Marches to me over the lawn; and the cat Elfie,
Furred like a musk-ox, coon-tailed, gold-leaf-eyed,
Looks at the paper boy without alarm
But yawns, and stretches, and walks placidly
Across the lawn to his ladder, climbs it, and begins to purr.
I let him in,
Go out and pick up from the grass the paper hat
Nestus has folded: this tricorne fit for a Napoleon
Of our days and institutions, weaving
Baskets, being bathed, receiving

Electric shocks, Rauwolfia. . . . I put it on
—Ah no, only unfold it.
There is dawn inside; and I say to no one
About—
            it is a note or two
That with a note or two would—
                        say to no one
About nothing: "He delivers dawn."

When I lie coldly
—Lie, that is, neither with coldness nor with warmth—
In the darkness that is not lit by anything,
In the grave that is not lit by anything
Except our hope: the hope
That is not proofed against anything, but pure
And shining as the first, least star
That is lost in the east on the morning of Judgment—
May I say, recognizing the step
Or tune or breath. . . .
                        recognizing the breath,
May I say, "It is Nestus Gurley."

The Great Night

(Rainer Maria Rilke)

Often I looked at you—stood at the window I had started
The day before, stood and looked at you. The new city still
Seemed something forbidden; the landscape, not yet won over,
Darkened as though I was not. The closest things
Didn't bother to make me understand. The street
Crowded itself up to the lamp post; I saw that it was strange.
Out there a room was clear in lamplight—
Already I was part; they sensed it, closed the shutters.
I stood there. And then a child cried. And I knew
The mothers in the houses, what they were—knew, suddenly,
The spring of all our tears, the spring that is never dry.
Or a voice sang, and went a little beyond
Whatever I had expected; or an old man coughed,
Full of reproach, as though his flesh were in the right
Against the gentler world. Then a clock struck the hour—
But I counted too late, and it got by me.
As a boy, a stranger, when at last they let him,
Can't catch the ball, and doesn't know any of the games
The others are playing together so easily,
So that he stands and looks off—where?—I stand, and suddenly
See that *you* have made friends with me, played with me, grown-up
Night, and I look at you. While the towers
Were angered, while with averted fates
A city encompassed me, and the unguessable hills
Were encamped against me, and in closing circles
Strangeness hungered round the chance-set flares
Of my senses: then was it, O highest,
That you felt it no shame to know me, that your breath
Went over me, that there passed into me
Your grave and from far apportioning smile.

The Grown-Up

(*Rainer Maria Rilke*)

All this stood on her and was the world,
And stood on her with all things, Pain and Grace,
As trees stand, growing and erect, all image
And imageless as the ark of the Lord God,
And solemn, as if set upon a State.

And she bore it; bore, somehow, the weight
Of the flying, fleeting, far-away,
The monstrous and the still-unmastered,
Unmoved, serene, as the water-bearer
Stands under a full jar. Till in the midst of play,
Transfiguring, preparing for the Other,
The first white veil fell smoothly, softly,

Over her opened face, almost opaque,
Never to raise itself again, and giving somehow
To all her questions one vague answer:
In thee, thou once a child, in thee.

Washing the Corpse

(*Rainer Maria Rilke*)

They had got used to him. But when they brought
The kitchen lamp in, and it was burning
Uneasily in the dark air, the stranger
Was altogether strange. They washed his neck,

And since they had no knowledge of his fate
They lied till they had put together one,
Always washing. One of them had to cough,
And while she was coughing she left the heavy

Sponge of vinegar on his face. The other
Stopped a minute too, and the drops knocked
From the hard brush, while his dreadful
Cramped hand wanted to demonstrate
To the whole household that he no longer thirsted.

And he did demonstrate it. Coughing shortly,
As if embarrassed, they went back to work
More hurriedly now, so that across the dumb
Pattern of the wallpaper their contorted shadows

Writhed and wallowed as though in a net
Until the washing reached its end.
The night, in the uncurtained window-frame,
Was relentless. And one without a name
Lay clean and naked there, and gave commandments.

Evening

(*Rainer Maria Rilke*)

The evening folds about itself the dark
Garments the old trees hold out to it.
You watch: and the lands are borne from you,
One soaring heavenward, one falling;

And leave you here, not wholly either's,
Not quite so darkened as the silent houses,
Not quite so surely summoning the eternal
As that which each night becomes star, and rises;

And leave you (inscrutably to unravel)
Your life: the fearful and ripening and enormous
Being that—bounded by everything, or boundless—
For a moment becomes stone, for a moment stars.

Childhood

(adapted from Rainer Maria Rilke)

The time of school drags by with waiting
And dread, with nothing but dreary things.
O loneliness, O leaden waiting-out of time. . . .
And then out. The streets are gleaming and ringing,
All the fountains flash up from the squares.
In the parks the world is enormous.
And to walk through it all in one's little suit
Not at all as the others go, have ever gone:
O miraculous time, O waiting-out of time,
O loneliness.

And to gaze far out into it all:
Men and women, men, men—black and tall
And going slowly, as if in their sleep,
Beside the sudden white and blue and red
Children; a house here, now and then a dog,
And one's fear changing silently to trust:
O senseless grief, O dream, O dread,
O bottomless abyss.

And then to play with top or hoop or ball
Beneath the paling branches of the park
Or sometimes, blind and wild in the reeling
Rush of tag, to brush against the grown-ups,
But to go home with them when it is dark
With little stiff steps, quiet, held fast to:
O knowledge ever harder to hold fast to,
O dread, O burden.

And to kneel beside the great gray pond
Hour on hour with one's little sail-boat,
Forgetting it because so many more,
Lovely and lovelier, glide through darkening rings,
And to have to think about the little pale
Face that shone up from the water, sinking:
O childhood, O images gliding from us
Somewhere. But where? But where?

Lament

(*Rainer Maria Rilke*)

All is far
And long gone by.
I believe the star
That shines up there
Has been dead for a thousand years.
I believe, in the car
I heard go by,
Something terrible was said.
In the house a clock
Is striking. . . .
In what house?
I would like to walk
Out of my heart, under the great sky.
I would like to pray.
And surely, of all the stars,
One still must be.
I believe I know
Which one endures;
Which one, at the end of its beam in the sky,
Stands like a white city.

The Child

(*Rainer Maria Rilke*)

Without meaning to, they watch him play
A long time; once or twice his profile
Turns and becomes a live, full face—
Clear and entire as a completed

Hour that is raised to strike its end.
But the others do not count the strokes.
Exhausted with misery, enduring their lives,
They do not even see that he endures:

Endures everything, now and always,
As—near them, as though in a waiting-room,
Wearily, dressed in his little dress—
He sits and waits till his time comes.

Death

(*Rainer Maria Rilke*)

There stands death, a bluish liquid
In a cup without a saucer.
An odd place for a cup:
Stands on the back of a hand. And one can see
Quite plainly, there on the glassy slope,
The place where the handle broke off. Dusty. And HOPE
On the side in used-up letters.

The drinker that drank the drink
Read it out, long, long ago, at breakfast.

This being of theirs!
To get rid of them you have to poison them?

Except for that, they'd stay? They munch away
At their own frustration so insatiably?
One has to pull the present from their mouths,
The hard present, like a dental plate.

Then they mumble. Mumble, mumble. . . .

. . . .
Star
Seen from a bridge once: O falling star,
Not to forget you. Stand!

Requiem for the Death of a Boy

(Rainer Maria Rilke)

Why did I print upon myself the names
Of Elephant and Dog and Cow
So far off now, already so long ago,
And Zebra, too. . . . what for, what for?
What holds me now
Climbs like a water line
Up past all that. What help was it to know
I was, if I could never press
Through what's soft, what's hard, and come at last
Behind them, to the face that understands?

And these beginning hands—

Sometimes you'd say: "He promises. . . ."
Yes, I promised. But what I promised you,
That was never what I felt afraid of.
Sometimes I'd sit against the house for hours
And look up at a bird.
If only I could have turned into the looking!
It lifted me, it flew me, how my eyes
Were open up there then! But I didn't love anybody.
Loving was misery—
Don't you see, I wasn't we,
And I was so much bigger
Than a man, I was my own danger,
And, inside it, I was the seed.

A little seed. The street can have it.
The wind can have it. I give it away.

Because that we all sat there so together—
I never did believe that. No, honestly.
You talked, you laughed, but none of you were ever
Inside the talking or the laughing. No.
The sugar bowl, a glass of milk
Would never waver the way you would waver.
The apple lay there. Sometimes it felt so good
To hold tight to it, a hard ripe apple.
The big table, the coffee-cups that never moved—
They were good, how peaceful they made the year!
And my toy did me good too, sometimes.
It was as reliable, almost, as the others,
Only not so peaceful. It stood halfway
Between me and my hat, in watchfulness forever.
There was a wooden horse, there was a rooster,
There was the doll with only one leg.
I did so much for them.
I made the sky small when they saw it
Because almost from the start I understood
How alone a wooden horse is. You can make one,
A wooden horse, one any size.
It gets painted, and later on you pull it,
And it's the real street it pounds down, then.
When you call it a horse, why isn't it a lie?
Because you feel that you're a horse, a little,
And grow all maney, shiny, grow four legs—
So as to grow, some day, into a man?
But wasn't I wood a little, too,
For its sake, and grew hard and quiet
And looked out at it from an emptier face?

I almost think we traded places.
Whenever I would see the brook I'd race it,
And the brook raced, too, and I would run away.
Whenever I saw something that could ring, I rang,
And whenever something sang I played for it.

I made myself at home with everything.
Only everything was satisfied without me
And got sadder, hung about with me.

Now, all at once, we're separated.
Do the lessons and the questions start again?
Or, now, ought I to say
What it was like with you?—That worries me.
The house? I never got it right, exactly.
The rooms? Oh, there were so many things, so many.
. . . Mother, *who* was the dog really?
That in the forest we would come on berries—
Even that seems, now, extraordinary.

Surely there're some other children
Who've died, to come play with me. They're always dying;
Lie there in bed, like me, and never do get well.

Well. . . . How funny that sounds, here.
Does it mean something, still?
Here where I am
No one is ill, I think.
Since my sore throat, so long ago already—

Here everyone is like a just-poured drink.

But the ones who drink us I still haven't seen.

The Winter's Tale

(Henrikas Radauskas)

Guess what smells so. . . . You didn't guess.
Lilies? Lindens? No. Winds? No.
But princes and barbers smell so,
The evening smells so, in a dream.

Look: a line goes through the glass
Bending quietly; and the hushed
Light, in the tender mist,
Is gurgling like a brook of milk.

Look: it's snowing, it's snowing, it's snowing.
Look: the white orchard is falling asleep.
The earth has sunk into the past.
Guess who's coming. . . . You didn't guess.
Princes and barbers are coming,
White kings and bakers,
And the trees murmur, covered with snow.

The Archangels' Song

(from Goethe's FAUST)

RAPHAEL:

The sun sings out, as of old,
Against the spheres' unchanging sound;
Yet once more, with thunderous footsteps,
He works out his predestined round.
Though no angel fathoms him, his face
Gives strength to them upon their way;
The inconceivably exalted works
Are glorious as on the first day.

GABRIEL:

Swift, past all understanding swift
Is the splendor of earth's whirling flight:
The brilliance of Paradise is changed
For the awful darkness of the night.
The ocean foams up, overwhelming,
The great rocks tremble with the force,
And rocks and ocean are swept onward
In the spheres' swift, eternal course.

MICHAEL:

In rivalry the tempests roar
From sea to land, from land to sea,
And, raging, forge out for the earth
Fetters of wildest energy.
Before the path of the thunderbolt
The lightnings of desolation blaze.
And yet thine angels, Lord, adore
The tranquil footsteps of thy days.

ALL THREE:
> Since none can fathom thee, thy face
> Gives strength to us upon our way,
> And thine exalted works, O God,
> Are glorious as on the first day.

Forest Murmurs

(*Eduard Mörike*)

Stretched out under the oak, in the wood's new leaves,
I lay with my book. To me it is still the sweetest;

All the fairy tales are in it, the Goose Girl and the Juniper Tree
And the Fisherman's Wife—truly, one never gets tired of them.

The curly light flung down to me its green May-shine,
Flung on the shadowy book its mischievous illustrations.

I heard, far away, the strokes of the axe; heard the cuckoo
And the rippling of the brook, a step or two beyond.

I myself felt like a fairy tale; with new-washed senses
I saw, O so clear! the forest, the cuckoo called, O so strange!

All at once the leaves rustle—isn't it Snow-White coming
Or some enchanted stag? Oh no, it's nothing miraculous:

See, my neighbor's child from the village, my good little sweetheart!
She'd nothing to do, and ran to the forest to her father.

Demurely she seats herself at my side, confidentially
We gossip of this and that; and I tell her the story

(Leaving out nothing) of the sorrows of that incomparable
Maiden her mother three times threatened with death.

Because she was so beautiful, the Queen, the vain one, hated her
Fiercely, so that she fled, made her home with dwarfs.

But soon the Queen found her; knocked at the door as a peddler,
Craftily offering the girl her wonderful things to buy;

And forgetting the words of the dwarfs, the innocent child
Let her in—and the dear thing bought, alas! the poisoned comb.

What a wailing there is that night, when the little ones come home!
What work it takes, what skill, before the sleeper awakes!

But now a second time, a third time, in disguise,
The destroyer comes. How easily she persuades the maiden;

Laces in the tender body, strangling it, till she has choked
The breath in the breast; brings, last, the deadly fruit.

Now nothing is any help; how the dwarfs weep!
The poor darling is locked in a crystal coffin, they set it

There on the mountain side in sight of all the stars—
And inside it, unfading forever, the sweet shape sleeps.

So far had I come: all at once, from the thicket behind me,
The song of the nightingale arose in radiant splendor,

Rained through the boughs like honey, sprinkling its fiery
Barbed sounds down over me; I shuddered in terror, in delight—

So one of the goddesses, flying above him unseen,
Betrays herself to a poet with her ambrosial fragrance.

But soon, alas! the singer was silent. I listened a long time
But in vain; and so I brought my story to its end.—

Just then the child pointed and cried: "She's here already,
It's Margaret! See, she's brought Father the milk, in her basket."

Through the branches I could make out her older sister;
Leaving the meadow, she had turned up into the wood.

Bronzed and stalwart, the maid; noon blazed on her cheeks.
We'd have frightened her if we could, but she greeted us first:

"Come along, if you like! Today you don't need any meat
Or soup, it's so warm. My meal is rich and cool."

And I didn't struggle. We followed the sound of the wood-axe.
How willingly I should have led, instead of the child, her sister!

Friend, you honor the Muse who, ages ago, to thousands
Told her stories, but now for a long time has been silent.

Who by the winter fireside, the loom and the work-bench,
Proffered to the folk's creating wit her delectable food.

Her kingdom is the impossible: impudent, frivolous, she ladles
   together
All that's unlikeliest, gleefully gives her prizes to half-wits.

Allowed three wishes, her hero will pick the silliest.
To honor her, now, let me make to you this confession—

How at the side of the girl, the sweet-spoken, the never-silent,
Catching me unawares, the passionate wish overwhelmed me:

If I were a hunter, a shepherd, if I were born a peasant,
If I handled an axe, a shovel—you, Margaret, would be my wife!

Never then would I complain of the heat of the day;
The plainest food, if you served it, would seem a feast.

Each morning, in its magnificence, the sun would meet me—
Each evening, in magnificence, blaze over the ripening fields.

Fresh from the woman's kiss, my blood would grow sweet as balsam;
Boisterous with children, my house would blossom on high.

But on winter nights, when the drifts pile high—by the fireside,
O Muse, maker of the stories of men! I would invoke thee.

THE WOMAN AT THE WASHINGTON ZOO   [255

Jamestown

Let me look at what I was, before I die.
Strange, that one's photograph in kindergarten
Is a captain in a ruff and a Venusian
—Is nothing here American?
John Smith is squashed
Beneath the breasts of Pocahontas: some true Christian,
Engraving all, has made the captain Man,
The maiden the most voluptuous of newts.
Met in a wood and lain with, this red demon,
The mother of us all, lies lovingly
Upon the breastplate of our father: the First Family
Of Jamestown trembles beneath the stone
Axe—then Powhatan, smiling, gives the pair his blessing
And nymphs and satyrs foot it at their wedding.
The continents, like country children, peep in awe
As Power, golden as a Veronese,
Showers her riches on the lovers: Nature,
Nature at last is married to a man.

The two lived happily
Forever after. . . . And I only am escaped alone
To tell the story. But how shall I tell the story?
The settlers died? All settlers die. The colony
Was a Lost Colony? All colonies are lost.
John Smith and Pocahontas, carving on a tree
We Have Gone Back For More People, crossed the sea
And were put to death, for treason, in the Tower
Of London? Ah, but they needed no one!
Powhatan,

Smiling at that red witch, red wraith, his daughter,
Said to the father of us all, John Smith:
"American,
To thyself be enough! . . ." He was enough—
Enough, or too much. The True Historie
Of the Colony of Jamestown is a wish.

Long ago, hundreds of years ago, a man
Met a woman in a wood, a witch.
The witch said, "Wish!"
The man said, "Make me what I am."
The witch said, "Wish again!"
The man said, "Make me what I am."
The witch said, "For the last time, wish!"
The man said, "Make me what I am."
The witch said: "Mortal, because you have believed
In your mortality, there is no wood, no wish,
No world, there is only you. But what are you?
The world has become you. But what are you?
Ask;
Ask, while the time to ask remains to you."

The witch said, smiling: "This is Jamestown.
From Jamestown, Virginia, to Washington, D.C.,
Is, as the rocket flies, eleven minutes."

The Lonely Man

A cat sits on the pavement by the house.
It lets itself be touched, then slides away.
A girl goes by in a hood; the winter noon's
Long shadows lengthen. The cat is gray,
It sits there. It sits there all day, every day.

A collie bounds into my arms: he is a dog
And, therefore, finds nothing human alien.
He lives at the preacher's with a pair of cats.
The soft half-Persian sidles to me;
Indoors, the old white one watches blindly.

How cold it is! Some snow slides from a roof
When a squirrel jumps off it to a squirrel-proof
Feeding-station; and, a lot and two yards down,
A fat spaniel snuffles out to me
And sobers me with his untrusting frown.

He worries about his yard: past it, it's my affair
If I halt Earth in her track—his duty's done.
And the cat and the collie worry about the old one:
They come, when she's out too, so uncertainly. . . .
It's my block; I know them, just as they know me.

As for the others, those who wake up every day
And feed these, keep the houses, ride away
To work—I don't know them, they don't know me.
Are we friends or enemies? Why, who can say?
We nod to each other sometimes, in humanity,

Or search one another's faces with a yearning
Remnant of faith that's almost animal. . . .
The gray cat that just sits there: surely it is learning
To be a man; will find, soon, *some especial*
Opening in a good firm for a former cat.

The Traveler

As she rides to the station
There is always something she has left behind.
Here is her hatbox; where is her hat?
Or she is blind—but the others are blind,
Not one thinks: Where are her eyes?
This plush smells—how does she smell it?
Her head hangs on a hanger in the closet
And calls as an engine calls, the engine
Cries as a head cries: *Shall I spare this city?*
The rails answer: *Raze it, raze it.*
She thinks as a child thinks:
When the sun sets, it is to count my loss.

Here in the station, in the other station,
On the track, appearing each instant,
That is made to her destination,
Her purse is heavier than she can know,
Her streaked breasts shake with a double heart.
When she steps at last to the stone of the station
Her arm drags, her step is slow.
She carries her head in her hand like a hatbox
Of money, of paper money:
A headful of money not even she will take.

When the moon rises, it is to count her money.
She sits on the bed of a bedroom counting her money:
Her look glazes, her breath is slow.
The wind moves to her
Softly, through parting curtains,

And a bill on the floor, a bill on the comfort,
As though they were living, stir.
When the wind says, *Shall I spare this city?*
She gives no answer.

A Ghost, a Real Ghost

I think of that old woman in the song
Who could not know herself without the skirt
They cut off while she slept beside a stile.
Her dog jumped at the unaccustomed legs
And barked till she turned slowly from her gate
And went—I never asked them where she went.

The child is hopeful and unhappy in a world
Whose future is his recourse: she kept walking
Until the skirt grew, cleared her head and dog—
Surely I thought so when I laughed. If skirts don't grow,
If things can happen so, and you not know
What you could do, why, what is there you could do?

I know now she went nowhere; went to wait
In the bare night of the fields, to whisper:
"I'll sit and wish that it was never so."
I see her sitting on the ground and wishing,
The wind jumps like a dog against her legs,
And she keeps thinking: "This is all a dream.

"Who would cut off a poor old woman's skirt?
So good too. No, it's not so:
No one could feel so, really." And yet one might.
A ghost must; and she was, perhaps, a ghost.
The first night I looked into the mirror
And saw the room empty, I could not believe

That it was possible to keep existing
In such pain: I have existed.

Was the old woman dead? What does it matter?
—Am I dead? A ghost, a real ghost
Has no need to die: what is he except
A being without access to the universe
That he has not yet managed to forget?

The Meteorite

Star, that looked so long among the stones
And picked from them, half iron and half dirt,
One; and bent and put it to her lips
And breathed upon it till at last it burned
Uncertainly, among the stars its sisters—
Breathe on me still, star, sister.

Charles Dodgson's Song

The band played *Idomeneo:*
  A child's felicity
Held Stendhal, sitting with the Empress
  Eugenie on his fat knee.

Clerk Maxwell's demon was possessed;
  He lay for half his days
And never moved a single molecule.
  Mill, haunted by the silent face

Of Bentham—it was made of wax—
  Read Wordsworth, and at last could weep.
I sought for love, and found it in girls' gloves:
  There's none outside, you know. "That bird's dead, Father,"

Said Darwin's son. Dejectedly
  The Father broke his spear, looked deep
Into the Cause of things: but it was only
  A hippopotamus asleep.

Deutsch Durch Freud

I believe my favorite country's German.

I wander in a calm folk-colored daze; the infant
Looks down upon me from his mother's arms
And says—oh, God knows what he says!
It's baby-talk? he's sick? or is it German?
That *Nachtigallenchor:* does it sing German?
Yoh, yoh: here mice, rats, tables, chairs,
Grossmütter, Kinder, der Herrgott im Himmel,
All, all but I—
        all, all but I—
                speak German.

Have you too sometimes, by the fire, at evening,
Wished that you were—whatever you once were?
It is ignorance alone that is enchanting.
*Dearer to me than all the treasures of the earth
Is something living,* said old Rumpelstiltskin
And hopped home. Charcoal-burners heard him singing
And spoiled it all. . . . And all because—
If only he hadn't known his name!

In German I don't know my name.
                I am the log
The fairies left one morning in my place.
—In German I believe in them, in everything:
The world is everything that is the case.
How clever people are! I look on open-mouthed
As Kant reels down the road *im Morgenrot*

Humming *Mir ist so bang, so bang, mein Schatz—*
All the nixies set their watches by him
Two hours too fast. . . .
                I think, *My calendar's*
Two centuries too fast, and give a sigh
Of trust. I reach out for the world and ask
The price; it answers, *One touch of your finger.*

In all *my* Germany there's no *Gesellschaft*
But one between *eine Katze* and *ein Maus.*
What's business? what's a teaspoon? what's a sidewalk?
Schweig stille, meine Seele! Such things are not for thee.
It is by Trust, and Love, and reading Rilke
Without *ein Wörterbuch,* that man learns German.
The Word rains in upon his blessed head
As glistening as from the hand of God
And means—what does it mean? Ah well, it's German.
Glaube, mein Herz! A Feeling in the Dark
Brings worlds, brings words that hard-eyed Industry
And all the schools' dark Learning never knew.

And yet it's hard sometimes, I won't deny it.
Take for example my own favorite daemon,
Dear good great Goethe: *ach,* what German!
Very idiomatic, very noble; very like a sibyl.
My favorite style is Leupold von Lerchenau's.
I've memorized his *da und da und da und da*
And whisper it when Life is dark and Death is dark.
There was someone who knew how to speak
To us poor *Kinder* here *im Fremde.*
And Heine! At the ninety-sixth *mir träumte*
I sigh as a poet, but dimple as *ein Schuler.*
And yet—if it's easy is it German?
And yet, that *wunderschöne Lindenbaum*
Im Mondenscheine! What if it is in Schilda?
It's moonlight, isn't it? *Mund, Mond, Herz,* and *Schmerz*
Sing round my head, in *Zeit* and *Ewigkeit,*

And my heart lightens at each *Sorge,* each *Angst:*
I know them well. And *Schicksal! Ach,* you Norns,
As I read I hear your—what's the word for scissors?
And *Katzen* have *Tatzen*—why can't I call someone *Kind?*
What a speech for Poetry (especially Folk-)!

And yet when, in my dreams, *eine schwartzbraune Hexe*
(Who mows on the Neckar, reaps upon the Rhine)
Riffles my yellow ringlets through her fingers,
She only asks me questions: *What is soap?*
I don't know. *A suitcase?* I don't know. *A visit?*
I laugh with joy, and try to say like Lehmann:
"Quin-quin, es ist ein Besuch!"
                            Ah, German!
Till the day I die I'll be in love with German
—If only I don't learn German. . . . I can hear my broken
Voice murmuring to *der Arzt: "Ich—sterber?"*
He answers sympathetically: *"Nein—sterbe."*

If God gave me the choice—but I stole this from Lessing—
Of German and learning German, I'd say: Keep your German!

The thought of *knowing* German terrifies me.
—But surely, this way, no one could learn German?
And yet. . . .
                  It's difficult; is it impossible?
I'm hopeful that it is, but I can't say
For certain: I don't know enough German.

The Girl Dreams That She Is Giselle

Beards of the grain, gray-green: the lances
Shiver. I stare up into the dew.
From her white court—enchantress—
The black queen, shimmering with dew,

Floats to me. In the enchainment
Of a traveling and a working wing
She comes shying, sidelong, settling
On the bare grave by the grain.

And I sleep, curled in my cold cave. . . .
Her wands quiver as a nostril quivers:
The gray veilings of the grave
Crumple, my limbs lock, reverse,

And work me, jointed, to the glance
That licks out to me in white fire
And, piercing, whirs *Remember*
Till my limbs catch. Life, life! I dance.

The Sphinx's Riddle to Oedipus

Not to have guessed is better: what is, ends,
But among fellows, with reluctance,
Clasped by the Woman-Breasted, Lion-Pawed.

To have clasped in one's own arms a mother,
To have killed with one's own hands a father
—Is not this, Lame One, to have been alone?

The seer is doomed for seeing; and to understand
Is to pluck out one's own eyes with one's own hands.
But speak: what has a woman's breasts, a lion's paws?

You stand at midday in the marketplace
Before your life: to see is to have spoken.
—Yet to see, Blind One, is to be alone.

Jerome

Each day brings its toad, each night its dragon.
Der heilige Hieronymus—his lion is at the zoo—
Listens, listens. All the long, soft, summer day
Dreams affright his couch, the deep boils like a pot.
As the sun sets, the last patient rises,
Says to him, *Father;* trembles, turns away.

Often, to the lion, the saint said, *Son.*
To the man the saint says—but the man is gone.
Under a plaque of Gradiva, at gloaming,
The old man boils an egg. When he has eaten
He listens a while. The patients have not stopped.
At midnight, he lies down where his patients lay.

All night the old man whispers to the night.
It listens evenly. The great armored paws
Of its forelegs put together in reflection,
It thinks: *Where Ego was, there Id shall be.*
The world wrestles with it and is changed into it
And after a long time changes it. The dragon

Listens as the old man says, at dawn: *I see*
—There is an old man, naked, in a desert, by a cliff.
He has set out his books, his hat, his ink, his shears
Among scorpions, toads, the wild beasts of the desert.
I lie beside him—I am a lion.
He kneels listening. He holds in his left hand

The stone with which he beats his breast, and holds
In his right hand, the pen with which he puts

Into his book, the words of the angel:
The angel up into whose face he looks.
But the angel does not speak. He looks into the face
Of the night, and the night says—but the night is gone.

He has slept. . . . At morning, when man's flesh is young
And man's soul thankful for it knows not what,
The air is washed, and smells of boiling coffee,
And the sun lights it. The old man walks placidly
To the grocer's; walks on, under leaves, in light,
To a lynx, a leopard—he has come:

The man holds out a lump of liver to the lion,
And the lion licks the man's hand with his tongue.

The Bronze David of Donatello

A sword in his right hand, a stone in his left hand,
He is naked. Shod and naked. Hatted and naked.
The ribbons of his leaf-wreathed, bronze-brimmed bonnet
Are tasseled; crisped into the folds of frills,
Trills, graces, they lie in separation
Among the curls that lie in separation
Upon the shoulders.
                              Lightly, as if accustomed,
Loosely, as if indifferent,
The boy holds in grace
The stone moulded, somehow, by the fingers,
The sword alien, somehow, to the hand.
                                        The boy David
Said of it: "There is none like *that*."
                                  The boy David's
Body shines in freshness, still unhandled,
And thrusts its belly out a little in exact
Shamelessness. Small, close, complacent,
A labyrinth the gaze retraces,
The rib-case, navel, nipples are the features
Of a face that holds us like the whore Medusa's—
Of a face that, like the genitals, is sexless.
What sex has victory?
The mouth's cut Cupid's-bow, the chin's unwinning dimple
Are tightened, a little oily, take, use, notice:
Centering itself upon itself, the sleek
Body with its too-large head, this green
Fruit now forever green, this offending
And efficient elegance draws subtly, supply,

Between the world and itself, a shining
Line of delimitation, demarcation.
The body mirrors itself.
                              Where the armpit becomes breast,
Becomes back, a great crow's-foot is slashed.
Yet who would gash
The sleek flesh so? the cast, filed, shining flesh?
The cuts are folds: these are the folds of flesh
That closes on itself as a knife closes.

The right foot is planted on a wing. Bent back in ease
Upon a supple knee—the toes curl a little, grasping
The crag upon which they are set in triumph—
The left leg glides toward, the left foot lies upon
A head. The head's other wing (the head is bearded
And winged and helmeted and bodiless)
Grows like a swan's wing up inside the leg;
Clothes, as the suit of a swan-maiden clothes,
The leg. The wing reaches, almost, to the rounded
Small childish buttocks. The dead wing warms the leg,
The dead wing, crushed beneath the foot, is swan's-down.
Pillowed upon the rock, Goliath's head
Lies under the foot of David.

Strong in defeat, in death rewarded,
The head dreams what has destroyed it
And is untouched by its destruction.
The stone sunk in the forehead, say the Scriptures;
There is no stone in the forehead. The head is helmed
Or else, unguarded, perfect still.
Borne high, borne long, borne in mastery,
The head is fallen.
                              The new light falls
As if in tenderness, upon the face—
Its masses shift for a moment, like an animal,
And settle, misshapen, into sleep: Goliath
Snores a little in satisfaction.

To so much strength, those overborne by it
Seemed girls, and death came to it like a girl,
Came to it, through the soft air, like a bird—
So that the boy is like a girl, is like a bird
Standing on something it has pecked to death.

The boy stands at ease, his hand upon his hip:
The truth of victory. A Victory
Angelic, almost, in indifference,
An angel sent with no message but this triumph
And alone, now, in his triumph,
He looks down at the head and does not see it.

Upon this head
As upon a spire, the boy David dances,
Dances, and is exalted.
                              Blessed are those brought low,
Blessed is defeat, sleep blessed, blessed death.

The Lost World

(1965)

To Michael di Capua

Next Day

Moving from Cheer to Joy, from Joy to All,
I take a box
And add it to my wild rice, my Cornish game hens.
The slacked or shorted, basketed, identical
Food-gathering flocks
Are selves I overlook. Wisdom, said William James,

Is learning what to overlook. And I am wise
If that is wisdom.
Yet somehow, as I buy All from these shelves
And the boy takes it to my station wagon,
What I've become
Troubles me even if I shut my eyes.

When I was young and miserable and pretty
And poor, I'd wish
What all girls wish: to have a husband,
A house and children. Now that I'm old, my wish
Is womanish:
That the boy putting groceries in my car

See me. It bewilders me he doesn't see me.
For so many years
I was good enough to eat: the world looked at me
And its mouth watered. How often they have undressed me,
The eyes of strangers!
And, holding their flesh within my flesh, their vile

Imaginings within my imagining,
I too have taken

THE LOST WORLD [279

The chance of life. Now the boy pats my dog
And we start home. Now I am good.
The last mistaken,
Ecstatic, accidental bliss, the blind

Happiness that, bursting, leaves upon the palm
Some soap and water—
It was so long ago, back in some Gay
Twenties, Nineties, I don't know . . . Today I miss
My lovely daughter
Away at school, my sons away at school,

My husband away at work—I wish for them.
The dog, the maid,
And I go through the sure unvarying days
At home in them. As I look at my life,
I am afraid
Only that it will change, as I am changing:

I am afraid, this morning, of my face.
It looks at me
From the rear-view mirror, with the eyes I hate,
The smile I hate. Its plain, lined look
Of gray discovery
Repeats to me: "You're old." That's all, I'm old.

And yet I'm afraid, as I was at the funeral
I went to yesterday.
My friend's cold made-up face, granite among its flowers,
Her undressed, operated-on, dressed body
Were my face and body.
As I think of her I hear her telling me

How young I seem; I *am* exceptional;
I think of all I have.
But really no one is exceptional,
No one has anything, I'm anybody,
I stand beside my grave
Confused with my life, that is commonplace and solitary.

The Mockingbird

Look one way and the sun is going down,
Look the other and the moon is rising.
The sparrow's shadow's longer than the lawn.
The bats squeak: "Night is here"; the birds cheep: "Day is gone."
On the willow's highest branch, monopolizing
Day and night, cheeping, squeaking, soaring,
The mockingbird is imitating life.

All day the mockingbird has owned the yard.
As light first woke the world, the sparrows trooped
Onto the seedy lawn: the mockingbird
Chased them off shrieking. Hour by hour, fighting hard
To make the world his own, he swooped
On thrushes, thrashers, jays, and chickadees—
At noon he drove away a big black cat.

Now, in the moonlight, he sits here and sings.
A thrush is singing, then a thrasher, then a jay—
Then, all at once, a cat begins meowing.
A mockingbird can sound like anything.
He imitates the world he drove away
So well that for a minute, in the moonlight,
Which one's the mockingbird? which one's the world?

In Montecito

In a fashionable suburb of Santa Barbara,
Montecito, there visited me one night at midnight
A scream with breasts. As it hung there in the sweet air
That was always the right temperature, the contractors
Who had undertaken to dismantle it, stripped off
The lips, let the air out of the breasts.

                        People disappear
Even in Montecito. Greenie Taliaferro,
In her white maillot, her good figure almost firm,
Her old pepper-and-salt hair stripped by the hairdresser
To nothing and dyed platinum—Greenie has left her Bentley.
They have thrown away her electric toothbrush, someone else slips
The key into the lock of her safety-deposit box
At the Crocker-Anglo Bank; her seat at the cricket matches
Is warmed by buttocks less delectable than hers.
Greenie's girdle is empty.

                    A scream hangs there in the night:
They strip off the lips, let the air out of the breasts,
And Greenie has gone into the Greater Montecito
That surrounds Montecito like the echo of a scream.

THE LOST WORLD

I. Children's Arms

On my way home I pass a cameraman
On a platform on the bumper of a car
Inside which, rolling and plunging, a comedian
Is working; on one white lot I see a star
Stumble to her igloo through the howling gale
Of the wind machines. On Melrose a dinosaur
And pterodactyl, with their immense pale
Papier-mâché smiles, look over the fence
Of *The Lost World.*
                    Whispering to myself the tale
These shout—done with my schoolwork, I commence
My real life: my arsenal, my workshop
Opens, and in impotent omnipotence
I put on the helmet and the breastplate Pop
Cut out and soldered for me. Here is the shield
I sawed from beaver board and painted; here on top
The bow that only Odysseus can wield
And eleven vermilion-ringed, goose-feathered arrows.
(The twelfth was broken on the battlefield
When, searching among snap beans and potatoes,
I stepped on it.) Some dry weeds, a dead cane
Are my spears. The knife on the bureau's

My throwing-knife; the small unpainted biplane
Without wheels—that so often, helped by human hands,
Has taken off from, landed on, the counterpane—
Is my Spad.

        O dead list, that misunderstands
And laughs at and lies about the new live wild
Loves it lists! that sets upright, in the sands
Of age in which nothing grows, where all our friends are old,
A few dried leaves marked THIS IS THE GREENWOOD—
O arms that arm, for a child's wars, the child!

And yet they are good, if anything is good,
Against his enemies . . . Across the seas
At the bottom of the world, where Childhood
Sits on its desert island with Achilles
And Pitamakan, the White Blackfoot:
In the black auditorium, my heart at ease,
I watch the furred castaways (the seniors put
A play on every spring) tame their wild beasts,
Erect their tree house. Chatting over their fruit,
Their coconuts, they relish their stately feasts.
The family's servant, their magnanimous
Master now, rules them by right. Nature's priests,
They worship at Nature's altar; when with decorous
Affection the Admirable Crichton
Kisses a girl like a big Wendy, all of us
Squirm or sit up in our seats . . . Undone
When an English sail is sighted, the prisoners
Escape from their Eden to the world: the real one
Where servants are servants, masters masters,
And no one's magnanimous. The lights go on
And we go off, robbed of our fruit, our furs—
The island that the children ran is gone.

The island sang to me: *Believe! Believe!*
And didn't I know a lady with a lion?
Each evening, as the sun sank, didn't I grieve

To leave *my* tree house for reality?
There was nothing there for me to disbelieve.
At peace among my weapons, I sit in my tree
And feel: *Friday night, then Saturday, then Sunday!*

I'm dreaming of a wolf, as Mama wakes me,
And a tall girl who is—outside it's gray,
I can't remember, I jump up and dress.
We eat in the lighted kitchen. And what is play
For me, for them is habit. Happiness
Is a quiet presence, breathless and familiar:
My grandfather and I sit there in oneness
As the Sunset bus, lit by the lavender
And rose of sunrise, takes us to the dark
Echoing cavern where Pop, a worker,
Works for our living. As he rules a mark,
A short square pencil in his short square hand,
On a great sheet of copper, I make some remark
He doesn't hear. In that hard maze—in that land
That grown men live in—in the world of work,
He measures, shears, solders; and I stand
Empty-handed, watching him. I wander into the murk
The naked light bulbs pierce: the workmen, making something,
Say something to the boy in his white shirt. I jerk
As the sparks fly at me. The man hammering
As acid hisses, and the solder turns to silver,
Seems to me a dwarf hammering out the Ring
In the world under the world. The hours blur;
Bored and not bored, I bend things out of lead.
I wash my smudged hands, as my grandfather
Washes his black ones, with their gritty soap: ahead,
Past their time clock, their pay window, is the blue
And gold and white of noon. The sooty thread
Up which the laborers feel their way into
Their wives and houses, is money; the fact of life,
The secret the grown-ups share, is what to do

THE LOST WORLD

To make money. The husband Adam, Eve his wife
Have learned how not to have to do without
Till Santa Claus brings them their Boy Scout knife—
Nor do they find things in dreams, carry a paper route,
Sell Christmas seals . . .

                    Starting *his* Saturday, his Sunday,
Pop tells me what I love to hear about,
His boyhood in Shelbyville. I play
What he plays, hunt what he hunts, remember
What he remembers: it seems to me I could stay
In that dark forest, lit by one fading ember
Of his campfire, forever . . . But we're home.
I run in love to each familiar member
Of this little state, clustered about the Dome
Of St. Nicholas—this city in which my rabbit
Depends on me, and I on everyone—this first Rome
Of childhood, so absolute in every habit
That when we hear the world our jailor say:
"Tell me, art thou a Roman?" the time we inhabit
Drops from our shoulders, and we answer: "Yea.
I stand at Caesar's judgment seat, I appeal
Unto Caesar."

               I wash my hands, Pop gives his pay
Envelope to Mama; we sit down to our meal.
The phone rings: Mrs. Mercer wonders if I'd care
To go to the library. That would be ideal,
I say when Mama lets me. I comb my hair
And find the four books I have out: *The Food
Of the Gods* was best. Liking that world where
The children eat, and grow giant and good,
I swear as I've often sworn: *"I'll* never forget
What it's like, when *I've* grown up." A prelude
By Chopin, hammered note by note, like alphabet
Blocks, comes from next door. It's played with real feeling,
The feeling of being indoors practicing. "And yet
It's not as if—" a gray electric, stealing
To the curb on silent wheels, has come; and I

See on the back seat (sight more appealing
Than any human sight!) my own friend Lucky,
Half wolf, half police-dog. And he can play the piano—
Play that he does, that is—and jump so high
For a ball that he turns a somersault. "Hello,"
I say to the lady, and hug Lucky . . . In my
Talk with the world, in which it tells me what I know
And I tell it, "I know—" how strange that I
Know nothing, and yet it tells me what I know!—
I appreciate the animals, who stand by
Purring. Or else they sit and pant. It's so—
So *agreeable*. If only people purred and panted!
So, now, Lucky and I sit in our row,
Mrs. Mercer in hers. I take for granted
The tiller by which she steers, the yellow roses
In the bud vases, the whole enchanted
Drawing room of our progress. The glass encloses
As glass does, a womanish and childish
And doggish universe. We press our noses
To the glass and wish: the angel- and devilfish
Floating by on Vine, on Sunset, shut their eyes
And press their noses to their glass and wish.

II. A Night with Lions

When I was twelve we'd visit my aunt's friend
Who owned a lion, the Metro-Goldwyn-Mayer
Lion. I'd play with him, and he'd pretend
To play with me. I was the real player
But he'd trot back and forth inside his cage
Till he got bored. I put Tawny in the prayer
I didn't believe in, not at my age,
But said still; just as I did everything in fours
And gave to Something, on the average,
One cookie out of three. And by my quartz, my ores,
My wood with the bark on it, from the Petrified
Forest, I put his dewclaw . . .
                                        Now the lion roars
His slow comfortable roars; I lie beside
My young, tall, brown aunt, out there in the past
Or future, and I sleepily confide
My dream-discovery: my breath comes fast
Whenever I see someone with your skin,
Hear someone with your voice. The lion's steadfast
Roar goes on in the darkness. I have been
Asleep a while when I remember: you
Are—you, and Tawny was the lion in—
In *Tarzan*. In *Tarzan!* Just as we used to,
I talk to you, you talk to me or pretend
To talk to me as grown-up people do,
Of *Jurgen* and Rupert Hughes, till in the end
I think as a child thinks: "You're my real friend."

III. A Street off Sunset

Sometimes as I drive by the factory
That manufactures, after so long, Vicks
VapoRub Ointment, there rises over me
A eucalyptus tree. I feel its stair-sticks
Impressed on my palms, my insteps, as I climb
To my tree house. The gray leaves make me mix
My coughing chest, anointed at bedtime,
With the smell of the sap trickling from the tan
Trunk, where the nails go in.
                              My lifetime
Got rid of, I sit in a dark blue sedan
Beside my great-grandmother, in Hollywood.
We pass a windmill, a pink sphinx, an Allbran
Billboard; thinking of Salâmmbo, Robin Hood,
The old prospector with his flapjack in the air,
I sit with my hands folded: I am good.

That night as I lie crossways in an armchair
Reading *Amazing Stories* (just as, long before,
I'd lie by my rich uncle's polar bear
On his domed library's reflecting floor
In the last year of the first World War, and see
A poor two-seater being attacked by four
Triplanes, on the cover of the *Literary
Digest,* and a Camel coming to its aid;
I'd feel the bear's fur warm and rough against me,
The colors of the afternoon would fade,
I'd reach into the bear's mouth and hold tight
To its front tooth and think, "I'm not afraid")

There off Sunset, in the lamplit starlight,
A scientist is getting ready to destroy
The world. "It's time for you to say good night,"
Mama tells me; I go on in breathless joy.
"Remember, tomorrow is a school day,"
Mama tells me; I go on in breathless joy.

At last I go to Mama in her gray
Silk, to Pop, to Dandeen in her black
Silk. I put my arms around them, they
Put their arms around me. Then I go back
To my bedroom; I read as I undress.
The scientist is ready to attack.
Mama calls, "Is your light out?" I call back, "Yes,"
And turn the light out. Forced out of life into
Bed, for a moment I lie comfortless
In the blank darkness; then as I always do,
I put on the earphones of the crystal set—
Each bed has its earphones—and the uneasy tissue
Of their far-off star-sound, of the blue-violet
Of space, surrounds the sweet voice from the Tabernacle
Of the Four-Square Gospel. A vague marionette,
Tall, auburn, holds her arms out, to unshackle
The bonds of sin, of sleep—as, next instant, the sun
Holds its arms out through the fig, the lemon tree,
In the back yard the clucking hens all cackle
As Mama brings their chicken feed. I see
My magazine. My magazine! Dressing for school,
I read how the good world wins its victory
Over that bad man. Books; book strap; jump the footstool
You made in Manual Training . . . Then we three
Sit down, and one says grace; and then, by rule,
By that habit that moves the stars, some coffee—
One spoonful—is poured out into my milk
And the milk, transubstantiated, is coffee.
And Mama's weekday wash-dress, Dandeen's soft black silk
Are ways that habit itself makes holy

Just as, on Sunday mornings, Wednesday nights, His will
Comes in their ways—of Church, of Prayer Meeting—to set free
The spirit from the flesh it questions.
                                                    So,
So unquestioned, my own habit moves me
To and through and from school, like a domino,
Till, home, I wake to find that I am playing
Dominoes with Dandeen. Her old face is slow
In pleasure, slow in doubt, as she sits weighing
Strategies: patient, equable, and humble,
She hears what this last child of hers is saying
In pride or bewilderment; and she will grumble
Like a child or animal when, indifferent
To the reasons of my better self, I mumble:
"I'd better stop now—the rabbit . . ."
                                                    I relent
And play her one more game. It *is* miraculous
To have a great-grandmother: I feel different
From others as, between moves, we discuss
The War Between the States. The cheerful troops
Ride up to our farmhouse, steal from us
The spoons, the horses—when their captain stoops
To Dandeen and puts Dandeen on his horse,
She cries . . . As I run by the chicken coops
With lettuce for my rabbit, real remorse
Hurts me, here, now: the little girl is crying
Because I didn't write. Because—
                                                    of course,
I *was* a child, I missed them so. But justifying
Hurts too: if only I could play you one more game,
See you all one more time! I think of you dying
Forgiving me—or not, it is all the same
To the forgiven . . . My rabbit's glad to see me;
He scrambles to me, gives me little tame
Bites before he eats the lettuce. His furry
Long warm soft floppy ears, his crinkling nose
Are reassuring to a child. They guarantee,

As so much here does, that the child knows
Who takes care of him, whom he takes care of.

Mama comes out and takes in the clothes
From the clothesline. She looks with righteous love
At all of us, her spare face half a girl's.
She enters a chicken coop, and the hens shove
And flap and squawk, in fear; the whole flock whirls
Into the farthest corner. She chooses one,
Comes out, and wrings its neck. The body hurls
Itself out—lunging, reeling, it begins to run
Away from Something, to fly away from Something
In great flopping circles. Mama stands like a nun
In the center of each awful, anguished ring.
The thudding and scrambling go on, go on—then they fade,
I open my eyes, it's over . . . Could such a thing
Happen to anything? It could to a rabbit, I'm afraid;
It could to—
           "Mama, you won't kill Reddy ever,
You won't ever, will you?" The farm woman tries to persuade
The little boy, her grandson, that she'd never
Kill the boy's rabbit, never even think of it.
He would like to believe her . . . And whenever
I see her, there in that dark infinite,
Standing like Judith, with the hen's head in her hand,
I explain it away, in vain—a hypocrite,
Like all who love.
                Into the blue wonderland
Of Hollywood, the sun sinks, past the eucalyptus,
The sphinx, the windmill, and I watch and read and
Hold my story tight. And when the bus
Stops at the corner and Pop—Pop!—steps down
And I run out to meet him, a blurred nimbus,
Half-red, half-gold, enchants his sober brown
Face, his stooped shoulders, into the All-Father's.
He tells me about the work he's done downtown,
We sit there on the steps. My universe

Mended almost, I tell him about the scientist. I say,
"He couldn't really, could he, Pop?" My comforter's
Eyes light up, and he laughs. "No, that's just play,
Just make-believe," he says. The sky is gray,
We sit there, at the end of our good day.

A Well-to-Do Invalid

When you first introduced me to your nurse
I thought: "She's like your wife." I mean, I thought:
"She's like your nurse—" it was your wife.

She gave this old friend of her husband's
A pale ingratiating smile; we talked
And she agreed with me about everything.
I thought: "She's quite agreeable."
You gave a pleased laugh—you were feeling good.
She laughed and agreed with you.
       I said to her
—That is, I didn't say to her: "You liar!"
She held out
Her deck of smiles, I cut, and she dealt.

Almost as the years have sprung up, fallen back,
I've seen you in and out of bed; meanwhile,
Hovering solicitously alongside,
This governess, this mother
In her off-whites—pretty as a nurse
Is thinly and efficiently and optimistically
Pretty—has spoken with an enthusiasm
Like winter sunlight, of the comprehensiveness of insurance.
If you want it to, it can cover anything.

Like the governor on an engine, she has governed
Your rashness. And how many sins
She has forgiven in her big child! How many times
She has telephoned in an emergency

For the right specialist!
After I'd left your bed she'd take me to the door
And tell me about your heart and bowels.
When you were up and talking she would listen
A long time, oh so long! but go to bed
Before we did, with a limp, wan, almost brave
"Goodnight!" You are a natural
Disaster she has made her own. Meanly
Clinging to you, taking care—all praise
And understanding outside, and inside all insurance—
She has stood by you like a plaster Joan of Arc.
Prematurely tired, prematurely
Mature, she has endured
Much, indulgently
Repeating like a piece of white carbon paper
The opinions of that boisterous, sick thing, a man.
I can see through her—but then, who can't?
Her dishonesty is so transparent
It has about it a kind of honesty.
She has never once said what she thought, done what she wanted,
But (as if invented by some old economist
And put on an island, to trade with her mate)
Has acted in impersonal self-interest.

Never to do one thing for its own sake!

Year in, year out, with what sincerity
You said anything, demanded everything,
And she, the liar!
Was good to you—oh, insincerely good,
Good for all the worst reasons. Good.
And she was nice to me, and I was nice
To her: I *wanted* to be nice to her.
She was wrong, and I was right, and I was sick of it.
It wasn't right for her always to be wrong
And work so hard and get so little: I felt guilty
Because I wasn't on her side. I was on her side.

THE LOST WORLD   [295

It was a terrible shock to me when she died.
I saw her cheeks red for the first time
Among the snowdrifts covering her coffin;
And you were up and talking, well with grief.
As I realized how easily you'd fill
This vacancy, I was sorry
For you and for that pale self-sufficient ghost
That had tended so long your self-sufficiency.

The X-Ray Waiting Room in the Hospital

I am dressed in my big shoes and wrinkled socks
And one of the light blue, much-laundered smocks
The men and women of this country wear.
All of us miss our own underwear
And the old days. These new, plain, mean
Days of pain and care, this routine
Misery has made us into cases, the one case
The one doctor cures forever . . . The face
The patients have in common hopes without hope
For something from outside the machine—its wife,
Its husband—to burst in and hand it life;
But when the door opens, it's another smock.
It looks at us, we look at it. Our little flock
Of blue-smocked sufferers, in naked equality,
Longs for each nurse and doctor who goes by
Well and dressed, to make friends with, single out, the *I*
That used to be, but we are indistinguishable.
It is better to lie flat upon a table,
A dye in my spine. The roentgenologist
Introduces me to a kind man, a specialist
In spines like mine: the lights go out, he rotates me.
My myelogram is negative. This elates me,
The good-humored specialist congratulates me,
And I take off my smock in joy, put on
My own pajamas, my own dressing gown,
And ride back to my own room, 601.

In Galleries

The guard has a right to despair. He stands by God
Being tickled by the Madonna; the baby laughs
And pushes himself away from his mother.
The lines and hollows of the piece of stone
Are human to people: their hearts go out to it.
But the guard has no one to make him human—
They walk through him as if he were a reflection.
The guard does not see them either, you are sure,
But he notices when someone touches something
And tells him not to; otherwise he stands
Blind, silent, among the people who go by
Indistinguishably, like minutes, like the hours.
Slowly the days go by, the years go by
Quickly: how many minutes does it take
To make a guard's hair uniformly gray?

But in Italy, sometimes, a guard is different.
He is poorer than a guard would be at home—
How cheap his old uniform is, how dirty!
He is a fountain of Italian:
He pulls back a curtain, shows you where to stand,
Cajoles you back to the Ludovisi Throne
To show you the side people forget to look at—
And exclaiming hopefully, vivaciously,
Bellissima! he shows you that in the smashed
Head of the crouching Venus the untouched lips
Are still parted hopefully, vivaciously,
In a girl's clear smile. He speaks and smiles;
And whether or not you understand Italian,

You understand he is human, and still hopes—
And, smiling, repeating his *Bellissima!*
You give him a dime's worth of aluminum.

You may even see a guard who is dumb, whose rapt
Smile, curtain-pulling-back, place-indication,
Plain conviction that he guards a miracle
Are easier to understand than Italian.
His gestures are full of faith in—of faith.
When at last he takes a magnifying glass
From the shiny pocket of his uniform
And shows you that in the painting of a woman
Who holds in her arms the death of the world
The something on the man's arm is the woman's
Tear, you and the man and the woman and the guard
Are dumbly one. You say *Bellissima!*
Bellissima! and give him his own rapt,
Dumb, human smile, convinced he guards
A miracle. Leaving, you hand the man
A quarter's worth of nickel and aluminum.

Well Water

What a girl called "the dailiness of life"
(Adding an errand to your errand. Saying,
"Since you're up . . ." Making you a means to
A means to a means to) is well water
Pumped from an old well at the bottom of the world.
The pump you pump the water from is rusty
And hard to move and absurd, a squirrel-wheel
A sick squirrel turns slowly, through the sunny
Inexorable hours. And yet sometimes
The wheel turns of its own weight, the rusty
Pump pumps over your sweating face the clear
Water, cold, so cold! you cup your hands
And gulp from them the dailiness of life.

The Lost Children

Two little girls, one fair, one dark,
One alive, one dead, are running hand in hand
Through a sunny house. The two are dressed
In red and white gingham, with puffed sleeves and sashes.
They run away from me . . . But I am happy;
When I wake I feel no sadness, only delight.
I've seen them again, and I am comforted
That, somewhere, they still are.

It is strange
To carry inside you someone else's body;
To know it before it's born;
To see at last that it's a boy or girl, and perfect;
To bathe it and dress it; to watch it
Nurse at your breast, till you almost know it
Better than you know yourself—better than it knows itself.
You own it as you made it.
You are the authority upon it.

But as the child learns
To take care of herself, you know her less.
Her accidents, adventures are her own,
You lose track of them. Still, you know more
About her than anyone *except* her.

Little by little the child in her dies.
You say, "I have lost a child, but gained a friend."
You feel yourself gradually discarded.
She argues with you or ignores you

Or is kind to you. She who begged to follow you
Anywhere, just so long as it was you,
Finds follow the leader no more fun.
She makes few demands; you are grateful for the few.

The young person who writes once a week
Is the authority upon herself.
She sits in my living room and shows her husband
My albums of her as a child. He enjoys them
And makes fun of them. I look too
And I realize the girl in the matching blue
Mother-and-daughter dress, the fair one carrying
The tin lunch box with the half-pint thermos bottle
Or training her pet duck to go down the slide
Is lost just as the dark one, who is dead, is lost.
But the world in which the two wear their flared coats
And the hats that match, exists so uncannily
That, after I've seen its pictures for an hour,
I believe in it: the bandage coming loose
One has in the picture of the other's birthday,
The castles they are building, at the beach for asthma.
I look at them and all the old sure knowledge
Floods over me, when I put the album down
I keep saying inside: "I *did* know those children.
I braided those braids. I was driving the car
The day that she stepped in the can of grease
We were taking to the butcher for our ration points.
I *know* those children. I know all about them.
Where are they?"

I stare at her and try to see some sign
Of the child she was. I can't believe there isn't any.
I tell her foolishly, pointing at the picture,
That I keep wondering where she is.
She tells me, "Here I am."
                                        Yes, and the other
Isn't dead, but has everlasting life . . .

The girl from next door, the borrowed child,
Said to me the other day, "You like children so much,
Don't you want to have some of your own?"
I couldn't believe that she could say it.
I thought: "Surely you can look at me and see them."

When I see them in my dreams I feel such joy.
If I could dream of them every night!

When I think of my dream of the little girls
It's as if we were playing hide-and-seek.
The dark one
Looks at me longingly, and disappears;
The fair one stays in sight, just out of reach
No matter where I reach. I am tired
As a mother who's played all day, some rainy day.
I don't want to play it any more, I don't want to,
But the child keeps on playing, so I play.

Three Bills

Once at the Plaza, looking out into the park
Past the Colombian ambassador, his wife,
And their two children—past a carriage driver's
Rusty top hat and brown bearskin rug—
I heard three hundred-thousand-dollar bills
Talking at breakfast. One was male and two were female.
The gray female complained
Of the plantation lent her at St. Vincent
"There at the end of nowhere." The brown stocky male's
Chin beard wagged as he said: "I don't see,
Really, how you can say that of St. Vincent."
"But it is at the end of nowhere!" "St. *Vincent?*"
"Yes, St. Vincent." "Don't you mean St. Martin?"
"Of *course,* St. Martin. That's what I meant to say, St. Martin!"
The blond female smiled with the remnants of a child's
Smile and said: "What a pity that it's not St. Kitts!"
The bearded male went for a moment to the lavatory
And his wife said in the same voice to her friend:
"We can't stay anywhere. We haven't stayed a month
In one place for the last three years.
He flirts with the yardboys and we have to leave."
Her friend showed that she was sorry; I was sorry
To see that the face of Woodrow Wilson on the blond
Bill—the suffused face about to cry
Or not to cry—was a face that under different
Circumstances would have been beautiful, a woman's.

Hope

To prefer the nest in the linden
By Apartment Eleven, the Shoreham
Arms, to Apartment Eleven
Would be childish. But we are children.

If the squirrel's nest has no doorman
To help us out of the taxi, up the tree,
Still, even the Shoreham has no squirrel
To meet us with blazing eyes, the sound of rocks knocked together,
At the glass door under the marquee.

At two in the morning
Of Christmas, there is a man at the glass
Door, a man inside the bronze
Elevator. We get off at four,
Walk up the corridor, unlock the door,
And go down stone steps, past a statue,
To the nest where the father squirrel, and the mother squirrel, and
    the baby squirrel
Would live, if the baby squirrel could have his way.

Just now he has his way.
Curled round and round in his sleigh
Bed, the child of the apartment
Sleeps, guarded by a lion six feet long.
And, too,
The parents of the apartment fight like lions.
Between us, we are almost twelve feet long.

Beside the harpsichord a lonely
Fir tree sleeps on a cold
Hill of gifts; it holds out branches
Laden with ice and snow.

Beyond it are paintings by Magnasco,
Ensor, Redon.
These are valued at—some value I forget,
Which I learned from—I cannot remember the source.

Here, from a province of Norway, a grandfather's
Clock with the waist and bust of a small
But unusually well-developed woman
Is as if invented by Chagall.
Floating on the floor,
It ticks, to no one, interminable proposals.

But, married, I turn into my mother
Is the motto of all such sundials.
The sun, shattering on them,
Says, *Clean, clean, clean;* says, *White, white, white.*
The hours of the night
Bend darkly over them; at midnight a maiden
Pops out, says: *Midnight, and all's white.*

The snow-cream my son is dreaming of eating
In the morning, is no whiter than my wife,
And all her lipsticks are like blackberries.
Looking into the cool
Dry oval of her face—snow tracked with eyes,
Lips, nostrils, the gray grained
Shadow of some sorrow, some repugnance
Conquered once, come back in easy conquest—
I read in it my simple story.
Breakfasting among apple blossoms, the first fiery
Rainbow that rings, in spring's and dawn's new dew,

The curly-locked Medusa, I—
                              I—
To put it in black and white,
We were married.
                    "A wife is a wife,"
Some husband said. If only it were true!
My wife is a girl playing house
With the girl from next door, a girl called the father.
And yet I *am* a father, my wife is a mother,
Oh, every inch a mother; and our son's
Asleep in a squirrel's nest in a tree.

(The mother of one of us
Disappeared while circumnavigating the earth.
The people of a saucer, landing on her liner,
Said: "Take us to your leader."
They were led to the mother.
When she had answered their unasked
Questions, they flew off—and to this day, in another
Star system many, many light-years away,
She governs the happy people of a planet.

My own mother disappeared in the same way.)

That? That is Pennsylvania Dutch, a bear
Used to mark butter. As for this,
It is sheer alchemy:
The only example of an atomic bomb
Earlier than the eleventh century.
It is attributed to the atelier
Of an Albigensian,
Who, fortunately, was unable to explode it.
We use it as a planter.

We feel that it is so American.

Sometimes, watching on television

My favorite serial, *A Sad*
Heart at the Supermarket:
The Story of a Woman Who Had Everything,
I look at my wife—
And see her; and remember, always with the same surprise,
"Why, you are beautiful." And beauty is a good,
It makes us desire it. When, sometimes, I see this desire
In some wife's eyes, some husband's eyes,
I think of the God-Fish in a nightmare
I had once: like giants in brown space-suits
But like fish, also, they went upright through the streets
And were useless to struggle with, but, struggled with,
Showed me a story that, they said, was the story
Of the Sleeping Beauty. It was the old story
But ended differently: when the Prince kissed her on the lips
She wiped her lips
And with a little *moue*—in the dream, a little mouse—
Turned over and went back to sleep.
I woke, and went to tell my wife the story;
And had she not resembled
My mother as she slept, I had done it.

She resembled a recurrent
Scene from my childhood.
A scene called Mother Has Fainted.
Mother's body
Was larger, now it no longer moved;
Breathed, somehow, as if it no longer breathed.
Her face no longer smiled at us
Or frowned at us. Did anything to us.
Her face was queerly flushed
Or else queerly pale; I am no longer certain.
That it was queer I am certain.

We did as we were told:
Put a pillow under her head (or else her feet)

To make the blood flood to her head (or else away from it).
Now she was set.

The sound she had made, falling,
The sound of furniture,
Had kept on, in the silence
Of everything except ourselves,
As we tugged her into position.
Now we too were silent.

It was as if God were taking a nap.

We waited for the world to be the world
And looked out, shyly, into the little lanes
That went off from the great dark highway, Mother's Highway,
And wondered whether we would ever take them—

And she came back to life, and we never took them.

The night has stopped breathing.
The moonlight streams up through the linden
From the street lamp, and is printed upon heaven.
The floor and the Kirman on the floor
And the gifts on the Kirman
Are dark, but there is a patch of moonlight on the ceiling.

The moonlight comes to the fir
That stands meekly, a child in its nightgown,
In the midst of many shadows.
It has come to its father and mother
To wake them, for it is morning
In the child's dream; and the father wakes
And leads it back to its bed, and it never wakes.

In the morning our father
In his false white, false red,
Took out his teeth and fed them to his reindeer,

THE LOST WORLD   [309

False reindeer, and gave us the presents his elves had made at the
   Pole
And gave Mother the money he had made at the Pole—
And explained it all, excused it all
With a cough, the smallest of all small
Coughs; but it was no use, it was unexplainable,
Inexcusable. What is man
That Thou art mindful of him?
A man is a means;
What, amputated, leaves a widow.
He was never able to make the elves real to Mother:
He was a shadow
And one evening went down with the sun.
I have followed in my father's light, faint footsteps
Down to some place under the sun, under the moon,
Lit by the light of the streetlamp far below.
Back far enough, down deep enough, one comes to the Mothers.

Just as, within the breast of Everyman,
Something keeps scolding in his mother's voice,
Just so, within each woman, an Old Woman
Rocks, rocks, impatient for her kingdom.

"I have a little shadow that goes in and out with me,
And what can be the use of him I—but that isn't fair,
He is some *use*," a woman in the twilight sings to me.

When the white nun handed to my white
Wife her poor red son—my poor red son—
Stunned, gasping, like the skin inside a blister,
Something shrank outside me;
I saw what I realized I must have seen
When I saw our wedding picture in the paper:
My wife resembled—my wife *was*—my mother.

Still, that is how it's done.
In this house everyone's a mother.

My wife's a mother, the cook's a mother, the maid's a mother,
The governess's—
                    why isn't the governess a man?
The things that *I* buy, even,
In a week or two they go over to my wife.
The Kirman, the Ensor, that grandmother's clock
Look by me with their bald,
Obsessional, reproachful eyes, a family
One has married into, a mother-in-law, a—
What is one's wife's mother's mother called?
Do all men's mothers perish through their sons?
As the child starts into life, the woman dies
Into a girl—and, scolding the doll she owns,
The single scholar of her little school,
Her task, her plaything, her possession,
She assumes what is God's alone, responsibility.

When my son reached into the toaster with a fork
This morning, and handed me the slice of toast
So clumsily, dropped it, and looked up at me
So clumsily, I saw that he resembled—
That he *was*—

                    I didn't see it.
The next time that they say to me: "He has your eyes,"
I'll tell them the truth: he has his own eyes.
My son's eyes look a little like a squirrel's,
A little like a fir tree's. They don't look like mine,
They don't look like my wife's.
                              And after all,
If they don't look like mine, do mine?

You wake up, some fine morning, old.
And old means changed; changed means you wake up new.

In this house, after all, we're not all mothers.
I'm not, my son's not, and the fir tree's not.
And I said the maid was, really I don't know.

The fir tree stands there on its cold
White hill of gifts, white, cold,
And yet really it's green; it's evergreen.

Who knows, who knows?
I'll say to my wife, in the morning:
"You're not like my mother . . . You're no mother!"
And my wife will say to me—
                              she'll say to me—
At first, of course, she may say to me: "You're dreaming."
But later on, who knows?

The Bird of Night

A shadow is floating through the moonlight.
Its wings don't make a sound.
Its claws are long, its beak is bright.
Its eyes try all the corners of the night.

It calls and calls: all the air swells and heaves
And washes up and down like water.
The ear that listens to the owl believes
In death. The bat beneath the eaves,

The mouse beside the stone are still as death.
The owl's air washes them like water.
The owl goes back and forth inside the night,
And the night holds its breath.

Bats

A bat is born
Naked and blind and pale.
His mother makes a pocket of her tail
And catches him. He clings to her long fur
By his thumbs and toes and teeth.
And then the mother dances through the night
Doubling and looping, soaring, somersaulting—
Her baby hangs on underneath.
All night, in happiness, she hunts and flies.
Her high sharp cries
Like shining needlepoints of sound
Go out into the night and, echoing back,
Tell her what they have touched.
She hears how far it is, how big it is,
Which way it's going:
She lives by hearing.
The mother eats the moths and gnats she catches
In full flight; in full flight
The mother drinks the water of the pond
She skims across. Her baby hangs on tight.
Her baby drinks the milk she makes him
In moonlight or starlight, in mid-air.
Their single shadow, printed on the moon
Or fluttering across the stars,
Whirls on all night; at daybreak
The tired mother flaps home to her rafter.
The others all are there.
They hang themselves up by their toes,
They wrap themselves in their brown wings.

Bunched upside-down, they sleep in air.
Their sharp ears, their sharp teeth, their quick sharp faces
Are dull and slow and mild.
All the bright day, as the mother sleeps,
She folds her wings about her sleeping child.

The One Who Was Different

Twice you have been around the world
And once around your life.
You said to my wife, once:
"Oh no, I've made all my long trips.
Now I'll make my short trips."

Is this a long trip or a short trip
Or no trip?

You were always happy to be different.
You queer thing: you who cooked
Straight through the cookbook; you who looked
As if the children next door dressed you in the attic
And yet came home from Finland fur
From head to foot: today you look regularly erratic
In your great lead-lined cloak
Of ferns and flowers,
Of maidenhair, carnations, white chrysanthemums,
As you lie here about not to leave
On the trip after the last.

Ah, Miss I———,
Hold not thy peace at my tears.

I hear moved—you unmoved, steadfast—
The earnest expectation of the creature
That comes up, and is cut down, like a flower:
"We shall not all sleep, but in a moment,
In the twinkling of an eye,

We shall be changed. When this corruptible
Shall have put on incorruption, and this mortal
Shall have put on immortality,
Then death is swallowed up in victory.
O death, where is thy sting? O grave, where is thy victory?"

The words that they read over you
Are all that I could wish.
If my eyes weren't open,
I'd think that I had dreamed them.
They seem too good for this former woman,
This nice dead thing that used to smile
Like a woodchuck that has learned to smile
When its keeper tells it: "Smile now!"
                                        Where's your smile
Now that the world is disassembling your features?
Is a smile like life,
A way things look for a while,
A temporary arrangement of the matter?

I feel like the first men who read Wordsworth.
It's so simple I can't understand it.

You give me the feeling that the universe
Was made by something more than human
For something less than human.

But I identify myself, as always,
With something that there's something wrong with,
With something human.
This is the sort of thing that could happen to anyone
Except—
        except—

Just now, behind the not-yet-drawn
Curtain (the curtain that in a moment will disclose
The immediate family sitting there in chairs)

I made out—off-stage looking on-stage,
Black under a white hat from Best's—
A pair of eyes. Too young to have learned yet
What's seen and what's obscene, they look in eagerly
For this secret that the grown-ups have, the secret
That, shared, makes one a grown-up.
They look without sympathy or empathy,
With interest.

               Without me.

It is as if in a moment,
In the twinkling of an eye,
I were old enough to have made up my mind
What not to look at, ever . . .
                       If a man made up his mind
About death, he could do without it.
He could shut his eyes
So tight that when they came to wake him,
To shake him and to say: "Wake up! Wake up!
It's time for you to die,"
He wouldn't hear a thing.
                 Oh, Miss I———,
If only I could have made you see it!
If only I could have got you to make up your mind
In time, in time! Instead of someone's standing here
Telling you that you have put on incorruption,
You would have lain here—I can see it—
Encased in crystal, continually mortal,
While the years rolled over you . . .
                    In my mind's eye
I can hear a teacher saying to a class
About the twenty-first or -second century:
"Children, remember you have seen
The oldest man that ever didn't die!"

Woman, that is.

A Hunt in the Black Forest

After the door shuts and the footsteps die,
He calls out: "Mother?"
The wind roars in the leaves: his cold hands, curled
Within his curled, cold body, his blurred head
Are warmed and tremble; and the red leaves flow
Like cells across the spectral, veined,
Whorled darkness of his vision.
                              The red dwarf
Whispers, "The leaves are turning"; and he reads
The dull, whorled notes, that tremble like a wish
Over the branched staves of the wood.

The stag is grazing in the wood.

A horn calls, over and over, its three notes.
The flat, gasped answer sounds and dies—
The geese call from a hidden sky.
The rain's sound grows into the roar
Of the flood below the falls; the rider calls
To the shape within the shades, a dwarf
Runs back into the brush. But smoke
Drifts to the gelding's nostrils, and he neighs.
From the wet starlight of the glade
A hut sends out its chink of fire.

The rider laughs out: in the branches, birds
Are troubled, stir.

He opens the door. A man looks up
And then slowly, with a kind of smile,

Acts out his own astonishment.
He points to his open mouth: the tongue
Is cut out. Bares his shoulder, points
To the crown branded there, and smiles. The hunter frowns.
The pot bubbles from the embers in the laugh
The mute laughs. With harsh habitual
Impatience, the hunter questions him.
The man nods vacantly—
Shaken, he makes his gobbling sound
Over and over. The hunter ladles from the pot
Into a wooden bowl, the shining stew.
He eats silently. The mute
Counts spoonfuls on his fingers. Come to ten,
The last finger, he laughs out in joy
And scuttles like a mouse across the floor
To the door and the door's darkness. The king breathes hard,
Rises—and something catches at his heart,
Some patient senseless thing
Begins to squeeze his heart out in its hands.
His jerking body, bent into a bow,
Falls out of the hands onto the table,
Bends, bends further, till at last it breaks.
But, broken, it still breathes—a few whistling breaths
That slow, are intermittent, cease.

Now only the fire thinks, like a heart
Cut from its breast. Light leaps, the shadows fall
In the old alternation of the world . . .

Two sparks, at the dark horn of the window,
Look, as stars look, into the shadowy hut,
Turn slowly, searching:
Then a bubbled, gobbling sound begins,
The sound of the pot laughing on the fire.
—The pot, overturned among the ashes,
Is cold as death.

Something is scratching, panting. A little voice
Says, "Let *me!* Let *me!*" The mute
Puts his arms around the dwarf and raises him.

The pane is clouded with their soft slow breaths,
The mute's arms tire; but they gaze on and on,
Like children watching something wrong.
Their blurred faces, caught up in one wish,
Are blurred into one face: a child's set face.

The House in the Wood

At the back of the houses there is the wood.
While there is a leaf of summer left, the wood

Makes sounds I can put somewhere in my song,
Has paths I can walk, when I wake, to good

Or evil: to the cage, to the oven, to the House
In the Wood. It is a part of life, or of the story

We make of life. But after the last leaf,
The last light—for each year is leafless,

Each day lightless, at the last—the wood begins
Its serious existence: it has no path,

No house, no story; it resists comparison . . .
One clear, repeated, lapping gurgle, like a spoon

Or a glass breathing, is the brook,
The wood's fouled midnight water. If I walk into the wood

As far as I can walk, I come to my own door,
The door of the House in the Wood. It opens silently:

On the bed is something covered, something humped
Asleep there, awake there—but what? I do not know.

I look, I lie there, and yet I do not know.
How far out my great echoing clumsy limbs

Stretch, surrounded only by space! For time has struck,
All the clocks are stuck now, for how many lives,

On the same second. Numbed, wooden, motionless,
We are far under the surface of the night.

Nothing comes down so deep but sound: a car, freight cars,
A high soft droning, drawn out like a wire

Forever and ever—is this the sound that Bunyan heard
So that he thought his bowels would burst within him?—

Drift on, on, into nothing. Then someone screams
A scream like an old knife sharpened into nothing.

It is only a nightmare. No one wakes up, nothing happens,
Except there is gooseflesh over my whole body—

And that too, after a little while, is gone.
I lie here like a cut-off limb, the stump the limb has left . . .

Here at the bottom of the world, what was before the world
And will be after, holds me to its black

Breasts and rocks me: the oven is cold, the cage is empty,
In the House in the Wood, the witch and her child sleep.

Woman

"All things become thee, being thine," I think sometimes
As I think of you. I think: "How many faults
In thee have seemed a virtue!" While your taste is on my tongue
The years return, blessings innumerable
As the breaths that you have quickened, gild my flesh.
Lie there in majesty!
                    When, like Disraeli, I murmur
That you are more like a mistress than a wife,
More like an angel than a mistress; when, like Satan,
I hiss in your ear some vile suggestion,
Some delectable abomination,
You smile at me indulgently: "Men, men!"

You smile at mankind, recognizing in it
The absurd occasion of your fall.
For men—as your soap operas, as your *Home Journals,*
As your hearts whisper—men are only children.
And you believe them. Truly, you are children.

Should I love you so dearly if you weren't?
If I weren't?
            O morning star,
Each morning my dull heart goes out to you
And rises with the sun, but with the sun
Sets not, but all the long night nests within your eyes.

Men's share of grace, of all that can make bearable,
Lovable almost, the apparition, Man,
Has fallen to you. Erect, extraordinary

As a polar bear on roller skates, he passes
On into the Eternal . . .
                              From your pedestal, you watch
Admiringly, when you remember to.

Let us form, as Freud has said, "a group of two."
You are the best thing that this world can offer—
He said so. Or I remember that he said so;
If I am mistaken it's a Freudian error,
An error nothing but a man would make.
Women can't bear women. Cunningly engraved
On many an old wife's dead heart is "Women,
Beware women!" And yet it was a man
Sick of too much sweetness—of a life
Rich with a mother, wife, three daughters, a wife's sister,
An abyss of analysands—who wrote: "I cannot
Escape the notion (though I hesitate
To give it expression) that for women
The level of what is ethically normal
Is different from what it is in men.
Their superego"—he goes on without hesitation—
"Is never so inexorable, so impersonal,
So independent of its emotional
Origins as we require it in a man."

Did not the angel say to Abraham
That he would spare the cities of the plain
If there were found in them ten unjust women?
—That is to say, merciful; that is to say,
Extravagant; that is to say, unjust as judges
Who look past judgment, always, to the eyes
(Long-lashed, a scapegoat's, yearning sheepishly)
Under the curly-yarned and finger-tickling locks
Of that dear-wooled, inconsequential head.

You save him and knit an afghan from his hair.

And in the cold tomb, save for you, and afghanless,
He leaves you to wage wars, build bridges, visit women
Who like to run their fingers through his hair.
He complains of you to them, describing you
As "the great love of my life." What pains it took
To win you, a mere woman!—"worst of all,"
He ends, "a woman who was not my type."

But then, a woman never is a man's type.
Possessed by that prehistoric unforgettable
Other One, who never again is equaled
By anyone, he searches for his ideal,
The Good Whore who reminds him of his mother.
The realities are too much one or the other,
Too much like Mother or too bad . . . Too bad!
He resigns himself to them—as "they are, after all,
The best things that are offered in that line";
And should he not spare Nineveh, that city
Wherein are more than sixscore thousand women
Who cannot tell their left hand from their right,
But smile up hopefully at the policeman?

Are you as mercenary as the surveys show?
What a way to put it! Let us write instead
That you are realists; or as a realist might say,
Naturalists. It's in man's nature—woman's nature
To want the best, and to be careless how it comes.
And what have we all to sell except ourselves?
Poor medlar, no sooner ripe than rotten!
You must be seized today, or stale tomorrow
Into a wife, a mother, a homemaker,
An Elector of the League of Women Voters.
Simply by your persistence, you betray
Yourselves and all that was yours, you momentary
And starry instances; are falling, falling
Into the sagging prison of your flesh,
Residuary legatees of earth, grandmothers

And legal guardians of the tribes of men.
If all Being showered down on you in gold
Would you not murmur, with averted breasts: "Not now"?

When he looks upon your nakedness he is blinded.
Your breasts and belly are one incandescence
Like the belly of an idol: how can a man go in that fire
And come out living? "The burnt child dreads the fire,"
He says later, warming his hands before the fire.
Last—last of all—he says that there are three things sure:
"That the Dog returns to his Vomit and the Sow returns to her Mire,
And the burnt Fool's bandaged finger goes wabbling back to the
        Fire."

Part of himself is shocked at part of himself
As, beside the remnants of a horrible
Steak, a little champagne, he confesses
Candidly to you: "In the beginning
There was a baby boy that loved its mother,
There was a baby girl that loved its mother.
The boy grew up and got to love a woman,
The girl grew up and had to love a man.
Because isn't that what's wrong with women? Men?
Isn't that the reason you're the way you are?
Why *are* you the way you are?"
                                You say: "Because."

When you float with me through the Tunnel of Love
Or Chamber of Horrors—one of those concessions—
And a great hand, dripping, daggered, reaches out for you
And you scream, and it misses, and another hand,
Soiled, hairy, lustful, reaches out for you
And you faint, and it misses: when you come to,
You say, looking up weakly: "Did you notice?
The second one had on a wedding ring."

May the Devil fly away with the roof of the house
That you and I aren't happy in, you angel!

And yet, how quickly the bride's veils evaporate!
A girl hesitates a moment in mid-air
And settles to the ground a wife, a mother.
Each evening a tired spirit visits
Her full house; wiping his feet upon a mat
Marked *Women and Children First,* the husband looks
At this grown woman. She stands there in slacks
Among the real world's appliances,
Women, and children; kisses him hello
Just as, that morning, she kissed him goodbye,
And he sits down, till dinner, with the paper.
This home of theirs is haunted by a girl's
Ghost. At sunset a woodpecker knocks
At a tree by the window, asking their opinion
Of life. The husband answers, "Life is life,"
And when his wife calls to him from the kitchen
He tells her who it was, and what he wanted.
Beating the whites of seven eggs, the beater
Asks her her own opinion; she says, "Life
Is life." "See how it sounds to say it isn't,"
The beater tempts her. "Life is not life,"
She says. It sounds the same. Putting her cake
Into the oven, she is satisfied
Or else dissatisfied: it sounds the same.
With knitted brows, with care's swift furrows nightly
Smoothed out with slow care, and come again with care
Each morning, she lives out her gracious life.

But you should gush out over being like a spring
The drinker sighs to lift his mouth from: a dark source
That brims over, with its shining, every cup
That is brought to it in shadow, filled there, broken there.
You look at us out of sunlight and of shade,
Dappled, inexorable, the last human power.
All earth is the labyrinth along whose ways
You walk mirrored: rosy-fingered, many-breasted
As Diana of the Ephesians, strewing garments

Before the world's eyes narrowed in desire.
Now, naked on my doorstep, in the sun
Gold-armed, white-breasted, pink-cheeked, and black-furred,
You call to me, "Come"; and when I come say, "Go,"
Smiling your soft contrary smile . . .
                              He who has these
Is secure from the other sorrows of the world.
While you are how am I alone? Your voice
Soothes me to sleep, and finds fault with my dreams,
Till I murmur in my sleep: "Man is the animal
That finds fault."
                    And you say: "Who said that?"

But be, as you have been, my happiness;
Let me sleep beside you, each night, like a spoon;
When, starting from my dreams, I groan to you,
May your *I love you* send me back to sleep.
At morning bring me, grayer for its mirroring,
The heavens' sun perfected in your eyes.

Washing

On days like these
What doesn't blow away will freeze.
The washing flops on the line
In absolute torment—
And when the wind dies for a moment
The washing has the collapsed abject
Look of the sack of skin
Michelangelo made himself in his *Last Judgment.*

Its agonies
Are heartfelt as a sneeze.

When Mama wrung a chicken's
Neck, the body rushed around
And around and around the yard in circles.
The circles weren't its own idea
But it went on with them as if it would never stop.
The expression of its body was intense,
Immense
As this *Help! Help! Help!*
The reeling washing shrieks to someone, Someone.

But as old hens like to say,
The world isn't chickenhearted.
The washing inhabits a universe
Indifferent to the woes of washing,
A world—as the washing puts it—
A world that washing never made.

In Nature There Is Neither Right
nor Left nor Wrong

Men are what they do, women are what they are.
These erect breasts, like marble coming up for air
Among the cataracts of my breathtaking hair,
Are goods in my bazaar, a door ajar
To the first paradise of whores and mothers.

Men buy their way back into me from the upright
Right-handed puzzle that men fit together
From their deeds, the pieces. Women shoot from
Or dive back into its interstices
As squirrels inhabit a geometry.

We women sell ourselves for sleep, for flesh,
To those wide-awake, successful spirits, men—
Who, lying each midnight with the sinister
Beings, their dark companions, women,
Suck childhood, beasthood, from a mother's breasts.

A fat bald rich man comes home at twilight
And lectures me about my parking tickets; gowned in gold
Lamé, I look at him and think: "You're old,
I'm old." Husband, I sleep with you every night
And like it; but each morning when I wake
I've dreamed of my first love, the subtle serpent.

The Old and the New Masters

About suffering, about adoration, the old masters
Disagree. When someone suffers, no one else eats
Or walks or opens the window—no one breathes
As the sufferers watch the sufferer.
In *St. Sebastian Mourned by St. Irene*
The flame of one torch is the only light.
All the eyes except the maidservant's (she weeps
And covers them with a cloth) are fixed on the shaft
Set in his chest like a column; St. Irene's
Hands are spread in the gesture of the Madonna,
Revealing, accepting, what she does not understand.
Her hands say: "Lo! Behold!"
Beside her a monk's hooded head is bowed, his hands
Are put together in the work of mourning.
It is as if they were still looking at the lance
Piercing the side of Christ, nailed on his cross.
The same nails pierce all their hands and feet, the same
Thin blood, mixed with water, trickles from their sides.
The taste of vinegar is on every tongue
That gasps, "My God, my God, why hast Thou forsaken me?"
They watch, they are, the one thing in the world.

So, earlier, everything is pointed
In van der Goes' *Nativity*, toward the naked
Shining baby, like the needle of a compass.
The different orders and sizes of the world:
The angels like Little People, perched in the rafters
Or hovering in mid-air like hummingbirds;
The shepherds, so big and crude, so plainly adoring;

The medium-sized donor, his little family,
And their big patron saints; the Virgin who kneels
Before her child in worship; the Magi out in the hills
With their camels—they ask directions, and have pointed out
By a man kneeling, the true way; the ox
And the donkey, two heads in the manger
So much greater than a human head, who also adore;
Even the offerings, a sheaf of wheat,
A jar and a glass of flowers, are absolutely still
In natural concentration, as they take their part
In the salvation of the natural world.
The time of the world concentrates
On this one instant: far off in the rocks
You can see Mary and Joseph and their donkey
Coming to Bethlehem; on the grassy hillside
Where their flocks are grazing, the shepherds gesticulate
In wonder at the star; and so many hundreds
Of years in the future, the donor, his wife,
And their children are kneeling, looking: everything
That was or will be in the world is fixed
On its small, helpless, human center.

After a while the masters show the crucifixion
In one corner of the canvas: the men come to see
What is important, see that it is not important.
The new masters paint a subject as they please,
And Veronese is prosecuted by the Inquisition
For the dogs playing at the feet of Christ,
The earth is a planet among galaxies.
Later Christ disappears, the dogs disappear: in abstract
Understanding, without adoration, the last master puts
Colors on canvas, a picture of the universe
In which a bright spot somewhere in the corner
Is the small radioactive planet men called Earth.

Field and Forest

When you look down from the airplane you see lines,
Roads, ruts, braided into a net or web—
Where people go, what people do: the ways of life.

Heaven says to the farmer: "What's your field?"
And he answers: "Farming," with a field,
Or: "Dairy-farming," with a herd of cows.
They seem a boy's toy cows, seen from this high.

Seen from this high,
The fields have a terrible monotony.

But between the lighter patches there are dark ones.
A farmer is separated from a farmer
By what farmers have in common: forests,
Those dark things—what the fields were to begin with.
At night a fox comes out of the forest, eats his chickens.
At night the deer come out of the forest, eat his crops.

If he could he'd make farm out of all the forest,
But it isn't worth it: some of it's marsh, some rocks,
There are things there you couldn't get rid of
With a bulldozer, even—not with dynamite.
Besides, he likes it. He had a cave there, as a boy;
He hunts there now. It's a waste of land,
But it would be a waste of time, a waste of money,
To make it into anything but what it is.

At night, from the airplane, all you see is lights,
A few lights, the lights of houses, headlights,

And darkness. Somewhere below, beside a light,
The farmer, naked, takes out his false teeth:
He doesn't eat now. Takes off his spectacles:
He doesn't see now. Shuts his eyes.
If he were able to he'd shut his ears,
And as it is, he doesn't hear with them.
Plainly, he's taken out his tongue: he doesn't talk.
His arms and legs: at least, he doesn't move them.
They are knotted together, curled up, like a child's.
And after he has taken off the thoughts
It has taken him his life to learn,
He takes off, last of all, the world.

When you take off everything what's left? A wish,
A blind wish; and yet the wish isn't blind,
What the wish wants to see, it sees.

There in the middle of the forest is the cave
And there, curled up inside it, is the fox.

He stands looking at it.
Around him the fields are sleeping: the fields dream.
At night there are no more farmers, no more farms.
At night the fields dream, the fields *are* the forest.
The boy stands looking at the fox
As if, if he looked long enough—
                              he looks at it.
Or is it the fox that's looking at the boy?
The trees can't tell the two of them apart.

Thinking of the Lost World

This spoonful of chocolate tapioca
Tastes like—like peanut butter, like the vanilla
Extract Mama told me not to drink.
Swallowing the spoonful, I have already traveled
Through time to my childhood. It puzzles me
That age is like it.

                Come back to that calm country
Through which the stream of my life first meandered,
My wife, our cat, and I sit here and see
Squirrels quarreling in the feeder, a mockingbird
Copying our chipmunk, as our end copies
Its beginning.

           Back in Los Angeles, we missed
Los Angeles. The sunshine of the Land
Of Sunshine is a gray mist now, the atmosphere
Of some factory planet: when you stand and look
You see a block or two, and your eyes water.
The orange groves are all cut down . . . My bow
Is lost, all my arrows are lost or broken,
My knife is sunk in the eucalyptus tree
Too far for even Pop to get it out,
And the tree's sawed down. It and the stair-sticks
And the planks of the tree house are all firewood
Burned long ago; its gray smoke smells of Vicks.

Twenty Years After, thirty-five years after,
Is as good as ever—better than ever,
Now that D'Artagnan is no longer old—
Except that it is unbelievable.

I say to my old self: "I believe. Help thou
Mine unbelief."
                    I believe the dinosaur
Or pterodactyl's married the pink sphinx
And lives with those Indians in the undiscovered
Country between California and Arizona
That the mad girl told me she was princess of—
Looking at me with the eyes of a lion,
Big, golden, without human understanding,
As she threw paper-wads from the back seat
Of the car in which I drove her with her mother
From the jail in Waycross to the hospital
In Daytona. If I took my eyes from the road
And looked back into her eyes, the car would—I'd be—

Or if only I could find a crystal set
Sometimes, surely, I could still hear their chief
Reading to them from Dumas or *Amazing Stories;*
If I could find in some Museum of Cars
Mama's dark blue Buick, Lucky's electric,
Couldn't I be driven there? Hold out to them,
The paraffin half picked out, Tawny's dewclaw—
And have walk to me from among their wigwams
My tall brown aunt, to whisper to me: "Dead?
They told you I was dead?"
                              As if you could die!
If I never saw you, never again
Wrote to you, even, after a few years,
How often you've visited me, having put on,
As a mermaid puts on her sealskin, another face
And voice, that don't fool me for a minute—
That are yours for good . . . All of them are gone
Except for me; and for me nothing is gone—
The chicken's body is still going round
And round in widening circles, a satellite
From which, as the sun sets, the scientist bends
A look of evil on the unsuspecting earth.

Mama and Pop and Dandeen are still there
In the Gay Twenties.
                          The Gay Twenties! You say
The Gay Nineties . . . But it's all right: they *were* gay,
O so gay! A certain number of years after,
Any time is Gay, to the new ones who ask:
"Was that the first World War or the second?"
Moving between the first world and the second,
I hear a boy call, now that my beard's gray:
"Santa Claus! Hi, Santa Claus!" It *is* miraculous
To have the children call you Santa Claus.
I wave back. When my hand drops to the wheel,
It is brown and spotted, and its nails are ridged
Like Mama's. Where's my own hand? My smooth
White bitten-fingernailed one? I seem to see
A shape in tennis shoes and khaki riding-pants
Standing there empty-handed; I reach out to it
Empty-handed, my hand comes back empty,
And yet my emptiness is traded for its emptiness,
I have found that Lost World in the Lost and Found
Columns whose gray illegible advertisements
My soul has memorized world after world:
LOST—NOTHING. STRAYED FROM NOWHERE.
   NO REWARD.
I hold in my own hands, in happiness,
Nothing: the nothing for which there's no reward.

New Poems

Gleaning

When I was a girl in Los Angeles we'd go gleaning.
Coming home from Sunday picnics in the canyons,
Driving through orange groves, we would stop at fields
Of lima beans, already harvested, and glean.
We children would pick a few lima beans in play,
But the old ones, bending to them, gleaned seriously
Like a picture in my Bible story book.

So, now, I glean seriously,
Bending to pick the beans that are left.
I am resigned to gleaning. If my heart is heavy,
It is with the weight of all it's held.
How many times I've lain
At midnight with the young men in the field!
At noon the lord of the field has spread his skirt
over me, his handmaid. "What else do you want?"
I ask myself, exasperated at myself.
But inside me something hopeful and insatiable—
A girl, a grown-up, giggling, gray-haired girl—
Gasps: "More, more!" I can't help hoping,
I can't help *expecting*
A last man, black, gleaning,
To come to me, at sunset, in the field.
In the last light we lie there alone:
My hands spill the last things they hold,
The days are crushed beneath my dying body
By the body crushing me. As I bend
To my soup spoon, here at the fireside, I can feel
And not feel the body crushing me, as I go gleaning.

Say Good-bye to Big Daddy

Big Daddy Lipscomb, who used to help them up
After he'd pulled them down, so that "the children
Won't think Big Daddy's mean"; Big Daddy Lipscomb,
Who stood unmoved among the blockers, like the Rock
Of Gibraltar in a life insurance ad,
Until the ball carrier came, and Daddy got him;
Big Daddy Lipscomb, being carried down an aisle
Of women by Night Train Lane, John Henry Johnson,
And Lenny Moore; Big Daddy, his three ex-wives,
His fiancée, and the grandfather who raised him
Going to his grave in five big Cadillacs;
Big Daddy, who found football easy enough, life hard enough
To—after his last night cruising Baltimore
In his yellow Cadillac—to die of heroin;
Big Daddy, who was scared, he said: "I've been scared
Most of my life. You wouldn't think so to look at me.
It gets so bad I cry myself to sleep—" his size
Embarrassed him, so that he was helped by smaller men
And hurt by smaller men; Big Daddy Lipscomb
Has helped to his feet the last ball carrier, Death.

The big black man in the television set
Whom the viewers stared at—sometimes, almost were—
Is a blur now; when we get up to adjust the set,
It's not the set, but a NETWORK DIFFICULTY.
The world won't be the same without Big Daddy.
Or else it will be.

The Blind Man's Song

(*Rainer Maria Rilke*)

I am blind, you out there. That is a curse,
An abomination, a contradiction,
A daily weight.
I lay my hand on my wife's arm,
My gray hand on her gray gray,
And she leads me through empty space.

You move and shove and think that you
Sound different from stone on stone.
You are mistaken: I alone
Am, am in torment, and bawl.
Inside me something interminably
Howls, and I can't tell what's howling,
My heart or my bowels.

You recognize the songs? You haven't sung them—
Not in this key, quite.
To you, at morning, the new light
Comes warm in your open house.
And you've a sense of seeing eye to eye,
And that tempts one to show mercy.

The Augsburg Adoration

Mozart, Goethe, and the Duke of Wellington
Spent the night at the Drei Mohren; so did we.
Did the Duke of Wellington find by his bed
Two bananas and two sugar-cubes, as we did?
Did the sparrows cheep, cheep, cheep to get the sugar?

And did Mozart sleep, next night, beside the highest
Spire in all the world—unfinished then? Ulm's emblem
Is a sparrow holding in its beak a straw.
You can buy it, in chocolate, at the bakeries.

Did Goethe see, among the cobblestones, the Roman
Manhole-covers marked SPQR? For the breath
Of those letters, the Senate and the People
Lived for us, indomitable as the sparrows
The bread-eating cats stalked in the ruins of Rome.

Travellers, we come to Rome, Ulm, Augsburg,
To adore something: the child nursing at the stone
Breast beside a stone ox, stone ass, a flesh-and-blood
Sparrow who nests in the manger. The Three Kings
Bring him stones and stones and stones, the sparrow
Brings a straw. The years have worn away the stone,
But the bird cramming food into the beseeching
Mouth in its nest of rubbish, is as perfect
As when the child first said of Mozart, Goethe,
And the Iron Duke: *One of them shall not fall*
On the ground without your Father. They have fallen
And the sparrow has not fallen. The straw-bearing

Sparrow at Ulm, at Augsburg, is indistinguishable
In its perfection from the sparrow who brought straw
To its nest, food to its young, in Rome, in Nazareth—
The green Forum's sparrows are the sparrows of home.

The Owl's Bedtime Story

There was once upon a time a little owl.
He lived with his mother in a hollow tree.
On winter nights he'd hear the foxes howl,
He'd hear his mother call, and he would see
The moonlight glittering upon the snow:
How many times he wished for company
As he sat there alone! He'd stand on tiptoe,
Staring across the forest for his mother,
And hear her far away; he'd look below
And see the rabbits playing with each other
And see the ducks together on the lake
And wish that he'd a sister or a brother:
Sometimes it seemed to him his heart would break.
The hours went by, slow, dreary, wearisome,
And he would watch, and sleep a while, and wake—
"Come home! Come home!" he'd think; and she would come
At last, and bring him food, and they would sleep.
Outside the day glared, and the troublesome
Sounds of the light, the shouts and caws that keep
An owl awake, went on; and, dark in daylight,
The owl and owlet nestled there. But one day, deep
In his dark dream, warm, still, he saw a white
Bird flying to him over the white wood.
The great owl's wings were wide, his beak was bright.
He whispered to the owlet: "You have been good
A long time now, and waited all alone
Night after long night. We have understood;
And you shall have a sister of your own,
A friend to play with, if, now, you will fly

From your warm nest into the harsh unknown
World the sun lights." Down from the bright sky
The light fell, when at last the owlet woke.
Far, far away he heard an owlet cry.
The sunlight blazed upon a broken oak
Over the lake, and as he saw the tree
It seemed to the owlet that the sunlight spoke.
He heard it whisper: "Come to me! O come to me!"
The world outside was cold and hard and bare;
But at last the owlet, flapping desperately,
Flung himself out upon the naked air
And lurched and staggered to the nearest limb
Of the next tree. How good it felt to him,
That solid branch! And, there in that green pine,
How calm it was, how shadowy and dim!
But once again he flapped into the sunshine—
Through all the tumult of the unfriendly day,
Tree by tree by tree, along the shoreline
Of the white lake, he made his clumsy way.
At the bottom of the oak he saw a dead
Owl in the snow. He flew to where it lay
All cold and still; he looked at it in dread.
Then something gave a miserable cry—
There in the oak's nest, far above his head,
An owlet sat. He thought: The nest's too high,
I'll never reach it. "Come here!" he called. "Come here!"
But the owlet hid. And so he had to try
To fly up—and at last, when he was near
And stopped, all panting, underneath the nest
And she gazed down at him, her face looked dear
As his own sister's, it was the happiest
Hour of his life. In a little, when the two
Had made friends, they started home. He did his best
To help her: lurching and staggering, she flew
From branch to branch, and he flapped at her side.
The sun shone, dogs barked, boys shouted—on they flew.
Sometimes they'd rest; sometimes they would glide

A long way, from a high tree to a low,
So smoothly—and they'd feel so satisfied,
So grown-up! Then, all black against the snow,
Some crows came cawing, ugly things! The wise
Owlets sat still as mice; when one big crow
Sailed by, a branch away, they shut their eyes
And looked like lumps of snow. And when the night,
The friend of owls, had come, they saw the moon rise
And there came flying to them through the moonlight
The mother owl. How strong, how good, how dear
She did look! "Mother!" they called in their delight.
Then the three sat there just as we sit here,
And nestled close, and talked—at last they flew
Home to the nest. All night the mother would appear
And disappear, with good things; and the two
Would eat and eat and eat, and then they'd play.
But when the mother came, the mother knew
How tired they were. "Soon it will be day
And time for every owl to be in his nest,"
She said to them tenderly; and they
Felt they were tired, and went to her to rest.
She opened her wings, they nestled to her breast.

A Man Meets a Woman in the Street

Under the separated leaves of shade
Of the gingko, that old tree
That has existed essentially unchanged
Longer than any other living tree,
I walk behind a woman. Her hair's coarse gold
Is spun from the sunlight that it rides upon.
Women were paid to knit from sweet champagne
Her second skin: it winds and unwinds, winds
Up her long legs, delectable haunches,
As she sways, in sunlight, up the gazing aisle.
The shade of the tree that is called maidenhair,
That is not positively known
To exist in a wild state, spots her fair or almost fair
Hair twisted in a French twist; tall or almost tall,
She walks through the air the rain has washed, a clear thing
Moving easily on its high heels, seeming to men
Miraculous . . . Since I can call her, as Swann couldn't,
A woman who is my type, I follow with the warmth
Of familiarity, of novelty, this new
Example of the type,
Reminded of how Lorenz's just-hatched goslings
Shook off the last remnants of the egg
And, looking at Lorenz, realized that Lorenz
Was their mother. Quacking, his little family
Followed him everywhere; and when they met a goose,
Their mother, they ran to him afraid.

Imprinted upon me
Is the shape I run to, the sweet strange

Breath-taking contours that breathe to me: "I am yours,
Be mine!"
                    Following this new
Body, somehow familiar, this young shape, somehow old,
For a moment I'm younger, the century is younger.
The living Strauss, his moustache just getting gray,
Is shouting to the players: "Louder!
Louder! I can still hear Madame Schumann-Heink—"
Or else, white, bald, the old man's joyfully
Telling conductors they must play *Elektra*
Like *A Midsummer Night's Dream*—like fairy music;
Proust, dying, is swallowing his iced beer
And changing in proof the death of Bergotte
According to his own experience; Garbo,
A commissar in Paris, is listening attentively
To the voice telling how McGillicuddy met McGillivray,
And McGillivray said to McGillicuddy—no, McGillicuddy
Said to McGillivray—that is, McGillivray . . . Garbo
Says seriously: "I vish dey'd never met."

As I walk behind this woman I remember
That before I flew here—waked in the forest
At dawn, by the piece called *Birds Beginning Day*
That, each day, birds play to begin the day—
I wished as men wish: "May this day be different!"
The birds were wishing, as birds wish—over and over,
With a last firmness, intensity, reality—
"May this day be the same!"
                          Ah, turn to me
And look into my eyes, say: "I am yours,
Be mine!"
            My wish will have come true. And yet
When your eyes meet my eyes, they'll bring into
The weightlessness of my pure wish the weight
Of a human being: someone to help or hurt,
Someone to be good to me, to be good to,
Someone to cry when I am angry

That she doesn't like *Elektra,* someone to start out on Proust with.
A wish, come true, is life. I have my life.
When you turn just slide your eyes across my eyes
And show in a look flickering across your face
As lightly as a leaf's shade, a bird's wing,
That there is no one in the world quite like me,
That if only . . . If only . . .
                              That will be enough.

But I've pretended long enough: I walk faster
And come close, touch with the tip of my finger
The nape of her neck, just where the gold
Hair stops, and the champagne-colored dress begins.
My finger touches her as the gingko's shadow
Touches her.
                    Because, after all, it *is* my wife
In a new dress from Bergdorf's, walking toward the park.
She cries out, we kiss each other, and walk arm in arm
Through the sunlight that's much too good for New York,
The sunlight of our own house in the forest.
Still, though, the poor things need it . . . We've no need
To start out on Proust, to ask each other about Strauss.
We first helped each other, hurt each other, years ago.
After so many changes made and joys repeated,
Our first bewildered, transcending recognition
Is pure acceptance. We can't tell our life
From our wish. Really I began the day
Not with a man's wish: "May this day be different,"
But with the birds' wish: "May this day
Be the same day, the day of my life."

The Player Piano

I ate pancakes one night in a Pancake House
Run by a lady my age. She was gay.
When I told her that I came from Pasadena
She laughed and said, "I lived in Pasadena
When Fatty Arbuckle drove the El Molino bus."

I felt that I had met someone from home.
No, not Pasadena, Fatty Arbuckle.
Who's that? Oh, something that we had in common
Like—like—the false armistice. Piano rolls.
She told me her house was the first Pancake House

East of the Mississippi, and I showed her
A picture of my grandson. Going home—
Home to the hotel—I began to hum,
"Smile a while, I bid you sad adieu,
When the clouds roll back I'll come to you."

Let's brush our hair before we go to bed,
I say to the old friend who lives in my mirror.
I remember how I'd brush my mother's hair
Before she bobbed it. How long has it been
Since I hit my funnybone? had a scab on my knee?

Here are Mother and Father in a photograph,
Father's holding me. . . . They both look so *young*.
I'm so much older than they are. Look at them,
Two babies with their baby. I don't blame you,
You weren't old enough to know any better;

If I could I'd go back, sit down by you both,
And sign our true armistice: you weren't to blame.
I shut my eyes and there's our living room.
The piano's playing something by Chopin,
And Mother and Father and their little girl

Listen. Look, the keys go down by themselves!
I go over, hold my hands out, play I play—
If only, somehow, I had learned to live!
The three of us sit watching, as my waltz
Plays itself out a half-inch from my fingers.

THE RAGE FOR THE LOST PENNY

(*1940*)

EINE KLEINE NACHTMUSIK

In my gay room, bare as a barn,
I sit like a rickety horse; in his unheeding night,
My daemon shifts, impatient, laughs at me
As I sit crying, lonely, out of luck,
Asks like a grey mouse: Am what? Why?
Thinks little of my loss, is careless if I die.

A year ago you owned me like a chair.
I lay on the poor beach by the crowded sea,
And your sleep-swollen face, secure and huge,
Hid for me, as it had hid so long,
The flat evil, the unmasked unmasking flesh
Of that sick dream the waking call a world.

The blank limbs dirtied with the east shore's sand
I saw and tried to love and could not love
Swim by me endlessly; and, past my glasses, half-concealed,
Tears slowly, senselessly, come one by one.
What world I have sleeps on . . . The absurd eyes
That watch the stranger crying in their midst—

Not amused, not pitying, that merely watch—
The eyes of man, helpless, indifferent,

Turned always inward, useless with the tears
That hide from him all pain except his own;
That cry to me—I see it—"Pity me!
I too was happy. And I too have lost

The little I could make my own, my life, my love—
Speak for me!" May they be plain to me! May I see
Past my eyes, past my world, past all I love—
So I speak . . . All's silent in my littered room:
My wish is here; and I sit wordless and alone,
Abashed at the wit that's more than I can bear.

Let me be blind! Or shut around me still
The crazy eyes, the crazy world, the crazy love
That spoke the one word to the foolish head
That that poor egg could bear and still not break—
The lie through which it guessed but could not see
What I see now: the night, the real night.

From

BLOOD FOR A STRANGER

(*1942*)

Muss es sein?
Es muss sein!
Es muss sein!

ON THE RAILWAY PLATFORM

The rewarded porters opening their smiles,
Grapes with a card, and the climate changing
From the sun of bathers to the ice of skis
Cannot hide it—journeys are journeys.

And, arrived or leaving, "Where am I going?"
All the travellers have wept; "is it once again only
The country I laughed at and nobody else?
The passage of a cell between two cells?"

No, the ends are hardly indifferent, the shadow
Falls from our beaches to the shivering floes,
The faces fail while we watch, and darkness
Sucks from the traveller his crazy kiss.

The tears are forming; and the leaver falls
Down tracks no wheel retraces, by the signs

Whose names name nothing, mean: Turn where you may,
You travel by the world's one way.

And the tears fall. What we leave we leave forever:
Time has no travellers. And journeys end in
No destinations we meant. And the strangers
Of all the future turn their helpless gaze

Past the travellers who cannot understand
That they have come back to tomorrow's city,
And wander all night through the unbuilt houses
And take from strangers their unmeant kisses.

LONDON

The wind wore me north, London I left a year.
—When the wind blows, boy, the bough is bare.—
When I came south in summer like a goose,
Leaves were more than I found left to lose.

I came to London, what did I find there?
I found my house full and my cupboard bare,
They sold my skillets and they stole my knives,
My wives have husbands and my husbands wives.

London, London, O where are you gone?
—No place is, child, man calls his own.
He tumbles all unwilling from the womb,
He reaches for a breast and gets a bone;

He calls his father God, his mother wife,
Of all the letters he knows only *I*.
And yet at last, man, you must learn to live,
Though you want nothing but to die.

THE LOST LOVE

When I woke up this morning
   I found I had dreamed of you;
You looked at me just as you used to
   (Just as you always do

In these dreams I need so often)
   And you said to me dryly, "Your face
Is older than when I knew you."
   I tried and could not say, "Yes."

"Your eyes are red with weeping,"
   You murmured tranquilly.
But when I could still say nothing
   You stretched your hand trembling to me

And whispered, "O my poor love—"
   And I felt a pang of such joy
Or pain that I cried, "I am dreaming."
   I awoke and it was day.

In my dream last night, I remember,
   Your face was sick and old;
Your voice shook; when I touched you
   My hand was cold.

1938: TALES FROM THE VIENNA WOODS

The reflections in the forest of the dying child
Are feverish and uneducated, and begin to tremble
At the footsteps of the ogre, who is night, and kind.
We do not move: the cries stop so soon.

The atoms are no longer conserved; annihilation
Is the tomorrow of the unwilling. The imperious wings

Are spread to the humble, who accept a rule
Conclusive as sleep; and the rattle of the waltzes

Sweeps high and guessed and gone over the crowds
Who will breathe glory for their day, and find no air
That night in the chambers of the clumsy spectre,
Who is lost; who cries all night: "I have lost my way—"

Because he is blind. What eyes could miss the road?
Look, look! By the signs of the bones,
The dreams in the glades of the shell-wood, and death's
Means in the disaster of all life, the dead,

Way by way, to the river of iron,
March in their long magnificence, their gazes flung
To the shattering future. Who hears the spectre
Who is blind and cries, "My way is gone"?

A LITTLE POEM

All night in the womb I heard the stories.
My brother was a fish, began, "O fish!"
And I listened till my gills began to fall.
There in the dark I levelled my pig's stare
At warm and wet, my limbs were ripened, and my wit
Was blood along the bough. "I am done now,"
I said to my brother, he said, "I know nothing."
So I fell first into this sink of time.

The world's word grew like butter on my tongue,
I cried out to my brother: "O go back!"
The child's fish, the pig inside its sea
Knew more than I. . . . But since he too was born,
I said no more, I told to that dumb ear
The first lie I had heart for; not the last.

I saw more than I had wit to bear,
I heard more than I had heart to hear—
A hand was laid upon me, not my own.
I saw, I said, *I see it not,* my heart was heavy
With blood, I heard, I said *I hear it not.*

My brother patted on his silted knee
A dumb wish budding into wives, a house
Where children coiled like smoke around a hearth
Crackling with popcorn in the Christmas night.
His beard was full of oil and guileless fingers,
The brides bounced on his stomach like a rug,
And he looked gayly into a moose's head

The babies mixed with Papa on the walls
Of all their elements. O his yes was the wish
Of people, the age cried, "Let our father sleep!"
My lean wife lay along me like a rule,
My child sat in my corner with a cap,
The butter hardened on my unpopped corn. . . .
I wept like a gargoyle to my empty squares,
I said, "O speak!" My brother smiled,
And I saw Nothing beckon from his lids,
The heart in his oiled breast was dumb as Time,
And his skull crackled with its empty blood.

Fat, aging, the child clinging to her hand,
She sits by the empty bandstand,
And whispers, gazing, to that mute form
The patient child cannot see.

So they all whisper to you—you smile your country smile
And listen dumbly; under the lace,

The schooled names—Maintenon, Montespan—
You lift your bleeding and speechless face.

The flame whirls up: time, and the scaffoldings
Swim like black phantoms through a darker waste—
The gutted balconies, bent under the moat,
Wake to some diver's peering and distorted face. . . .

So the drowning globe contracts for her.
Inhuman, lunar, like a shocked dream,
Some cracked and glutting image of the past
Welters along the margin of the sea.

Poor Asphaltine! take fern for epitaph.
The kings pass, nodding over the horses' heads—
How many a mile of leather, bone, and hair,
Red rust and powdery blood, I know not . . . we were once

Sheltered by the trees' spirits, and the crumbling vine,
The old bear, humble, tentative—these were to us
Images that were meaningless; we fell, we fell.
Gas, the machine-guns enfilading the square,

The shell-torn tenements—some shot-down bomber
Blazing here, under the searchlights' long-drawn lines—
Here are our commentators; under the gliding flare,
Shapeless, masked, your eyes glassed in,

You stare at us grimly; as the years grate by,
You look aghast at us—you lift your head,
Blinded and deafened, sick with the bursting smoke,
And laugh out with joy. O king of the age!

A POEM FOR SOMEONE KILLED IN SPAIN

Though oars are breaking the breathless gaze
Of the summer's river, the head in the reeds
Has its own success; but time is brimming
From the locks in blood, and the finished heart

Gasps, "I am breaking with joy—" and joy
Suffuses with its blood the difficult fields
Where the dogs are baying. "I am not angry,"
Thinks the fox. Nor is death. And the leaves

Of the light summer are too new to joy
To think that their friend is dying, and their whispers
Are not patient but breathless, are passionate
With the songs of the world where no one dies.

THE ICEBERG

The pressure as it crushes gags the moan;
One must have air to weep; and these have none.
The blood trembles in their eyes for light,
The blood rages in their ears for sound.
(The black is silent in the lower sea.)
These see with their hands; and their hands are frozen.

What they feel it is impossible to guess.
Their life is death for us: what we reason
From what we see, by the light they feel as warmth,
Is something we speak of and cannot conceive.
To the steel beetle tubes give light, a line brings air:
There is nothing neglected for his ignorance.

"There is no sign of any end," the diver phones.
"Already motion is impossible, and life

Extinct by our standards: the abyss
Affords no air, heat, food, or light."
Death haunts him: crushed into faces by the deep
The berg gapes in the thousand looks of men.

Their frown is iron: the perplexed unchanging stare,
The mute tetanic rigor (great Necessity
Stamped on the blinding faces of the sea)—
"What? What?" thinks the diver, hopelessly,
Drunk with the puzzles his descent creates,
The sick ambiguous wisdom of the sea.

Drawn back, blood bubbling, he blinks crazily,
Stumbling so heavily the air-borne jeer;
Thought runs like water from the melting heads
That tower from the iceberg into air.
Mad, various with heat, the rotting flowers
Laugh icily: an extravagance of summer, of the star

That shines partially on air, on ice, on sea;
The mitigating sunlight carves in air
Skills, legend, cultures—a morality!
The diver (before he dies) can judge between
The conscious and witty evil of the air,
The witless and helpless evil of the sea.

Because of me, because of you,
More things happened than I know:
The star's distention, the detonation
Of the instant and endless collocation
Of the wicked unlikely spinsters—and Mother;

The singular protein, the abstract cell,
Elaborated, industrial,
Grew feet and fat to keep from falling
In inland air or ever feeling
The limiting ice of the glacial sea;

The gangling and abortive fathers
Worked out their odds-on lives before us
And laughed at the actuaries' end;
Despised, evaded, or endured
The novel virus, the unique star;

Grew witty, mutant, and courageous,
And never faltered, because they knew
Their blood meant more than us and now:
The unstable and haggard intimation
Of a wiser speech and a stranger's face.

THE BAD MUSIC

I sit, sit listening; my lashes droop
And the years come close around me like a crowd
Of the strangers I knew once; and they say nothing,
And I see at last that they were never mine.
The breast opening for me, the breaths gasped
From the mouth pressed helplessly against my wrist
Were lies you too believed; but what you wanted
And possessed was, really, nothing but yourself:
A joy private as a grave, the song of death.

. . . These are lies, too? I sit here like a fool
And think half-tenderly, as my lips curve:
What do you know? How can you say it?
You were something, you loved something—
And where have they gone? What are you now?

There is no answer. I don't cry now,
So I don't cry; and I don't laugh—
What's happening to all of us is in its way
Laughable—why don't I laugh? Why don't we laugh?

It's bad music; but it's what we hear. . . .
It's night here; outside my big windows
The students come home from carolling, the candles
Wink out and on and out, like mixed-up stars.
I sit here like a mixed-up star:
Where can I shine? What use is it to shine?
I say; and see, all the miles north inside my head,
You looking down across the city, puzzling.
You always cried. And now are you trying

Instead, to be lucky? To be happy, really,
Where your small light is seen and shining
High over the millions who breathe and wait and sparkle
With the rain's globes, the worlds that roll like laughs
To the dark stream and its immediate sea?
Of those millions how many know or love at all
You, Anna? A few; so few. Enough.
This world holds more than we can see or say,
And it stuffs us like a goose before it kills us.

1789–1939

A man sick with whirling,
A sensibility brutal as a thumb.
Even the idiots clench their spoons,
Rap and call: Great changes have come.

Blood sticks to the platters;
The hangman holds the judge's seat.

Wisdom is choked with violence,
The heads can only vacillate.

Necessity like a marionette
Flops in the dust; the knitters yawn
Or hold the yarn its blood has drenched
Before the trunk—the head grins like a dog.

Call up the legions! that monstrous child,
Fathered by Reason, the despair of Time,
Who once like an idol overstrode
The streets that glittered with his blood,—

Climbs to the long roll of the drums,
Wearying, wearying, lifts his huge head
To see with helpless and darkening eyes
The tyrant standing among his torturers.

THE WAYS AND THE PEOPLES

What does the storm say? What the trees wish,
If they can manage to wish it. I am the king of the dead,
Says the hero strongly to his won field.
And it's true, too. Nobody hears him.

And wisdom has sorts—ones even the intelligent
Can understand if they wish; love is the limit that love
Approaches and approaches. And the skinny digger
Picks up among the caves the partial shard

She loves better than all our brilliance. On it the leopard,
In ochre and not foreshortened, manages quietly
After its own millennia, the quick
Stare of the dead one, in that dawn, among its deer.

Remember, each cupful of air has its vector,
And the backward seedling can always say:
It may be so; and I certainly vary;
And it's you who're taking the great wind's way—

And it knows what it says will always be taken
As the simple answer of the helpless love
Of the dwarfs in the forest for the glittering virgin
Who is dying and glass on her marvellous bier.

THE REFUGEES

In the shabby train no seat is vacant.
    The child in the ripped mask
    Sprawls undisturbed in the waste
Of the smashed compartment. Is their calm extravagant?
  They had faces and lives like you. What was it they possessed,
  That they were willing to trade for this?

The dried blood sparkles along the mask
    Of the child who yesterday possessed
    A country welcomer than this.
Did he? All night into the waste
  The train moves silently. The faces are vacant.
  Have none of them found the cost extravagant?

How could they? They gave what they possessed.
    Here all the purses are vacant.
    And what else could satisfy the extravagant
Tears and wish of the child but this?
  Impose its cancelling terrible mask
  On the days and faces and lives they waste?

What else are their lives but a journey to the vacant
    Satisfaction of death? And the mask
    They wear tonight through their waste

Is death's rehearsal. Is it really extravagant
  To read in their faces: What is there that we possessed
  That we were unwilling to trade for this?

Love, in its separate being,
Gropes for the stranger, the handling swarm,
Sits like a child by every road
With begging hands, string-dwindled arms;

Must be chafed, clothed, nourished, questioned,
Its button glances, dunce's ways
Wrenched and rasped till through them shines
Love's logical obsessive face;

Till of the simpleton's country scorners
From grey-sored urchin to blinking miner
Not one sticks hostile, holds out still
Against love's ten-foot gentle stature.

From the tamer, the crammer, the trainer,
The torturers' shredding hours,
Who would have dreamed for a minute
That love and love's perfection flower?

Where love moved, a home-sick stranger,
By bare shires and foreign shores,
Earth crackles with love's repeated look:
The subject's glance, the heart each shares

To be ignorant, to be innocent,
Welcome the warship sent for the exile,
Divine in his words the perfected world
Of—grown giant, gracious—the exposed child;

Yield the great keys, the graves, and the charter—
In the bared head, over the soldiers' song,
See sparkling, rising and murderous in their grace,
The emblems of that butchered king;

And up the choked mouth and closing way
The doomed men cry: He is one of us.
But, necessary, triumphant, beautiful,
Love laughs and is not magnanimous.

The hanged man on the gallows,
Warmed by fire and fed with dew,
Would cry if he could with every breath:
"Would I were yet as you!"

As it is he hangs there breathless
And thinks as the world walks by
The words it spoke and doubted: "There
Save for God's grace go I!"

And yet his mouth is stuffed with gold:
There's stored up after death
For dead men what no living man
Has hoped for or has guessed.

A PICTURE IN THE PAPER

(I upset someone in a badminton tournament and had my picture in the newspaper; this poem is about the picture. The tournament was held in a brightly lighted gymnasium, in a city, at night.)

There I was, here I am: a foot in air,
Looking up, going up, in the simple instant
The spring uncoils, the smash begins
Within the magnesium's enchanted stare.
Lovely to hang like a star or dancer,
To win, be sighed for—watched by friends,
To play in the floodlights' novel dream;
But even here the eyes are anxious,
Are still ascending, are lifted higher
To something else that's out of the picture.

Even the fixed, star's, paper features
Are tortured by that enormous knowledge:
The frame is cracking, breaks once more
Before the real world's terrible stare.
The philosopher's waking lucid minute
Runs like flame through the innocent systems;
The end of all our love and labor,
The instantaneous wonderful matches
Dance in the dunce's bleeding hands.
The real magician lifts his wand.

But who knows now what he is willing?
Tonight, while they play, the loved, the lighted
See pressed to the windows of their sphere
The great eyes, the dying elaborate faces
That speak at last, that thrust like flowers
Their cries, their gaunt intolerable gazes
Into the innocent world of light.

The old bonds are broken; tonight we lift
Our faces to darkness, the inhuman eyes—
The Forms of the stranger. The giants are calling.

The cow wandering in the bare field,
Her chain dangling, aimless,—
The Negro sitting in the ashes,
Staring, humming to the cat,—

Their greyed figures, muffled in snow,
Perhaps, outside the starred window,
At that hour when the sun has rusted away,
Range themselves in the only order they know—

These are the inhabitants of the country of the mind,
Or only the marching motion of the mind,
But still, this is what the mind gives the mind.
Standing there, familiar, brutal, and resigned,

A few trees, gelatinous, evergreen,
Powdered and leaden, creaking in one's age's snow—
That is, the mind's aging, the sky's covering snow—
Speak, bend, so vacantly as to seem

The thirsty images of a dream.
I summon them, then, from the old darkness
Into this wooden room, dripping and warm,
To chorus for you their bad charm

Because I knew their true living forms.
And how shall I make you, mossy, bearded, mournful,

A stuffed father on a Christmas night,
Cry out in pride and blessedness: O children!

When you and I were all,
Time held his trembling hand,
Fall's leaves lay long, the snows
Were grave on wire and wand;
Along the echoing ways
Our steps were lucky on the stone;
And, involved in our embrace,
Man's intent and mercy lay
Dazed through love's exacting day.

Bones' beggar with his cup
Might rattle where he sat,
And every limb or look
Look thin where love looked fat;
Their pocked and scaling brick
Was marble with our snow;
The blind man's cane, the scarecrow's stick
Creaked as spryly to our ears
As drumsticks to an orphan's jaw.

What will had we to mend
Or wish, except to suck
The springs of our enchanted sleep?
"The ranges sprawl like sacks,
Their locked limbs indolent with snow,"
The travellers wrote, who had not guessed
That we were what they saw.
And us what step, what kiss could wake
Whose world and sleep were one embrace?

So when our time was told
To stir, to speak, to stare below,
Among the sights we had not seen
What misery we saw!
We saw little love, we saw
The world that no men name;
All night or innocence or blood
Sickens at in its worst sleep
We watched done and praised by day.

What love's quick tongue could shape,
What love's shameless hands could mend,
We had no heart for; our own acts
Were sodden with acts' common end.
We made out in man's face the guilt
Ours were shot with; our intent
To change, to bless, to nourish, thinned
Till our shrunk glances shone instead
To praise the sleeping and the dead.

The towel and the ewer scraped
The blood from our consent; our kiss
Was acquiescence, but we knew
The dooms would fall no less if its
Wet sanction were untendered. We
Might stammer to the magistrates, "You too
Are housed and nourished with that crime;
And who is there that hears but is
Its and the world's accessory?"

FOR THE MADRID ROAD

Stranger, the wages that we earned
For the skills you need not learn
Waste if you will; the traversed road
Is interrupted with our blood. . . .

The private guilt, the general grave
Are debts of yours; or so men say.
Believe what you will. Here where
The gunners looked, our lives ago,
Set if you like the stones that show
Here men's dooms were satisfied,
Here we and the strangers died. . . .
We perished, if you like, for you;
We died that—that you may die.
But when were lives men's own? Men die
For man's life, man; that men may miss
The unessential ills—but these
Are man's responsibilities.

THE AUTOMATON

In the emplacements of the wood,
By the pierced aqueduct, I lay and wept.
I heard the wind run through the drums
Or, held in the marsh the oil made, moan.

Since I was what was left, I spoke;
Since I was what I was, I signed;
Next day I tore the treaties up.
That night I saw the dead men walk

With baskets through the yellow wood.
Night's will grew keener, and a cry
Or dying whisper wakened me;
Along the wires, as I crept by,

The faint wind whispered fitfully.
Someone laughed, and something shone;
Discolored by the gibbous moon,
A troop of corpses huddled there,

A corpse held upright by the wire
Seemed meditating some command,
His helmed head held so low it brushed
The pierced mask strapped against his breast.

In their midst a great shape rose,
The slave and remnant of the slain,
Its senseless limbs awaiting
The word the dead men puff to say—

Unconquered, inexhaustible,
The genius of a world's desire,
And cast at that world's judgment
Into the world-consuming fire—

Unquestioning and pitiless
Among the ruined and strengthless dead,
It lifts above the bloody field
Its powerful and lifeless head.

Over the florid capitals,
Up midnight's staring sky
Past sign and plane and spire
The graphed beasts shudder by.

Love in the candle's world,
The twinkling sphere of time,
Shines lasting as a tear
In sleep's unloving eye;

But love comes wet with its caress
To its own nightmare of delight,
And love and nothingness possess
The speechless cities of the night.

KIRILOV ON A SKYSCRAPER

Something gnaws inside my head
That changes everything I see:
An indolent and cloudy time,
The treasures of a barbarous scene,—

What use the crow's malignant look
Or joints as aching as a song
To show that aimless dignity
And ease that even an eye can own?—

The faces by the parapet,
Infected with their gazing, glare
As savagely as though they'd build
Another Eden, and a fruit

To reave from us the knowledge that we got.
What's good or evil to the man
So soon diminished to a doll,
Too rapid to catch a window's stare?—

His love, his mother, ranged at them—
Too fast! too fast! They gaze at, in their hour,
One instant in one instant's world—
Mortality distending like a flower.

Up in the sky the star is waiting,
On a range in the night of the sea
The divers toil; but deep in its attic,
The metaphysician's smile is fading,
The maid lets fall her mystery.

The green spring and fevers of their joy
Are slowed by some different stress or time,
The great year like an unsolved crime
Whistles in each: *Is it you? Is it me?*

And the future that beats through the leaders' worlds
Like some famous heart, the heroic endings
That spin like flowers from the dyes unfurled
For the proclamation of their love
Blaze up like film—are now not lending
One impulse to the actual makers;
In the jets, the lenses, piecemeal, fantastic,
The future already stirs like a spore,
Erects to our incredulous stare

The unknown organ, the tentacles
That bend to us in their long caress.

THE WINTER'S TALE

The storm rehearses through the bewildered fields
Its general logic; the contorted or dispassionate
Faces work out their incredulity, or stammer
The mistaking sentences. Night falls. In the lit
Schoolroom the hothouse guests are crammed
With their elaborate ignorance, repeat
The glib and estranged responses of the dead
To the professor's nod. The urgent galleries
Converge in anticipation on the halls
Where at announced hours the beauty,
Able, and Laughable commence patiently
The permanent recital of their aptitudes:
The song of the world. To the wicked and furred,
The naked and curious, the instruments proffer

Their partial and excessive knowledge; here in the suites,
Among the grains, the contraceptives and textiles,
Or inside the board cave lined with newspapers
Where in one thoroughly used room are initiated,
Persevered in, and annihilated, the forbidding ranges
Of the bewildered and extravagant responses of the cell;
Among all the inexhaustible variations—of milieu,
Of compensation and excess, the waltz-theme shudders,
Frivolous, inexorable, the inadequate and conclusive
Sentence of our genius.
Along the advertisements the blisses flicker,
Partial as morphine, the terminal moraine
Of sheeted continents, a calendar of woe.

We who have possessed the world
As efficiently as a new virus; who classified the races,
Species, and cultures of the world as scrub
To be cleared, stupidity to be liquidated, matter
To be assimilated into the system of our destruction;
Are finding how quickly the resistance of our hosts
Is built up—can think, "Tomorrow we may be remembered
As a technologist's nightmare, the megalomaniacs
Who presented to posterity as their justification
The best armies that the world ever saw."
Who made virtue and poetry and understanding
The prohibited reserves of the expert, of workers
Specialized as the ant-soldier; and who turned from their difficult
Versions to the degenerate myth, the cruelties
So incredible and habitual they seemed escapes.

Yet, through our night, just as before,
The discharged thief stumbles, nevertheless
Weeps at its crystals, feels at the winter's
Tale the familiar and powerful delight;
The child owns the snow-man; the skier
Hesitant along the stormy crest, or wrenching
His turn from the bluff's crust, to glide

Down the stony hillside past the robbers' hut
To the house of the typhoid-carrier; the understanding
Imperturbable in their neglect, concentrating
In obscure lodgings the impatient genius
That informs all the breasts; the few who keep
By lack or obstinacy scraps of the romantic
And immediately adequate world of the past—the
Strangers with a stranger's inflections, the broken
And unlovely English of the unborn world:
All, all, this winter night,
Are weak, are emptying fast. Tomorrow puffs
From its iron centers into the moonlight, men move masked
Through streets abrupt with excavations, the explosive triumphs
Of a new architecture: the twelve-floor dumps
Of smashed stone starred with limbs, the monumental
Tombs of a whole age. A whole economy;
The fiascoes of the metaphysician, a theology's disasters,
The substitutes of the geometer for existence, the observation
Of peas and galaxies, the impatient fictions
Of the interminable and euphuist's metaphor exploding
Into use, into breath, into terror; the millennia
Of patience, of skills, of understanding, the centuries
Of terms crystallizing into weapons, the privative
And endless means, the catastrophic
Magnificence of paranoia; are elaborated into
A few bodies in the torn-up street.
The survivor poking in the ruins with a stick
Finds only portions of his friends. In this universe
Of discourse the shameless and witless facility
Of such a conclusion is normal, and no one thinks:
"What came before this was worse. Expected so long,
Arrived at last, tomorrow is death."

From the disintegrating bomber, the mercenary
Who has sown without hatred or understanding
The shells of the absolute world that flowers
In the confused air of the dying city

Plunges for his instant of incandescence, acquiesces
In our death and his own, and welcomes
The fall of the western hegemonies.

JACK

The sky darkened watching you
And the year sinking in its journey
Seem to you the slit beanstalk
And the goose crumpled in its pen.

The river, the spilt boats,
And the giant like a cloud falling
Are all pieces in your mind
Of a puzzle that, once joined,

Might green again the rotting stack.
Now, the oven's stiff creaking
Vexes you, but lifelessly,
Shameless as someone else's dream;

The harp crying out as you ran
Seems, rustling, your daughters' yellow hair . . .
As, bound in some terrible wooden charm,
You sit here rigid and aghast,

Sometimes, in your good memory,
The strait princess, the giant's simpler wife
Come torn and gazing, begging
The names you could never comprehend,

And in the narrowing circle, sitting
With the world's puzzle rusting in your hands,
You know then you can never regain
The land that the harp sang so loudly.

ESTHETIC THEORIES: ART AS EXPRESSION

Poems, like lives, are doing what we can
And very different from what we know.
They start surprisingly, like blood in bones.
The unlucky wake up bleeding at the nose
For no reason *they* can see; a shallow cut
Elicits from them the disquieting jet
Of blood, of blood; they usually die.
But poets thrive on it, as if the muses
(Like Dr. ——— in some worn-out memoir)
Found bleeding adequate for anything;
Becoming in time, almost, autonomous.

It would be nice if this were all.

Dried, or preserved in jars, and certified
By experts of some bureau of the State,
It would be found invaluable, like pots,
To show all sorts of things about an age:
What the people worshipped, whom they ate.
For centuries the reconstructed cultures
That festered uncertainly in someone's heart
Would pale and warp among the glances
And desiccation of a gallery
Where children in sterile coveralls would falter:
"The diseases glitter darkly, like a jewel."
One sees *der Übermensch* endow
A Chair of Paleohaemolysis.

And one can work it out in terms of tears.

But blood is nothing, tears are nothing: pain,
The evil the dumb schools traverse like a sea—
Are equally the ground of everything, the Cause
The humblest of our cries comes huddling from.
The poem is not distinguished in its source;

The wise will class its nurture with a qualm;
And who has comprehended the determiners
That smoke like dry ice from the witches' brew:
The spirit curling from the careful page
To call the hair up on another age?

DUMMIES

O the dummies in the windows!
Their big round arms are fair as milk,
They look through lashes, comb back locks
Of glittering embroidery silk.

How can the weak designer bear
The strength of that constructed face?
Resist when his own eyes give back
Their great consenting gaze?

Yet through that wax dream at last
Press a new world's different bones,
Eyes look, with their silk lashes gone,
A love and terror all their own.
Love laughs, when through our made world breaks
A stranger's real and difficult face.

AN ESSAY ON THE HUMAN WILL

The innocents tug blindly at the yielding
And sinewy tissues of their lives,
Or distractedly determine, if they can,
Where ignorance leaves off, and luck begins;
But, think what they will, they end in skillets.
The knife is tempered to the shrewdest lamb.

There is something magnificent in so much pain:
Heaven lowers so steadily upon the meadows
Where the glum sheep try bitterly to graze
They are lent the warped dignity of Esquimaux
Whose short and scanty spans are wrung
From the harshest extravagance of malice,

It seems to dwellers of the warmer zones.
The lambs wring nothing: they are wrung.
It is simply pathetic: the tragic flaw
May lead to stockyards, but the flawless too
Are swept in the common current of their kind
To the Pole's indifferent and stunning hand.

Fish also strike at anything, and flop
For hours or minutes on the thinnest line.
"It is as if God destined me for death,"
The carp's eyes mutter in the restaurant.
(And the huge mouth in the mottled
And whiskered dusk of the blue face

Is drawn into a terrible smile
Of effort, of misunderstanding and—remorse.)
It is hard for them to be objective.
Like heroes, they are astonished at their fate
And think that it is something they have done.
Like Virtue, the will is praised and starves.

THE SEE-ER OF CITIES

When the train whistles, it wants to say
Take me, take me. What for? which way?
The people ask; *to places, to places,*
Say the rails, say the wheels. *To houses, to faces,*
The poster says, so harsh and gay—

But who believes it? The fool of every street,
Craning for each new joke the heavens float
Across his browning bushes and tight throat,
Knows more than *that;* cries, "Your America
Is here around you"; pointing to your skull.

Time has (my Lord!) new senses for old saws:
That signboard with its bland *For Diamonds
Dig Up The Yard,* has changed to *No Way Out.*
"Great Goethe was a child," the children think;
"Ice at the pole, gas at the equator—

"Tears are the only object of these eyes."
And—and how can I go on playing, they are right.
What did I ever see but you? What are the lands
But the same senseless ground? the crazier figure
Stares back from each: that great Gestalt

Black with the blood of the imposer's breast,
The sure and treacherous and final sum
Of sea, soul, city—from Dan to Omsk
I walked this planet, and I found
Nothing but my own footsteps on the ground.

A DESCRIPTION OF SOME
CONFEDERATE SOLDIERS

The torn hillside with its crooked hands
Where Tom lay beneath the banks of light
Grows shadier, and through its shades
The sun looks seldomer. The laurels are faded.

Ah, how it blazed! the splintered leaves
Burned against your forehead, and your tongue
Grew thick with wisdom; till you laughed, and fled
Like a shadow from that senseless shape.

Then that pale life—scars on the tree—
Where, listlessly, among the mushrooms of your hill,
You stared at your comrades—fatal waxworks!—
And saw, pale, virtuous, half-concealed,

Hovering over each leafy and swollen cheek,
The blue transparency of a smile.
This was the last of that furious speech—
The lustre, the wreathing of the shade.

Strewn like sweat, like dropped jewels,
They lay there; their ringed mouths gaped
Like wounds about to speak, their eyes
Shrank back from those curved faces,

Staring, coagulated with light.
Tell how you were hunted by cunning death,
That night when, stumbling, soaked with blood,
You sank there with open mouth

Until the hunters came, and kneeling there
Lifted you, and saw covering your face
That greedy and imperishable arrogance. . . .
Man's choice, and man's magnificence

Grow monstrous, and unclouded by
The empty measure of his breath.
How can the grave hold, a statue name
Blood dried in that intolerable glare?

They stand like shattered and untopped columns,
The barbarous foliage of an age
Necessity instructed and destroyed.
There is no hesitation in those eyes.

THE HEAD OF WISDOM

(This poem is written for Katherine Louise Lyle Starr, who was born May 16, 1940. The head is Beethoven's.)

The little Will comes naked to its world
    Without a rag of wit;
Church, State, the crazy categories
    Crowd to the straw where it
Weeps under the family's fondling;

The shepherds baa, the Magi smell like camels,
    Hark, how Herod's agents sing!
No godmother comes giftless to the foundling:
    Child, is there anything
In your whole universe to spare you

Its witless and officious blessing?
    "Do, do," your mother nags,
Your father gives his senseless laugh, or mutters
    His sour hits while he wags
A dry head at each new day's errors;

State sets a rifle in that aimless hand;
    The manufacturers
Bid for the labors of its fruitless years;
    "Obey, or hell is yours,"
Church tells; and your Hell's apologists—

King, priest, philosopher, the lean professors—
    Tell, tell, and tell. You see.
Learn it all—the lies, the hunger, and the blood:
    The peoples' history;
What we said; and all that we knew instead;

Learn it; but wisdom is more than knowing
    What we knew, what we said,

The famous errors of the famous dead.
   The maned and erring head
Holds, under the truth, under the lies,

Something stronger than either; the great stare
   Of the magnificent eyes
Dazzles, is dazzled with more than tears;
   No surprise
Warms the ruined face: the wilderness

Of confusion, of desolation, the helpless laughter
   Of the wise break free
From the mouth open in the dying face—
   Child, *here* is history,
Here is knowledge, is wisdom—see! see!

1938: THE SPRING DANCES

These loves are the helpless or wanted bliss
Of the white girls on their easy stair;
Light stains the orchids of the blind breast.
The dancers kiss under the flawless branches,

And the horns' waltz is loud in the forest
Of luck and money, the grateful lawns
Are the Way of the scrubbed and aimless shepherds
Who laugh in the moonlight hired for their hours.

These are the ends of our state, the ingenuous
And iron inheritors, the waltzers of the sphere
That is pressed slowly on to the darkness
And hard conclusions of the real sea.

FEAR

The running peoples on their bloody way
Articulate your rank, the jeering names;
It is you repeated in the shaking lights
The child hangs sprawling in his vacant sky.

You are uttered in the simple and forgetful words
The homing seaman, the soldier falling to his stage
Pronounce in commentary on their state.
The child rocking in her empty room,

Patient, sleepless, haunted by your dreaming shape—
Helpless and suffering in a tale
She herself at last tells carelessly,
She serves a symbol for this world,

The passion of our ending world.
Within that slanting-shadowed fire-hung flowering room,
Fear, branched and netted, jetting by her hands,
Struck out its strangling change within her breast.

And now the windows, shaken and obscured with snow,
The rusting statue, ermined, argent, ice-encrusted, hoar,
Whisper: "Child, what you and your kind
Have accomplished is nothing. Be like us, absolute."

Yet doubt ends the metaphysician, and darkness
Prepares in its labyrinth the iron kiss
That persuaded the heroes; does love lie
Indeed, for the hunter, in that final pit?

A child's words, swollen with weakness and pain,
Could paint our sawn and mortal world,
And scorn that sawdust-gushing wound
Tended with pity and unmending love;

But it's unfed and in the end betrayed,
Sucked hollow by those gazing sheep-like forms,
That dreaming and inhuman world,
The forest of a winter night.

THE MACHINE-GUN

The broken blood, the hunting flame,
The pierced mask and the flowering shell
Are not placated—nor the face
That smouldered where the searchlights fell;

Our times lie in the welded hands,
Our fortune in the rubber face—
On the gunner's tripod, black with oil,
Spits and gapes the pythoness.

THE CHRISTMAS ROSES

The nurse is at the tree, and if I'm thirsty no one minds.
Why don't they finish? . . . If it's metastasizing
I wish that it would hurry. Yesterday it snowed.
The man they took before me died today.
When I woke up I thought I saw you on the bed,
You smiled at me and said, "It's all all right,"
And I believed you and went back to sleep.
But I was lucky: the mortality's so high
They put it in a foot-note or don't mention it.

Why don't you write to me? . . . The day nurse sits and holds
The glass for me, but yesterday I cried
I looked so white. I looked like paper.
Whiter. I dreamt about the pole, and bears,
And I see snow and sheets and my two nurses and the chart

I make all by myself with my thermometer
In red that's like the roses that are like the blood
That's gone, that's gone for good—and what's left's spoiled,
The silly culture I keep warming for my death.

How could I believe you, how could I believe them?
You were lying, and I am dying; and you knew. . . .
I dreamed it, I woke and laughed at it; and then I saw
That there was nothing else that could be so,
I knew, I knew. And now I know you never meant
The least letter of the poorest kiss
You thought about and gave me; you and life were tired of me,
You both thought—quickly, quietly, in a dream—
To kill me, to be rid at last, for good, for good,

Of that blind face that still looked up to you
For love, and then pity, and then anything.
And now I'm dying and you have your wish.
Dying, dying; and I have the only wish
That I had strength or hope enough to keep,
To die: to lie here ruined and dumb and done,
And lose at last what I have left to lose, the shame
And need and pain, the unendurable desire:
What I was given for a world. . . . Now when I see myself

Even in my own thoughts or dreams or—or desire,
It's only as a nuisance, Want out of a play
There begging in your bed; but it's I who am in bed
Really, O isn't it?—and it's not right, not right
Even to die so badly, once you loved me, too,
And I'm not angry now, I'm dying now, I—
Come to me! come to me! . . . How can I die without you?
Touch me and I won't die, I'll look at you
And I won't die, I'll look at you, I'll look at you.

CHE FARÒ SENZA EURIDICE

"Had I my will," the shrill wind sang,
"Thou child of mine—" I kept on riding
Into the forest of the foolish deer,
And I saw the turrets above the stair
Of the white cascade, the long meanders
Of the silting stream in the valley's bliss.

The red corpse by its pool was the spring
Of the fishers who tore from the cracked blood
The heart I wept for; sunlight caked
The lips of the fountain, the swimmers raised
Their dry smiles from the summer's bed.
All night the leaves spoke thirstily.

In my child's dream the ravished limbs
Were stuffed with my torment, and my tears beat
Like blood in the rash breasts. The milk of death
Ran from your loosed lips, sleep ate
Your love in a wink, you slumbered for all time
In my murderous arms. Who could have dreamed

There grew, those years, under the thousand deaths
Of the sleepy trunk, under the beast's innocent
And ruinous limbs—death? your real death?
You grinned like a dog in your anguish, your blood sprang
To the hands of the strangers, the fishers of the river
Of death; when, dying, you called my name,

I held you once more, my lips like birds
Were breasts to your tears, the nurse and stanchers
Of the smashed vessels, the angry and matchless blood—
I? My ears were wax to you, my lips gnawn
By new limbs, my eyes blind with their own delight—
I slept in a stranger's arms while you died.

From

LITTLE FRIEND, LITTLE FRIEND

(1945)

. . . Then I heard the bomber call me in:
"Little Friend, Little Friend, I got two
engines on fire. Can you see me, Little
Friend?"
    I said "I'm crossing right over you.
Let's go home."

THE DREAM OF WAKING

. . . in the bottom of a boat, badly wounded, crying and
stroking the face of the other, who was dying; and say-
ing, "Come on now, you'll be all right. You'll be all right."

Something is there. And teacher here at home
Curled fast on the quilt like Kitten, saying Come
You'll be all right, you'll be all right—is gone,
And the water trembles upward into light,
And the light's smile breaks, is laughter—it is me
And the room and the tree: oh, morning, morning.

And the frost is starry, like the sun between my eyes
In my lashes so they open: and the white
Is the breath the night breathed, there like mine;

My *clouds are cover and my nightgown and the breath*
That prints me on the window; and my sun
Is gold all mixed with air, is my own life—

So he wakes? No, wakes from; and the teacher cat
Is the nurse of the world, *his* clouds are plaster brown with blood,
And he is back for good: the boat is bodies
And the body broken in his broken arms
And the voice, the old voice: *Please don't die*—
His life and their death: oh, morning, morning.

MOTHER, SAID THE CHILD

Mother, said the child, *the boughs all talk*
All night, they say that all of us—
No, no, she answered; who has heard them speak?
They stand there silently. . . . Or perhaps walk

Up through the grasses, said the child, *and stare*
At me there sleeping; and the leaves all stir—
The wind, she answered; when have the leaves waked?
Sleep on, my life. . . . Tonight your murderers

Have found me, said the child; *one calls, Come back!*
But I wake here in moonlight, pale and old—
No, no, she answered; how can that be so?
You lie home sleeping. . . . And your cheeks are black

With blood, said the child; he flung back his white head
And cried, *Come warm me with your crazy limbs*—
And the mother laughed, and opened her cold arms
And pressed to his dead mouth the blood of the dead.

SOLDIER [*T.P.*]

(T.P. means Title Pending: the interviewer writes this, in pencil, on the recruit's Form 20, and his job title is filled in by another worker, an expert in these things.)

When the runner's whistle lights the last miles of darkness
And the soldier stumbles into the hard green clothes
(From the night where his earth is the dream of a stranger
And the years are stripped from his heart like a sigh;
Where death and life and their child are—civilian)
And stands for his hour there in the cold green lines
That are always waiting for something, or waiting;
There wakes in the cropped dusty head, one supposes,
In the blistered hands, in the soft uneasy eyes,
The smell of the ages where no one is dying
And the old dog stirs in his sleep in the sun:
The world where they marry and live in houses.

But his house and his wife are—pending; and the life
That was his to starve in, to waste as he chose,
Has no option now: the iron unchanging
Chance that had governed his price like a plate's
Is smashed for an instant, as the atoms' wills
Are fused in the grim solicitude of State.
Yet it is not You the sergeants hoarsely
Curse at there where the travelling sand
Obscures the relief-map of the parade-ground.
That You may be, perhaps—as Justice
May be, may be; *this* world's justice
Is here, is now—as you too are, soldier.

What have you learned here? To bear, and be silent.
To do what I must, as I must: that is, to die.
What are the soldier's answers? Yes, sir;
No, sir; no excuse, sir. . . . *But (sir) there is no room there, to die—*

To die or to live. . . . Hush, no one is listening.
Ask as you please, there is no one here to reply.
Here what they teach is other people's deaths;
Who needs to learn why another man should die?
Who has taught you, soldier, why you yourself are dying?
And there is no time, each war, to learn.
You must live or die as the dice are thrown on a blanket;
As the leaf chars or is kindled; as the bough burns.

THE LEARNERS

When the planes come in all night, and the lights reach, wavering,
Into the empty barracks, for the crews—the old, old crews—
And the faces, shapeless at waking, stare from the rainy turrets
For the faces—the old, lost faces; and, slowly, the blind light greys
That dream of the old wars; and the lines brood listlessly
Beside the pools of the runway, in the thin unending rain—
The dead lines; when you remember
Will you care then—dead in someone else's dream—
That you lived, that you died? Waking at twilight to the haunting
    brain
That is your world now, ghosts, have you learned anything?

THE DIFFICULT RESOLUTION

Night after night the dead moon lit
Mortar and sentry, and the whole strand
Lay stripped of its cottagers, the night's dead
Who escape once more to their habitual
Graves from the terrible life of the island,
To the dreams along whose beaches laps
The owned and amniotic sea.

They know their life, brilliant with the light and play
Riches afford each impulse, the distractions of sunlight

And surf and summer, engaging with the elaborated
Ejaculations of dancers, the laughs of nurses—
Terrible because it is still life: the mother
Thinks, "Enough. I may die"; and the girl speaks
Publicly of love, and means her death.

Under the grave limbs, the accessible grace
Of the new flesh, the cell's old anguish
Works extravagantly: we learn to think,
"My wish unsatisfied, my need unknown;
My intent, and the world's, incommensurable;
And happiness, if there is happiness, inaccessible—
Let me sleep, let me perish!" In the warm darkness
The sleeper whispers at last: "The grave is my mother."

There is the knowledge you and I unlearned.
We heard, a few nights, the unhousing sea,
No womb now of ours; the wind from the darkness
Laughed to us endlessly, a will of the world.
Yesterday's peoples, those storms like an indignation
Of Europe's, implacable with its pressures and anguish—
Over the dark sea and centuries, the strangers coming

To die in the ranges of the empty land—
Who remembers those nameless? The needs and death
Of Yesterday on the bed of straw, by the wall of logs,
Who existed only that you might lavish
Your magnificent and unenduring smile
On the phosphorescence of bathers, the rockets wandering
Up to the cold galaxy—my own face

Looking and unendurable in the young night?
Today, the child lies wet and warm
In his big mother; tomorrow, too, is dumb,
The dry skull of the cold tomb. "Between?"
Between I suffered. "And are content at last
To know no more of that desire, of that intolerable

Anguish: the degradation and the limits of your kind?
That is what you learned from the wind, from the darkness

That was never still, that moved all night
Toward day and its death—star wandering
To other star, a stranger, a new sky?"
No, no! The wind, the night—
Those knew no will to sleep, no hope of death.
Blind strength, the harshness and agony of purpose—
The true, the sure will of that living world

Stretched taut around us like a crazy womb—
I learned that then; I too felt for my instant
The waves of that constriction, the rejecting lips
Wet still with the tides that formed us, with the blind
Determiners of that blind mother: the great beast
Convulsed with its passion for it knows not what,
That gives and takes away and gives and in the end destroys

All that has loved it or has found it bearable;
That weeps—weeps at us, not once for us; that at last
Twists us to pieces, slings us away, merciless with its despair
At us and at itself: the universe we judge.
Remember what you learned then: that you are powerless
Except to know that you are powerless, to learn
Your use and your rejection, all that is destroying you—
And to accept it: the difficult resolution.

THE SOLDIER WALKS UNDER THE TREES
OF THE UNIVERSITY

The walls have been shaded for so many years
By the green magnificence of these great lives
Their bricks are darkened till the end of time.
(Small touching whites in the perpetual

Darkness that saturates the unwalled world;
Saved from the sky by leaves, and from the earth by stone)
The pupils trust like flowers to the shades
And interminable twilight of these latitudes.

In our zone innocence is born in banks
And cultured in colonies the rich have sown:
The one is spared here what the many share
To write the histories that others are.
The oak escapes the storm that broke the reeds,
They read here; they read, too, of reeds,
Of storms; and are, almost, sublime
In their read ignorance of everything.

The poor are always—somewhere, but not here;
We learn of them where they and Guilt subsist
With Death and Evil: in books, in books, in books.
Ah, sweet to contemplate the causes, not the things!
The soul learns fortitude in libraries,
Enduring patience in another's pain,
And pity for the lives we do not change:
All that the world would be, if it were real.

When will the boughs break blazing from these trees,
The darkened walls float heavenward like soot?
The days when men say: "Where we look is fire—
The iron branches flower in my veins"?
In that night even to be rich is difficult,
The world is something even books believe,
The bombs fall all year long among the states,
And the blood is black upon the unturned leaves.

In the first year of the first war called the *World*
I watched a world blaze skyward into States,
And faced across the trenches of a continent
The customers whom I was shipped to kill.
Then Each taught Each to give up for the All
His joys, his reason, and his blood;
And those who had lived for profit marched to die
For all the sad varieties of Good.

All integers alike—the young and old, the poor and poor—
Were shadowed past distinction by the deaths
The States sowed over continents like salt.
Those years the flesh was levered from our bones.
The atom scratching in the gutted sty
Lost faith in that outmoded evil, good;
And guessed, the rifle steady at his back,
The functions of a variable: to die.

The westering lives were steadied to a north
A little distant from that sombre pole
The centuries had dreamed was Chance or Fate;
We learned—our poor wits sharpened with their blood—
That last cold center of our wish was Trade.
Where our blood ran the German books are red;
Because we died a bank in Manchester
Ships textiles to the blacks the Reich had taxed.

AN OFFICERS' PRISON CAMP SEEN
FROM A TROOP-TRAIN

It is some school, brick, green, a sleepy hill,
That blazes from the train's turn in its wire.
Nightly the guns are set, the cold guards yawn,

The lights burn for the sleepless prisoner
Who works like a gopher through the dirt of time
To climb this midnight back to his own war.

At first he waited: read, slept, or heard the lies
They told him always—the interminable defeats—
Till he began to see—next year, next year—
What he remembered from his childhood, Peace:
The marks papering a wall, the hungry weeping,
The machine-guns pulsing in the workers' streets.

Numb, filthy, shivering, he sees again
The stars dim behind the eternal lights of man
And sobs. It is, as it has been, the joy of men
To escape from another's evil to their own.
Here, so like, so different, is all that you had planned.
Think, as you tremble in the new world's air,

That more than seas, than continents, the years
Lie absolute between you and those wars
You wished, worked out, and thought at last were yours.
Here, here around you are your colonies;
Here in the midnight of the alien wilderness
The mastering races forge their destiny and yours.

Teach me the meaning of my world too well
For you or it to be endurable to me;
Last, till the states, the years, end here with you
To cough their blood out on the neutral earth.
Die, soldier, while the guns learn everything
From your thin body pinned against the light.

LOSSES

(1948)

IN THE CAMP THERE WAS ONE ALIVE

*(This is a concentration camp burned by its guards, deserted
by its prisoners, and not yet occupied by the Allies.)*

Flakes pour to the black dead
    At Lasen, by the wire.
The child, in his charred cave,
    Watches the shaking fire

Struggle to him in torment
    Till, stumbling, the shades sink back
Into his helplessness; his shaking
    Limbs shrink to nothing, crack

Under the beams that pin him.
    He hears, beneath the hiss
Of snow, a step on snow, the vague
    Murmur of many voices.

They have come; and he calls to them
    In gladness—
                It is the dead.
They speak softly, he understands
    Nothing, and inches his head

Back over to them; but he sees
 Nothing, he hears nothing. He moans
In his last loneliness—and the voices
 Ring in his ears, the stones

Are flung from the hammering feet
 Of the dead who cry
The child's name over and over.
 He laughs out in joy

And wrenches with all his strength
 Against the timbers, cries:
"I'm coming." The voices are fainter,
 The footsteps die as he dies.

ORESTES AT TAURIS

(Iphigenia and Orestes were children of Agamemnon and Clytemnestra. When the Greek fleet, on the way to Troy, was delayed by contrary winds at Aulis, Agamemnon killed Iphigenia as a sacrifice. Later versions of the myth have her snatched from the altar by Artemis, who makes her a priestess at Tauris, in the Crimea. Coming home after the fall of Troy, Agamemnon was murdered by Clytemnestra and her lover Aegisthus. Orestes, at Apollo's command, killed his mother and Aegisthus. He was pursued from country to country by the Furies, and finally was required, in expiation for his crime, to bring back to Greece that image of Artemis to which the Tauri sacrificed the strangers cast up on their shores.)

Sailing to Tauris: the pitchy cave,
The corpse bobbing, bleached, limp as oil.
Days, hung at the wind's aging breast—
The sail had no shade, the place of the sun
No shape to tell you where he rode—

You fell like a dream; or, looking down,
Smiling, the laurel darkening your face,
You saw Them watching, Their pale mouths opened,
Like shadows under the gliding sea. . . .
One night you began to rot in your dream
And held your sister, wet in your arms,
Who wept with lips that fell apart in fat.
You woke with a sob, rippling with sweat,
And ran to the helmsman, and turned his face;
He spoke in the gods' tongue, forsaking you,
His nostrils distended, drugged with the scent
Of the dried blood scaling from his lips—
That hair, prettier than a horse's mane!
And you cried "Lord!"—flung out your arms,
And looked into eyes so fierce and luminous
You woke with a hollow and tumbling cry.
A bird came by your head, her wings thudding,
The mast shook, the shields fell rattling to the deck,
The ship struck.
            There, rocking, till day,
Your ship broke in that shallow way.
The waves friended with the urging wind
Flowed to your ship where she began
To rot and scale—grey foam lumped thick as bees
Gathered along her beak, spun up the oars
That hung there creaking; and she heeled
Half-over to those towering crests—waves wore at her,
She wallowed shoreward, struck again, and stuck
There on that shelf, head fast against the rocks
That reached for her, stern back along the shoal
That streamed like a snow-plume from them,—
Fast, with chopped oars and grinding beak,
Her snake's head twisted back, and trailing oars;
And as each wave burst, the plunging spray
Broke round you and clustered on you in such clouds
You looked like men whom darkness overtakes
In harshest winter, when snow falls so thick

They look like ghosts among the silent flakes
And hardly speak. So you stood mute
With hanging head, or looked indifferently
Along the smoking flats, or where a stream
Crept pricked with bony weeds; and your gaze failed
On all that water. . . .

                Last, that day, dwarfed warriors
Crept along that floor, faceless with air,
A long time on the finger ridges,
Patient and necessary as a star.
The sand foamed with prints. Where they rode,
Stamped there on the edge of the world
Striped with the livid flutings of the sky,
They seemed as many as the night-seen swarms
Of journeying strangers, when from far on high
Their shrill song falls. So that day you heard
The neighing of horses and the sound of iron
And shouts—no Argive shouts!
Some dismounted and walked on the sand,
Waving to you, lifting their long cries
That seemed so strange to you—the surf's sounds strewn
Along the beaches, spoke in that savage tongue.
Standing in a chariot, shading her eyes with her hand,
A woman in a dyed cloak, holding a flat wand,
Gazed out at you, solitary among the swells.
The riders stared at her, or called to her
Till she stretched out her arms and sang:
The veils of mist, of foam riding the wind,
Rolled seaward, or sank slowly to the sea,
And the shore glittered in the fiery light.
Her voice came floating across the waves.
Then from the sea-depth voices groaned,
And you looked down, shrieked out to see
The black ship breaking, half-sucked-down.
Stripped off the mantle! flung down the sword!
Diving into the whirlpool, that cauldron
Loud with a thousand shouts, shields'-sound, the shields

Showing a last time their ornaments,
An oar up-ended in the sea's triumph—
You and your men sounded like birds with your cries:
Helpless, pale as fish,
Drawn down strangling, swept to the salt flats,
Trying to stand, trembling, clutching at
The spiked flowers of the reeds.
Some they speared (with what imperious gestures!);
And you, last left of them, lay senseless there
And rose half-senseless from the running sand
And tried to stand, and staggered and sank back,
Standing for one instant—imperishables!—
Holding out to them your pressed hands.

Afterward you remembered them looking down,
Standing so that the last foam of the wave
Swirled round, or ended at, their feet:
Doom looking at you, under the helmet's rim—
Over it, the trembling feathery plumes.
The journey inland: your wrists were bound.
Standing in the chariot, staring back
Through long locks the wind floats back,
You watched the long train, the low sun
Gilded your salt skin, your burning face.
Riders called to you, waving their shields to you—
The scarves waved, the wheat bent as you passed.
You sat trying to hold up your head
Or pressed your chin to the car's rim,
Felt it so cold, you gave a child's sigh.
Struggling through the first gasps of darkness,
The riders came past; you peered at them—
Limp hands, slow stride, wet beating sides—
And then the winding road, the weedy road,
Two haystacks like wheaten snow-men
Standing like glaciers by the flood.
How cold the drops flung from the hooves
Felt as you halted at the ford!

Wide and dark seemed the water, the sky darkening;
Weeping, listening to the sound of that water,
You lay by the gravels and the broken shells
The low waves lapped along; when the bird whistled,
You shuddered and fell asleep, and never saw
The frogs and water-rats and all those birds
That crept up through the reeds and stared at you;
And in their midst the Furies sat
And watched you with Their drowsy look, and patiently
Watched the horses drink with long sucking draughts
Or peered at the carved handles of the shields.
And as They stared at you, a mournful cry
Sprang from your lips and from the leaves
The Furies fondled with Their hands. . . .
When they shook you awake, you moaned like a dog
And lay with stretched mouth and struggling limbs—
How bright the torches were! Then someone came to you
And held out water in a cup, and lifted you;
You looked at her senselessly, and shook your head.
Yet when she pressed it to your lips you gulped at it,
And it was so thick and bitter with some drug
Your teeth rang on the rim, you gave a long shudder,
Snatched it, and poured the rest out on the ground—
Then you looked up at her and laughed.
Her head began to swim away, you fell asleep.

How long had you slept? You woke to the late day.
Clouds blazed in the sunlight, the whole plain
Bent to the sigh of that steady wind.
You looked astonished at the image there
That crouched like a hunted and misshapen thing,
Swathed with the hides of horses, fox-furs, and the skins
Of some long-horned, long-furred, and long-tailed beast.
A fleece with its knotted and dragging fringe.
Around, the maidens dressed like bears
Pressed rank on rank; and past them old men stood
In fresh-washed flax, and held out in their hands

Green branches, green rye-woven crowns.
On poles around, their long hair stirring in the wind,
Some heads stood drying. One had rotted there so long
Shreds of its face hung fluttering like a beard;
And others, tanned like leather, stuffed with straw,
Their combed hair twisted back, looked piteously
From jewels sewn in their lids, into your eyes,
As though to beckon you to their blind world.
A man came walking through their midst, with clumsy steps.
A long, white, and heavy coat, high shapeless boots,
A broad-sleeved and knee-long coat, and great peaked hood:
Such garments, white as salt, hung covering him.
Come to the goddess, he swayed and stood
Two heads above her, huge as some high stone,
And then unstrung and broke the bow he held
With hands still hidden in his coat's great sleeves,
And spoke; but in a voice so tremulous
You stared, and saw under the high hood
No face at all: an egg of bandaging.
Then as he stripped the stiff skins one by one
From the black goddess who gazed passively
Past your still face and travelling eyes,
You saw her splintered arms and hacked-out breasts—
And yet the knife-scarred wood seemed still to bear
A rough and sooty bark. That bark, that skin was blood.
Then you knew you were dreaming; when the white man laughed
You laughed aloud—laughed senselessly until you saw,
Under the chest's stiff basketwork and loose-spun cloth,
An old man's withered face and twinkling eyes.

And so you came to her. Ah, lamentable it seemed
To lurch like a beast, with harsh forced steps,
To a wooden altar, there groan out
Unpitied words—and no more known as words. . . .
Sidelong, and timidly, the maidens looked
Who came to you; lashed like a sail upon a pole,
You struck with your head against the hands

That wound the furs along your limbs, or hid
Even the ropes that bound you with their flowers,
Long ribbons, leaves, and garlands hanging down.
You still spoke a while, and then for pity ceased
And wept at yourself; and strange it was to see
The dancers with their masks and swords and leaves,
And hear no music, no, nor sound except
Their feet against the turf and their intaken breath
Or your own moans and painful gasping breath. . . .
A sigh waved their ranks; they stood there silently.
You heard a sound, a sound, a long whispering sound,
Then silence; then you waited a long time
While your skin changed and your whole body changed,
And still there was no sound; until you sensed
A sort of warmth against your flesh, and suddenly
Felt someone breathing there, a feathery touch.
Sweat sprang from your limbs! your heart leapt!
You felt your life halt, your weak lids grate fast:
When you opened them she was standing before you.

Gold hung from her arms, dark gold clasped round
Her haggard face; what beasts worked red with gold
Twisted their antlers past her tangled hair?
Rays like a fan's shrivelling ribs
Curved from her lips to color her burnt cheeks;
Her lips were dyed; and through dyed lashes peered
Eyes with a bird's pitiless and gloomy stare.
So she looked; and yet in all that press
At Argos or Mycenae, or in all the isles
You never saw her like: a face so fair!
She wet your hair, and smoothed it with her hands,
Water ran down your face, and it looked pale
Under those dark and darkening locks; you shook them free,
And how ghastly it looked—your pale anxious face!
You trembled like a knife; was it thirst, then,
That you felt stirring, clapping its wings
In your dry breast and shrivelling throat?

And in your anguish, the heavy foam
Lay on your lips like a smile; until they came unstuck
With a short wordless shriek, your head lolled back,
And in your fit your eyes looked yellow
As the bone eyes of an orphan's doll
He makes from rags he finds, and sticks,
And splinters from a bone the house-dogs gnaw.
And surely, bound as you were, half-hid
In flowers and long leaves, you looked
More like a bush or some low branchy tree
Than like a dead man hanging at the side
Of his own death. A man came out, uprooted you,
And stripped the lashings off, and let you fall,
And you sat stiffly in the trampled grass
And did not move, you could not move,
And the man touched you and you fell.
He looped round cords, and stretched and pegged them fast,
And you lay staring to that endless sky—
You saw the sword blaze. She bent over you
And sobbed aloud, and raised it in both hands;
Then shuddered and shrank back, and loosened it—
You were still silent, and looked at her blindly.
And when she calmed herself, and picked it from the ground,
And once more raised it; when between you and her face
The sword's line came—what did you see then, Orestes?

The head sprang up, spun once, and fell.
The hairs that trailed back toward the trunk
Began to rise and shudder in the wind.
Then she trembled and turned aside,
Her hands were weakened, she loosed the sword
And moved back blindly, bent to lift the head;
But as she reached to take it, its lips curled
For a little in their trembling smile,
The lashes trembled, the bright eyes
Looked at her meltingly. The mouth said: Sister!
She stood there with her hand outflung

And stared at the head; her lips shook,
She stammered to herself the heavy word. . . .
She once had stood and seen her slayers round
And left living. None living had left *her* hand.
Borne over the cloudless or shadowy deep,
Friendless, or friended with arms, and armored friends,
They swept to the garland and the wand,
Long-lined, through long years, and all to that end!
How strange to stand like a child, and tremble
At a headless body—one more head
To stuff and smoke and set on an empty stake;
And if in the long nights of the long winter
It still stares at you with its aching smile,
And when you name it, and lean to it longingly,
Its eyes seem to cloud in the firelight
And it turns from you, slowly, in the stinging smoke—
What is it but one more head? If it seems to you
The whole world and the way to a world
Lost in one instant, under the plunging sword—
Now once more your fingers shine with blood.
The maidens lift their jars, pour through your hands
Water that falls past stained; and after strew
Bright shells and sea-sand on that sodden ground.

An end for the children of a king,
The king of that age. And under foreign eyes
And far from their own home—from Argos, or from any town
In all the Greek land; too far for any Greek
To have come to aid, or bear back word of them:
For in another season, months before,
He must have boarded ship, and spread his sails,
Set out long-voyaging, and many days
Sailed the Aegean, till at length he came
Past Scyros, and far-seen Lemnos, to those straits
Where passed the Boeotian prince, that hungry year
His mother and her servants parched the seed
(He from the altar and his father's sword

Fled on the Ram, to Colchis; out of love for him
His sister fled, and by the Chersonese
Fell like a star); so, quitting her small sea,
Set forth upon the Euxine and, worn, wandering
Along those houseless shores until he seems
The dying autumn, or some wandering god—
He gains that savage coast; come there by night,
Goes all alone, silent, leaving his ship
Moored, set for sailing, in some shadowy cove;
And then bears inland, walking all that night
Among the marshes with their shivering reeds
And night-blanched and misshapen flowers—swims
With slow strokes through some little stream
Dappled with stars and, at the western brim,
The sinking moon. . . . The late night quickens,
Over the stagnant waters of the marsh
An iron light flows; far away, with faint harsh cries
Some birds fly up. So dawns the day
The traveller walks through, and at eve he sees,
Naked and grim among her worshippers,
The image of the Taurian Artemis.

This was the image Orestes came to take—
And beside it his head and body lay.

So the traveller might have come; but no man came,
No man lay hidden there— or saw,
Parting the grasses with a silent hand,
Under the long light of the level sun,
The people, silent, watching with grave faces
Their priestess, who stands there
Holding out her hands, staring at her hands,
With her brother's blood drenching her hands.

From

THE SEVEN-LEAGUE CRUTCHES

(1951)

THE OLIVE GARDEN

(*Rainer Maria Rilke*)

He went up under the gray leaves
All gray and lost in the olive lands
And laid his forehead, gray with dust,
Deep in the dustiness of his hot hands.

After everything this. And this was the end.
—Now I must go, as I am going blind,
And why is it Thy will that I must say
Thou art, when I myself no more can find thee.

I find Thee no more. Not in me, no.
Not in others. Not in this stone.
I find Thee no more. I am alone.

I am alone with all men's sorrow—
All that, through Thee, I thought to lighten,
Thou who art not. O nameless shame . . .

Men said, later: an angel came.

Why an angel? Alas, there came the night
And leafed through the trees, indifferently.

The disciples moved a little in their dreams.
Why an angel? Alas, there came the night.

The night that came was no uncommon night;
So hundreds of nights go by.
There dogs sleep; there stones lie.
Alas a sorrowful, alas any night
That waits till once more it is morning.

For men beseech: the angels do not come,
Never do nights grow great around them.
Who lose themselves, all things let go;
They are renounced by their own fathers
And shut from their own mothers' hearts.

UNCOLLECTED POEMS

(1934-1965)

O weary mariners, here shaded, fed,
Dull as the wave, old hostages to sleep,
Well-bearded, eloquent, the world's hands,
Take what the kind sea brings to your feet—
Shells, rays, tributes of the unsparing deep.

Here, perhaps, the shaved pinnacles of sand,
Containing so much worth, will be abashed—
Clouds torn by the storm and night of heaven
Come home to you, rest dripping by your shores—
And bend, magnificent, docile, proud,

The palms to lay their branches in your hands.
Your dwelling-place is full of leaves and murmurs,
And coldly, beaten and drunk, the waves come in
And hold their arms and voices to your land

So that one night the mermaid's bitter cries
Sound through your blind and monstrous dreams,
And as you struggle in the whelming deep,
She gasps her green life out upon the sands.

[1934]

The man with the axe stands profound and termless,
Fixed in the progression of foregone regret—
Yet how forgotten? for he who stands in time is timeless,
The axe swings forever, it will never relent.

Tears will corrupt his fading rancour
And drowsy memory turn again its foreknown pain—
The shuddering hand will hide the shuttered window.
Sigh the last term, the axe strikes again.

Mindless and heedless, the corrupt and fading flowers
Of your bitter wit and sore content
Among the grasses wreathe the forgotten virtues
That make him weep, who can never relent.

[1934]

Above the waters in their toil
Where the land song slowly came
The forms within their caverns wept
As fancies in the grottoed isles

Resuming the semblance of their fear
Had seen the wavering moon reveal
The hooded Electra sheet her eyes
With water islands and the smoke

Bending palely, the wind's burden . . .
And as she wept, the petals of the dew
Rose from her skin and from the leaves
The furies fondled with their hands.

[1934]

The swallows' twisting southward-turning flock,
Whirling upon itself, above an empty house,
I turn from, in forgetfulness and indifference.

That short-haired man, wrapped in his sheet,
Who sat and watched the rafted wood
Blown sea-swept toward the Eleatic shore.
The sea-bird twisting to its rest—
Here, let us imagine, first devised
The formal antinomy of the world,
And set it out, satisfying, profound. . . .
The waters and the wing-hung gull
Still erred outside, and gulled his eyes.
The wind stuck colder than his cloak.

What wool can blanket you, what rotting stack
Play straw-house to the winter's siege?
The cold wind and her spotted snow
Ride brindled down one moment-lifted gaze;
This pool, air, or earth-engendered flame
Set in the coils of durance—ah, poor siblings!
Greedy be, treacherous, distrustful, you quick hostages—

Cold came the wind; the winter goddess by the sea,
The blued sea-nymphs, trembling, fleecy, were a-cold.
Headland, promontory, the white smooth-mantled line
Loomed seaward, awing, slow, those blind deities
He had beguiled—this distortion,
This patchwork, this bloody agglutination,
The creaking stasis, the memorial gape;
That glazed-over and livid face,
Its lashes lowered to shut out
The storm howling, puffed, venomous—
The poor exigency, the unlucky decline.

You too, beside the silent traveler,
Tracing his slow steps, giddy with sleep,
Over some winding and night-hidden track
Along the uncertain margin of the deep—
Pricked up with suet, the bright mistletoe,
And drenched with willfulness and pride,
A lizard under their chalked faces,
O God, with what a malicious eye—

But see, the people trotting through the snow
To take you in, the shepherd with his cheese.
How apple-cheeked and warm the house
You drowse in—how easy now to disbelieve
That fanged inarticulate confusion—and see,
Once more, wide as the goat-herd's prongs, the horned antinomy.

Passing confusedly and silently across the sky,
Peoples of the marshes, the gradual abyss,
They wander to some estuary, some consummation
Sunk to under the crumbling wave—
To die in the stormy night, to plummet
Insensate, icy; or, like the lost pilot,
To stare over the long reaches of the sea
And feel, still gnawing in your breast,
The invincible and treacherous resolution—
Or, weltering, smashed, strangling, cry out to see
The rocket's livid and streaming memorial.

[1934]

And did she dwell in innocence and joy,
Loved, cared-for, a happy child? Not only in the mind,
When, swollen and wicked, she forgot her state;
As though, condemned in an old time,

The guards, the dumb spinners bending to their yarn,
Were changed into the guardians of her thought,
And sat in meditation by time's formal stream,
Webbed, eloquent, and loving to their child;

But she must strangle in some hooded doom,
Sheet in vain rhetoric their reader names,
And, falling, lament the kingdom of the clouds,
And afterwards struggle blindly to regain

The most ignorant and most savage moment of her life.
Think her, even, the justification of her age,
Pitiful, full of virtue, contented, new,
Sent down the unpainted corridors of the blind:

And in the end she's undone by violence.
The night, a snow-owl bending from the north,
Horned, light-eyed, stooping to his prey
To beat her down with snowy wings,

Stands glaring by her twisted form
And rends her in that instant by the wall
Where she lay swept with dumb content.
She lived in splendor and in light;

And, if she died corrupted, in the world's end,
And that other, in misery and fantasy,
Satisfied her shaved and corrupt heart
With greed and longing, the empty clusters of delight,—

The world's evil? Stand there waxen in the snow,
Kind-hearted, ignorant, obstinate, secure; the
Child of the world. Can one show
The way of blessedness to the unsaved?

[1935]

THE INDIAN

Among the shades and cries of the night
I dreamed I wandered—by a stranger's shore
I wept, and weighed the cumbering pack.
Cartridges are more than furs: I saw their light
Gleam for a moment in those fading eyes.

I kept the scalps, the cartridges—the bolts
Of madras blanched by a fiercer sun
Swept from my wives' long shoulders; I still felt
A prescience in the rifle's sound,
A new world rising out of the smoke.

[1936]

OLD POEMS

I knew you once so well I know you still—
Neglectful now-not-loving I; yet what now seem
Anxious and haggard ways, you have because I had—
My blood that dried on you, and left you stained.
You shone once iron and violent as blood,
And like old blood, grew shriveled, black, and thin;
How can I love you—I think ruefully—
Whose beauties seem so harsh, and faults so plain?

And they reply: Think you to a later self
Yours any less will look? or wiser seem?
Blind to them you are; will later to later more;
And more times, O more times will groan
As anxiously. I mean more than songs: all doing done,
Once done, seems best undone—O well 'tis done!

[1936]

AN OLD SONG

A shoe that I forgot to tie
Vexes me, and here I sit
Staring at it; passers-by,
Take your stand and gaze at it,
You remember more than I.

The mirror's lamentable change
And the old dispersing world—
If I remember after all,
There is nothing I would change,
There is nothing in that world

I would change, or live again.
How still the grave looks! in those depths
Even a soul might think it might escape
Even its punishment, or praise, or might endure
The altering ages in that altered shape;

And how could He judge? or judging, condemn
Those who, taken from His sight,
Nurtured in the coarse establishment of Time,
Fell, in loneliness and arrogance,
To haunt the empty portals of the night?

[1936]

When Achilles fought and fell,
Joy or pity filled each breast.
When I saw the bomber fall,
My heart felt iron within my breast.

Man looks weak beside the girder—
By the bomb's sight, what is man?
Men have made themselves an image
That does not glass, but judges, man.

[1937]

Falling in love is never as simple
As love and the lady novelists say;
Love's least sneeze may take, may rankle,
The thousand nights be as bad as a day.
Instead of responding like an apple,
You fall in your own unfortunate way.

That first year I used to look
At your one face with hesitation,
Almost distrust my sense and my luck
When I thought of the unknown loving nation
Who dreamed of me as their one lack;
But love kept growing on his odd rations.

I learned your face by finger-tip,
By the nightmare's galactic rigor,
By greedy look, the sucking lip,
Learned that love had nothing to fear for;
Is safe as a bank—I thought, and was tricked;
Because love is dangerous as a mirror.

Love never changes; or, *Love's first minute
Past noon is night*—the authorities read;
But love never answered to their description,
Was as desperate or fat as the circulars said.

Love sobbed, surrendered, shrieked *I've been framed*—
But at twelve-fifteen love was never dead,

At two sat up, examined his jail,
Took broth at four, and by six had escaped
With a musical saw or was out on bail.
Love fluctuates like a ticker-tape:
Makes his wet farewells, the sirens wail—
And returns next day in next year's shape.

But now—this year, today, at twelve, while love
Groans for the news-reels: *I'm nearly done*—
Your face wipes out next year's disguises,
Keeps repeating softly, *I'm the only one:*
Which is love's way of saying it's hard to end
What you and love should have never begun.

[1937]

A DIALOGUE BETWEEN SOUL AND BODY

Soul: You're the can and I'm the salmon,
        You're the feathers, I'm the goose,
        You're the shell and I'm the oyster—
        Love me, leave me, I can't lose.

Body: I'm hearing voices—can it be
        My own tongue's talking back to me?
        You armless, eyeless, witless wonder,
        What would you do without me?

Soul: The dancer's best without the fan,
        The horse's best without the flies;
        It's your tongue that makes me stutter,
        I'm astigmatic with your eyes.

Body: Darling, you're like the poor old lion,
               Gaped-at, told-of, the pride of the zoo,
               Who puffs and roars till he thinks he's made
               The crowds, the cage, and the whole world too.

Soul: How long till you see through it?
               The whole thing's nothing but a show
               I made one year—and when I tire
               You will be the first to go.

Body: You must learn now what you'll learn
               As I draw your final breath:
               We live each other's life,
               We die each other's death.

Soul: If it's because I'm sick of it
Body: Or that our end has come at last,
Soul and Body: There's one thing we agree on—
               . This world is failing fast.

[1937]

Enormous Love, it's no good asking
The rocketing burst, the point-blank stare
From the eligible and half-stunned owner
Of the sweepstakes virtue, the pitchblende star—

To win by meekness and inclination
The told-about Real and the light-year feeling,
Be accused and forgiven for a dwarf's devotion
By the biggest hole in the punched-out ceiling:

Too much to ask—too much to find
One mortgaged farmer, one asteroid

To graft and cherish the ailing sprig
And laugh at the dispossessing void;

O ancient Love, sun, single out
The aimed-at organ, the jinnee's anger,
The cave of the sleeper: detonate
The consummation of the Stranger.

[1937]

A NURSERY RHYME

Here we are: the Bowl, the thousands,
This is the team we've got to beat.
They're warming up. But something's wrong.
You feel it? No? Then take a seat.

They're using a shift I haven't seen.
What are the rooters yelling?
Things have a look I hardly like.
Perhaps we should go. You're still not willing?

Then destiny must have blinded you.
For behind you, in their sallow lines,
The noosed ones cough; a foot from your face
The carrot-haired barber halts and grins;

The orphan laterals the warden's head
To a manic who gains eleven yards,
Runs to the stands and assaults a nurse,
Is beaten to shreds by the fretting guards;

First down: the giant from the criminal side
Cuts the umpire half in two with a cleaver,
Is clipped by the badly demented passer
Who finds he's lost his last receiver;

The frothing thousands yell *Water! Water!*
Rain bottles and bombs on the cartwheeling leaders,
The racing-plane with the kidnapped star
Is down in flames in Section R;

The ravished Scout—no, not today.
Let's stop pretending it's Judgment Day.
Because each of you knows as well as I
What it is I'm trying to say;

The spinster who's never attended a seance
As well as this year's Conference quarter,
The crystal-gazer in an Arkansas tent
Spells it in dreams to the great reporter;

While you're eating peanuts or loving Aquinas
It sticks to you like the back of your head;
The bill's presented before you're born,
Marked *Payment Still Deferred* when you're dead;

I could call it Love—but whoever liked it?
A Star—it's enlightened no one yet;
The puzzle that you and I and the cat
Are the answers to—and wrong at that;

The riddle that no one has even posed,
That you were never made for solving;
That you slash or finger until you feel
Your wits, your wife, and your world dissolving;

So say what you like, do what you please,
It's not important except to you—
The ones who can satisfy the conditions
Are other and odder and after you.

[1940]

Ski-rails run down the sugar-loaf,
Beards garnish every stone.
The calculus of an ice-cube
Supplants for the time our own.

Last week's notion was a pond
Or soddener—but ice!
Ah, there's the thing, thought Thursday,
And Friday waxed the skis.

The new lamb freezes, does it?
Coughs star the boundless slums.
But through my new, my red wool shirt
My hand and quick head come.

Back along the glistening hill
The tracks shoot long and dark and dead,
The future's blank untroubled fields
Stretch absolute ahead.

Tomorrow always comes, the poles
Print like Euclid in the flour—
Older the birds', the hare's impression:
Love, love knows no tomorrow.

Can any love cling faster
Than here along the headlong slope
Where all day the live man carries
The dead man through the snow?

Man's writ runs no further
Than a red shirt in the snow.
The bones had a bloody mother?
Next year will never know.

[1941]

(This is supposed to be a parody of Miss Marianne Moore's poetry. I hope that it is accurate, admiring, and a little critical.)

THE COUNTRY WAS

all hills and all interesting—in one field
by a barn, by a haystack, were two 'real
    brand new lambs',
        three ewes too 'uncertain of their
election' to judge at all or require
    much more than
        lambs—believed in by another
        lamb, perhaps, but not by other

things. The 'impossible once-or-twice-seen'
freak flower 'marred by dew', smashed by tears, seems
    healthy by
        this starveling fantastic sawdust
changeling rag-Sambo scare-crow cur, with its
    embryo's
        generalized pink pig's head—un-
        suited for earth, as anyone

but an ewe knows. Yet obviously no one
could 'harm seriously or curse at' so in-
    nocent a
        virgin—much less 'seethe, butcher, and
so forth and so forth', as poor Couperin
    wrote strongly:
        meaning tenors. One thinks all three
        his mother and uncertainly

prances to each in his jointless graceless
ungainly knock-kneed stagger, as if fac-
    ing nothing
        but joy: the maturing half-wit

perfecting in these scrupulous scales its
    cadenza,
        the overwhelming responses
        of the horned ram. The other raises

his head an inch and lets it drop with a
conclusiveness familiar to the ewes graz-
    ing by the
        barn and to the understanding
farmer as birth, but not yet as hackneyed
    to the lamb,
        who would perhaps not recognize
        birth either. 'Just as advertised'

by the champion of Oxford and other
lost causes such as the classics, as the
    man who 'saw
        life steadily and saw it whole',
Sophocles got 'about twenty' firsts, still
    thought: Better
        to be dead than alive but best
        of all not to have been born. Test

this response with the dead lamb and it rings
like a bell: iron. The live lamb's sprawling
    bright gait is
        learned, exact, and in a way
magnificent, but after all play, a
    prepara-
        tion rather than the essential
        life of sheep—dumb, but theirs and real.

[1942]

TIME AND THE THING-IN-ITSELF
IN A TEXTBOOK

I read it quickly: all the old clichés
In simpler terms for students with no time
Or inclination for a definition
Of what they know, they think, too well already: time.
(Like skaters to whom ice is only space
That pays the swiftest foot with certainty)
They go too fast to doubt or be convinced,
And write, *K. says its mode perception.*
In my head, these days, the mode is Reason.

Let me examine all more carefully: *the Thing
Is*—"You go too fast already,"
Caws Reason, like a rook or Robert Browning;
"For *thing* is singular, implies plurality—
If Thing were all, who'd think to call it *thing?*
And how say *the* unless the thing is picked
From something else: this presupposes space
And qualities—we pick it out by *some*thing.
And that *is,* that *is!* I cannot bear that *is!*"

I could bear more than that, I think.
With so much Reason there is no philosophy.
There's such a thing as going much too slow.
Just one's own warmth will wear through any ice
If one sits fishing long enough: the fisher
Falls to the Nothing whence he drew his fish
And never reappears except in textbooks,
Where he and his fish acquire a ghastly sheen
As though—as though the fish, at least, were rotten.

[1942]

MAN

The cranes along the scaffolding are gorged
With matter, the neutral useful stuff
We eat or carry on our bones all day—
That pains or dies and never sheds a tear.
But the bricks—blank, senseless, identical—
By repetition and arrangement have assumed
A shocking life: the building's bad,
Thugs maul the laborers the bankers sweat,
The statue on the pediment is Chance,
The whole vulgar beyond belief; and yet a kind
Of majesty informs the crazy spire,
The gilt tendrils of the wigged head
Are brighter than the birds, the life that litters them—
And the clouds smile like Heaven on their falseness.

Man is magnificent to man; *je le sais bien.*

[1942]

THE ISLANDS

Man, if I said once, "I know,"
Laugh at me, stuff in my angry mouth
Your rueful and foolish laughter. Man is a stone.

Lips own love; did I say once, "I love"?
I said a word. When the hands told they were love,
I bled and I was beautiful. Man is a knife.

When I said blood, I say I bled.
Is man no more than pain? Speak for me, scars.
Knife holds for me no blood but mine—

When I told I could wish for more than you,
Death, I was dreaming I had died.
Next year's skull perplexed me like a kiss,

I felt my veins contorted with the tongue
That ran through them like my world's crazy will;
My breath cracks into sleep, time eats my fat,

Friends fall and my mouths fail, I brim to death
—Man's hands were wishes, all my wives were iron,
Death shades me like a sword, and I am kissing—

I sweat to my sea like a floe; blue, blue
Were all the islands of my sleep, I wake, I see—
I saw as I lay dying that unbroken sea.

[1943]

THE NOVEMBER GHOSTS

The rain slants from the clouded light
Where I pass wetted, pale with cold,
Along the old way aimlessly.
The bell's sounds quieted by the wind
I count with trembling spotted hands
And work my stiffening face.
So he I sing of passes, murmurs:
"And I must wander in the storm."

The Queen of Night's bright face
Or the old man bending with his sticks:
In warmer years, you watched them rise
Past wet stacks, the fields' half-silvered straw;
Mixed with the west wind and veiling airs,
You might have heard, hampered by the weeds' saw,

The rattle of Night oiling her worn gear—
Imagined her, soft in her sickle, crescent car.

Who loved you then? A cloud? A star.
Beckoning to you from the blind train
Of the old glittering queen,
She trailed her firefly-light line
Across the sky's night-backed pane—
Not knowing your eyes could discern
Only you, dew-bedecked, luckless, yearning,
Looking back at you from the crooked pane.

[1943]

THE LABORATORY

In the technician's thicket
The Arabian nightmares swarm;
　　I warmed up agar
　　And changed their water
And counted the creatures till my head swam.

Confirmed by the sawdust and chicken-wire,
The ingenious rodents waited
　　To die on the rations
　　And odd preparations
The instructors and children created.

I killed enough frogs to stock a bog
Or embarrass a famishing stork,
　　And after the first
　　I felt no remorse—
It was only a part of the work.

I started habitually realizing
Why the hangman feels no misgivings;

The sexton too
Sees nothing new
In the face the clods are falling to:

When the cross is exchanged for a cipher
And the scales are replaced by a rake,
    Says the Hog to the Dove:
    "Won't you be my love?—
And we can be married tonight by the Snake."

[1943]

SCHERZO

To sit on a chair, to eat from a table,
Is right, is polite, is comfortable—
    Or so they say;
I say so too, I suppose I know it,
If I didn't, still, I suppose I'd do it—
    It's a way.

The errors one's acquaintances call life,
The drab habitual disasters
Of paupers dropped from märchen into Europe—
The woodman frozen with both feet in air
As stiff as compasses beneath the bomber
The banker sent as succor to his winter:
I read about them sitting in my chair.

And am them; we are all corrupted.
Each year I talk more like the other fools,
Like less, lie more, am almost liked—
What does it matter? All that I love dies,
Even my wishes perish in the winter
That darkens for our time above the lands.
The snow falls on the unjust and unjust.

If I wish for a life, if I wish for my death,
In the cells where I am dying,
  Does it matter? Why care?
Does anyone care? Get up from your chair—
Is anything better? Who cares?
  It is over.

[1944]

AN INDIAN MARKET IN MEXICO

The bees are eating the candy,
The big dogs sleep like furs
In the aisles where the children handle
The babies or cats whose mothers
Are selling or stealing some food . . .
It is there: and, bad or good,
It works like a universe.

To say bad to their good, to bargain
For a people's life like a plate,
Is as easy as life for the strangers,
Cold, fair, and fat
As the cats asleep on their strings . . .
As they stare at a thin stray cat
The caged birds clap their wings.

[1945]

THE MILLER

On bank and brake the moonshine quakes,
  The fox steals past the stream
That curls to where the mill-rat wakes
  From the miller's dream.

The fish fly in the mill-pond's black
        The black of the mother-otter,
The mill-rat stares above the sack
        At the miller's water

Where the miller's girl bobs absently
        In her own night;
And the wheel turns, the wheel spins free
        Until the daylight.

[1945]

TO THE NEW WORLD

The leaves are struck and dance, the bird is blown
Along the summer's burned and homeward breast;
Berg and blind sea, the scrawled and lapping foam,
The coal and portraits of the galleries
Are lost in the hills of firs: the bird flaps west.

Through the wet green I hear the axes' iron,
I see the spindles coupling in the glade—
The tied face pitiless above the native flame.
The stone of ages scales from my ruined eyes;
The rifles ring like clocks from their stockade.

The new eyes are dry as coins; the corn is gold
To the gold eyes, and all its arms are iron;
These tendons thresh a continent like steam.
Trapped, sawn, or failing westward with a sigh,
The atoms tremble from their bankrupt dream.

On stones and sand a government reserves
For some few, halting and bewildered braves,
Their grannies spinning out an age on mush

And bony children with a threadbare ball,
The peoples find asylum for the life

(Dull haunter of the unattaching eyes)
That veined, from ice to ice, a hemisphere.
What bloods bought my redemption! what lives cleansed
The iron hands, the pure demanding eyes
I turned back to the evil of my birth!

Yet surely I bought an Eden with that blood,
The peoples died to feed a final Life,
The world's heart beating in its wilderness. . . .
Who dreamed that it might burst, the bird stoop home,
The leaves plunge eastward to outranging death?

[1945]

THE STREET HAS CHANGED

I

In the city that ruled me
The heads turn to another head.
I am forgotten like a year.
Was I good? was I happy?
Who is there to care?
I was a dream, a dream, the dream of the dead.

II

Had you sucked no more sense than I
From that undifferentiating misery
The new beast draws home
Old to his old blood: to blood brackish, not with tears
But with the salt of that first hopeful sea

That saw commence as one and new
The old and separate you and me?

III

What were you? It is too late to learn
And it does not matter. I thought you
Mine, that was not true, I thought you
All that I had, all that I could ever
Wish to have or have, and that was true.
And that does not matter either. What were you?
What does it matter? I love you
And who knows now, who would care if he knew?

[1945]

                                                    NEWS

Children, come to my knee.
I am old, I forget
More things than I can say.
What is the news today?
No news today, no news today.

There is always news—a town
Burning, a man shot down.
Men salt the lands with man;
The blood rusts a man's hand.
That is no news today.

No news, no news. . . .
But were I to say
I have seen mercy: the sun lapping
The bared head, the empty hand—
Why, who would believe you today?

[1945]

"THE GERMANS ARE LUNATICS"

Of course, of course! Who else would die
For profits from some thankless colony,
And rot beneath the curt outlandish stone
For markets long since settled as our own?

Would any sane man starve, or go to war
For treaties we were anxious to deplore?
A well man sell his liberties for bread—
And stock or bomb the cities of the dead?

What one of them, if he'd a grain of sense,
Would perish for his crazy tenements?
What fool would kill his neighbor for the thanks
Of governments of other people's banks?

[1945]

THE DEAD

If after the manner of men I have fought
with beasts at Ephesus, what advantageth it
me, if the dead rise not?

    The maze under the loess
Takes its tribute still. The pilgrims come and go
In Weimar, all the graves at Rome are green;
Here Abel lived a month, there Mendel kept his spade.
The world throws in its sack another skull.

    Knossos, Vienna
Are tumuli, the rust of the leaf-shaped sword.
The bulls that roared to its bare-breasted galaxy,
The starred faïence of the thalassocracy
Are the stamping waltzers of a Hapsburg wedding;

The Turks sweep up in their rout
The deaf ghost weeping for its graceless Karl.
The red brain unreels into its labyrinth
The thread of blood; and the beast's betrayer dreams
Over the horned, man's corpse—a Saviour.

And he too is history:
The charnel of the saved, the whitening
Sepulchre of the betrayed—of man's old agony:
All that is loved and does not love, that rises
Unmoved from the last contraction of his limbs.

Mazed in that great tomb
The soul grasps its last thread; beside the cypress tree
It chooses from the springs the spring of Memory,
Cries: "I am a child of Earth and Starry Heaven,
But my race is of Heaven alone." But its race is of Earth alone.

[1946]

A GHOST STORY

The fox lifts his head from the feathers
  And stares to the goose in the sky;
A song drifts from the bars of the tower
  To the sow asleep in her sty.

The crushed or folded flower
  Is grey in the grey of the moon;
The moonlight dreams of moonlight.
  The vacant whorls of the tune

Ripple like wheat to the shepherd
  From the light in the empty tower.
He nods, and the blurred moon sets.
  The voice laughs over and over,

The ticking shriek of the crickets
  Fades; and a long, light sigh
Trails over the lonely valley,
  The leaves stir absently.

[1947]

THE CLOCK IN THE TOWER
OF THE CHURCH

*(In the last years of the tenth century, over most of Europe,
work on public buildings was discontinued, since the Second
Coming of Christ was expected in the year 1000.)*

How patient man is in his time! The day
Is short to him, the hand moves past his hand
Into the hour, wheels whir, and the iron
Dwarfs run from darkness, reach into the sun
That blazes without patience on the stone
Where shepherds graze, or look up for the star
That sighed their change, once: this with patience.

The time is short, now: so the workers said
In the last years of the millennium.
In '80, '90, the last building stopped.
The weather-cock, poised like a rock
Upon this church, mocks the unvarying
Peter; crossed in death, set upside-down
In stone, the grey head yearns up to its grave.
The passionate impatience of the stone
Has calmed the carvers (who wait; wait and die)
And stars, or a bearded comet heralding
The Coming, flame in the concluding skies.

By '04 the men have come back to the stone.

But patience! patience! cry the messengers
Winged past time, impatient as the light
That fires the carvers of the messengers—
And the bird floats to the shadow of the hand
Set in the gesture of Creation.
Gnarled, weathered, whitening into stone,
The slow hands hammer at their stony Hand:
The seeds of light are flung to the abyss.
Rains fall, the winds come; and the years
Are centuries. The child asks, "What is that?"
The angel's wings are featherless as bats',
The Hand wears to a flipper of the stone—
How can the cock, a rod of rust,
Crow at the cracked lump that was Cephas, once?

The figures of salvation are worn down
Into these Roman numerals, the Hand
Revolves in the senseless circle of the world.
At sunset black dwarfs run into the sun,
Gesture, withdraw into damnation.

[1947]

OVERTURE: THE HOSTAGES

The teacher, the preacher, my mother, a mouse
Sit snarled in the circle the cat has stitched
In the barn; and they shift all day in their rope
Till one of them cries, his neighbor hums,
And one knits in her head; but the pigeons glide
From their nests in the eaves, to the shades that clock
The time of death. The boots of the grey
Guards tick on the stone. But the wood's wild eyes
Peer in from the green glades roped with light,
From the paths that ribbon the sighing wild;
And the shapes move, at the back of sight,

From the pit where they mined the stones of the graves,
From the rails where the hand-car rusts in the shaft,
From the field where the tame fox plays by the trap.
They have fired their volley over the fat
Cold limbs of their major, dead a day—
But no one comes; and the captives wait
For life, for death—so the pigeons say—
And hear, from the square where the guns are set,
These shots that herald the end of day.

[1947]

LAMENT OF THE CHILDREN OF ISRAEL
IN ROME

(Ferdinand Gregorovius)

Very bitter were the sorrows
Of our fathers, who in exile
Hung their harps upon the weeping
Willows of the flat Euphrates:
But beside the Tiber's flood,
Pressed behind these stifling gratings,
We hang up our wailing zither;
Judah's children, we—in Rome.

We last children of those slaves
The Romans led here, once, from Canaan,
In their triumph over Zion—
Those who sank waist-deep in shame;
We orphans of the Holy City
Build forever, stone on stone,
Our own pyramid of sorrow
Here above the Roman rubble.

For two thousand years we mourned
Beside this stream, whose yellow waves

Rush savagely, in wild confusion,
Past the ghetto's dreary walls;
With our fathers' wailing courage,
One in grief, we have endured:
We weep, as they have wept,
Eternally, to this same stream.

Nation after nation fell;
But we cling, like the undying
Green ivy to these ruins—cling
To Octavia's shattered halls,
The witnesses of our dishonor
When our motherland's despoiler,
When Jerusalem's destroyer
Stood to judge the seed of Judah.

Alas! for us, in narrow alleys,
In rooms the sunlight could not reach—
Not even fit to hold our anguish—
Pharaoh piled another Goshen;
And there came to gape upon us,
To mock our bitter agony
Sneering Brothers, haughty Fathers,
In their glances hate and death.

Like the Messenger who passes
Through the streets, to chalk the marks
Of death upon the houses: Here
And here they die; so fever wanders—
Plague on plague, in their full power,
Dread and toil at every hour,
And our shame—all bound together
With the gnawing ache of hunger.

In the street outside, the laughing
Crowds surge, packed from wall to wall,
And the gay floats roll among

The masked and glittering throngs;
In its gold-embroidered silk
Each house is dressed for holiday—
From balcony and window, Joy
Strews, as spring strews, flowers, flowers.

Then the roses—ah! of Sharon
We remember: how they withered,
How the blossoms fell in clusters
From the almond-wand of Aaron.
Zion's daughter, stripped of jewels,
Maid of Rome: into the ashes
You must bow your head, in silence—
In a silence full of tears.

We think of our abandoned daughters.
We remember how the lashes
Scourged our fathers to their judgment
Through the people's mocking laughter.
We think how the blood of Judah
Stained the threshold of St. Peter's.
We see, still, the livid frightful
Glare of the flames about the stake.

Now, in the sweat of our faces,
Day after day, we sit before
Our doorsteps; and all our toil
Lengthens with our bitter zeal—
And from every hole and corner
We hunt out our rags and patches,
For with loathing hands, the world
Throws us its refuse, only.

Alas, the rags make us remember
Solomon: all earthly glory
Breaks to pieces—and at last,
Like these rags here, falls to nothing.

Oh, the bracelets that adorned you,
Zion's daughters! All are gone,
All your glittering dress is tarnished,
All that was is rags and tatters.

So we sigh, and sew the tatters
In this rubbish of the Romans,
And we think: As this has shattered,
So Rome must also—and must perish.
But we still, in mockery,
Cling fast, like the undying
Green ivy to the ruins—
For, alas, it is a ruin!

No more, from the Arch of Titus,
Can the marble pictures grieve us:
Candlesticks, the Temple's tablets,
And the Jordan's holy waters;
Long ago, in filth and dust,
Thy gods, O Rome, have perished—
But Jehovah's holy emblems
Shine forth after a thousand years.

The grass springs above the rubble
Of the temple of the Father, Jove;
And down into the dust have fallen
The palaces of every Caesar:
But here, in spite of Time and Death,
To Thine everlasting glory
Thine old altars rise unbroken—
Lord of Times, of Life, Jehovah!

By the waters of the Tiber
We set up, with silent weeping,
Poorly, and with unhewn stones,
The sanctuary of Thy temple;
And we traced upon the walls

Thine emblems, Lord, that we might still
Remember, when they met our gaze,
Thy house's old magnificence.

And we sons of Abraham,
The faithful brotherhood, have met
Once more, before the Holy Ark,
In the Sabbath's quiet hour;
And we bear before the face
Of Elohim, the seven fold
Light of the seven fold lamp—
The unchanged, undying light.

Then we chorus, with the tongues
Of our fathers, to the harps,
In harmonies our sorrow sharpens,
David's Psalms, still unforgotten:
Till the tears begin to flow—
And once more, from our hearts,
The pain of a thousand years
Melts into hope for the Messiah.

[1948]

A PERFECTLY FREE ASSOCIATION

(*Mayday: the radio telephone distress signal used
by ships and aircraft*)

The torn-up newspaper
Out under the tree is blossoms
Or the first snow of May.
This year, those years
There was snow on the first of May.
The blossoms turned black and fell from the branches
The way a man falls from the door of a transport:

The black, writhing lump
Bursts suddenly, is gay
With the silk of the shrouding canopy—
Friends blossom by, a light tank, mortars,
And they fall through the light wind, roll
Head over heels through the grass of the meadow,
And scratch for themselves a sort of shallow
Pit or grave, and lie
Waiting there in the earth of their grave.
                                        The wave
The wind makes over the grasses
Runs for a thousand miles, then birches
Run by huts, by tractors, for a thousand miles:
Then there is a field or square of the files
Of the men who fell from the plane.
They march in leather
By tanks, beneath fighters:
Red Square.

On the first of May
There was a sort of fighting in my soul
That would not let me sleep: I got up early
And walked out into the meadow with its row
Of graves; there was not one Maypole
And the cups of the flowers brimmed with snow.
May Day! May Day!
In the gray night, almost day,
There is snow in flurries,
And the tower at the field on the edge of the marshes
Looks into the snow that hides the sea
And hears, from the homing fighter,
The fairly scared, the fairly gay
Voice saying, *Mayday! Mayday!*
Then there is a position, static,
And the voice ends on *May*—

[1949]

THE PRINCESS WAKES IN THE WOOD

It darkened; I was cold.
Where is it now, the night?
Between my head and the tree
Someone has spread gold.
Very soon I shall understand
All this: but now I see.
I am floating here in light.
. . . But all this comes to me through thee.

I close my eyes, and the tree
That trembled all night in my breast
Is—
    where is it now, the tree?
One branch, one dark belief
Is left in my loosed hand
To crumple in light to light.
The day weighs down the land.
. . . But all this comes to me through thee.

All our ways lead back to the world.
I who was—everything; I do not know—
Am now—I am—
    I do not know.
I woke here, here is a world
And a world; and between them a world . . .
Night that lowered to my breasts its stars,
Child—child of the worlds, of this first sun:
In thee all these—all these, and I, are one.

[1950]

Each year, just as the blossoms
Fall, and the buds curl from the boughs,
I hear from the sky a wondering voice:
The brass bird that drowses
All year on the turning house
Has felt in his veins, once more, a green
Start: a shudder of awe
Runs through him—the new life
That comes, in the spring, to everything but our lives.

From their setting of eggshells, the nestlings
Call fiercely up to a sky
That rains, like the hours, blessings
Into their straining bills: to live, to die.
All or none: it is all one.
"The real sun

Is the eye of the beholder,"
Says the beholder, turning the page
That will someday be turned by the wind;
"Each year I am a year older
And the people in the street are a year younger."
The world is always the same age.

[1951]

THE TOWER

He runs his eyes out idly, sliding
Above the city's grey diminished blocks,
The patch of earth he has the claim of seeing.
His world runs off and ends in hearsay:
The strangers waving from the isles of space,
A cry or word that floats up from the past;

And even his heart beats, *Child, I am not you.*
He hears what he has heard: the cries of strangers.

This tower where he works shows him as great
In a little world, his hand blots out a town;
Men are uneasy where his shadow falls.
And all the pigmies sweating in their fields
Are like him, truly—but on what a scale!
There where the runners measure out their inch
What breast grows huge enough to take his head?
Lord, I am lonely in this world you made me.

Man, is it possible for you to learn
You are not Gulliver? To learn it from the man
Who stares from the great fields to the tower's mite
And sees the unnoticing stars sail by
So far away that his sigh thinks
That they are less than his least wish—no use
Except to make him wish, to spite him? . . .
And, Gulliver, what does it matter what you wish?

But wish. . . . What is your life but a wish—a cry
Unheard, unanswered, indifferent? A man plunges
Story on story, past a thousand windows,
Blank eyes of empty offices; or if someone's there,
Why should he look? If someone sees,
Why should he care? And, care or not,
What can he do? The man is falling.
But care while you can: you too are falling.

[1951]

THE FORSAKEN GIRL

(after Eduard Mörike)

Ere the cock has crowed,
　The least star dwindled,
I kneel here at the hearth
　Till the fire has kindled.

The warm light is beautiful,
　The flames soar eagerly.
I stare unseeing
　Sunk in my misery.

All at once I remember:
　The whole night through,
Dear one, wicked one,
　I have dreamed of you.

As I remember,
　The tears come one by one.
So the day begins—
　If only it were done!

[1952]

THE AUTHOR TO THE READER

I've read that Luther said (it's come to me
So often that I've made it into meter):
*And even if the world should end tomorrow
I still would plant my little apple-tree.*
Here, reader, is my little apple-tree.

[1962, in *A Sad Heart at the Supermarket*]

THE CHIPMUNK'S DAY

In and out the bushes, up the ivy,
Into the hole
By the old oak stump, the chipmunk flashes.
Up the pole

To the feeder full of seeds he dashes,
Stuffs his cheeks,
The chickadee and titmouse scold him.
Down he streaks.

Red as the leaves the wind blows off the maple,
Red as a fox,
Striped like a skunk, the chipmunk whistles
Past the love seat, past the mailbox,

Down the path,
Home to his warm hole stuffed with sweet
Things to eat.
Neat and slight and shining, his front feet

Curled at his breast, he sits there while the sun
Stripes the red west
With its last light: the chipmunk
Dives to his rest.

[1964]

THE FIRE AT THE WAXWORKS

(Henrikas Radauskas)

In the basement of the waxworks the old guard puts on his
glasses. He reads the story of a golden bird that rises each night from
the treasure buried in a forgotten tomb. The book and the pipe fall

from his hands; the bird, having flown into his dream, swoops down and, ringing like a harp, flings itself over the basement in pieces of gold.

The fire's orange hands creep out from under the bed and gag him; he tries to get up, falls without having screamed; and swimming up slowly, they break through the ceiling with soft blows; instantaneous as a pianist's fingers, skim down the gallery.

The faces of the wax figures begin to glow as they do in surrealist paintings; and the famous poet who, alive, couldn't bear to have a woman near him, sees how with a melting breast, a king's mistress, breaking in two at the waist, leans toward him faster and faster.

He shrieks in a posthumous voice. Making a dreadful face, he falls into her arms and, swimming out of their burning clothes, the two lazily coalesce into a puddle of melted wax.

[1965]

IN A HOSPITAL GARDEN

(Henrikas Radauskas)

Through a hospital window
The chloroform from a broken bottle
Flows into the twilit garden,
And the feet of the poplar fall asleep
And its arms get lost in a dream.

The petals of the wild roses
Gasp for air like fish.
A bush shudders, starts to fall,
Tries to hang on with its branches
To a low cloud, collapses.

And the nightingale
Cannot any longer count to three:

The tune, in its third trill, goes to pieces,
Falls into the yellow pond
—And all at once the garden is lighted.

Beside my suspended casket
I burn like a wake candle,
And I run down into the bottomless
Box, and the weathervane
Thrashes about in its turret, creaking feverish
Prayers to scare away the chloroform
From the poplar, the rose, the nightingale;
And then, having forgotten my name,
It spins round and round, hysterical,
Squeaks at the top of its voice, and strangles.

[1965]

UNPUBLISHED POEMS

(1935-1965)

My aunt kept turnips in a flock—
Did you ever hear of such strange stock?
They'd the funniest wool you ever did see;
It looked like turnip greens to me.

Turnip greens, oh turnip greens!
There's nothing I love like turnip greens!

[1935–1936]

A SUMMER NIGHT

In the room, our old room, barred with moonlight,
I yawn till my jaws crack. In night
Your specter floats up from the back of sight,
I shut my eyes. The crickets shriek on: *See.*
I see you, now that you aren't here. Before
You were and I saw nothing. . . . I shut my eyes.

A year ago I owned you like a chair.
We lay in the coarse sand by the crowded sea
And my sleep-swollen face, secure and huge,
Still hid for you, as it had hid so long,
The faces, the unmasked unmasking flesh
Of that last dream the waking call a world.

Your big face, dirtied with the shore's gray sand,
That I loved and tried to love and could not love
Rises to me, falters. The overmastering
Tears roll over it. I shut my eyes.
So you wept, I cared; still . . .

                              The absurd eyes
That watch the stranger crying in their midst—

Not amused, not pitying, that merely watch—
The eyes of man: These change to your dog's eyes
That say: "We don't see. We don't *mind*. We hurt."
And then change, in death, to comprehension.
I shut my eyes . . . *See. See. See. See.*
The world shrills. And I see.

[1938?]

                                                    HE

I sit all day outside a bank,
A box of pencils by my padded stumps,
Or walk with glasses, cup, and cane
Through what the newsboys say is day.

On country roads, in blood and fur,
My trunk repeated like a stammered word
Says, Driver, think too well of me
And feel your made world break like ice.

I am the sense under the kissed face
You press to in the glass; alone and knitting
I wait in the room you will never leave.
You cover me like flesh, like ivy; and I wait

Like a word you do not know, in a novel
You are going to read: a word that you will know.

There is no need to run; you cannot escape
From what you cannot know. Yet run, yet look,

While you can run, while you can look—
Die while you can die. Tomorrow
You will be afraid no longer, you will awaken
And whisper in your new voice, "I am He."

[1939]

Dear Mr. Jarrell:
It seems that the twenty-fourth floor is complaining of lost students who are hunting you. Could you put your name and office hours on your door?
Thank you.

The English Office
[University of Texas, at Austin]

RANDALL JARRELL, OFFICE HOURS 10-11

Mr. Jarrell: Come back and you will find me just the same.
    Hunters, hunters—but why should I go on?
    Learn for yourself (if you are made to learn)
    That you must haunt an hourless, nameless door
    Before you find—not me, but anything.

Lost Students: It never seemed to me that I was lost.
    You were, perhaps; at least, no one was there.
    I missed you; why should I go back?
    I am no hunter, I say. I was sent
    And asked to find—not you, not anything.

English Office: Each of them is lost, and neither hunting;
                And they stand still around a crazy door
                That tells a truth, or lie, that no one learns.
                Here is a name, an hour for you to use:
                But name, or come, or come not, as you choose.

[1939?]

THE TREE

When I looked at the tree the bough was still shaking,
So surely there was a bird
That lit for an instant and left its motion
To the dead wood.

But the bough has ceased; what the tree remembers
Who is there to tell?
I have not changed, I have not forgotten . . .
I am waiting still.

[1939?]

THE DREAM

"What dreams you must have had last night,"
   My wife exclaims with a smile.
"Really, you threshed and muttered
   So loudly, for such a while

"I made up my mind to wake you.
   What was it you were dreaming?"
I yawn and stretch as I answer,
   "I can't remember a thing.

"What did I say?" "Why, nothing—
   I couldn't make out a word.

You whimpered the way a puppy will.
　It was awfully absurd."

I laugh and agree; and all the time
　The thought spins round in my head:
"If you'd guessed why I was crying
　Or what it was I said

"Would you too weep? or speak? or dream
　The dream that troubles me?
Does she know? What would she do?"
　And we smile uncertainly.

[1939-1940?]

THE NORTHERN SNOWS

I miss my volley; walking back to serve
I think, "Good God, that was a sorry—"
The *sorry* is enough: the red clay turns grey-green,
The wind and cold light from the unlucky Hill
Blow over me again, and I see Morey
Turn from the net with his loud laugh, and vanish;
And the rest vanishes. They flame up with a word
And with a look, a word, sink back to darkness.
It is a ghost, a world, a glance can lay.

What flickers its instant in the Texas sun
Was the last flutter of my happiness,
The crazy luck, the sufficient kingdom of the child.
I whirled down the hillside to the foxes' mill;
The skaters twisted by the Bishop's dam
(I waved to the farmer with the scarf you knitted);
And, bored, desperate, alone, I still was happy
At my mere being—at remembering
That my unhappiness was for a year, a term,

A day and night's ride on the whistling train.
My misery was something that I wouldn't count.
When I ate dinner with the ragman, when I landed
The plane the first time, when I wrecked the car—
When I dreamed that you had touched me, woke,
And found the grey mouse fretting at my arm—
The glow and urgency of desperation
Suffused it, something was always wrong, the sand
Whirled from the hourglass, the glass was cracking,

The time, the time broke in my freezing hands.
—Winter we played in the short gym under lights
With the dead balls, I stroked my volleys like a fool.
The wind came up the bare hill with a whoop.
The snow fell and fell and fell, your letters came,
And I read them, read them; and we skied
Through the graveyard to the golf-course, the chocolate
And cheese were lumpy in my shirt and throat.
It sticks there still: a lump, a lump.

And what could you know about it all? You lived
And worked and changed five hundred miles away;
If you had known, still, what could you have done?
The accidents are too much in the end.
"What did I *do?*" I can't help thinking,
And like a child I answer, "Nothing—"
The good and evil fall on us like snow.
I was warm for my while, and it was to my will.
But the winter comes; and we bear it
In one way or another, as we will.

[1939–1940]

I loved you, too. There was no use. I had no time,
No heart, nothing for you. All night in my ward
A child—no, nurse brought slides, the child kept screaming,
Screaming . . . You are nothing to me, forget me.
The boy is dying, dead now; here, too, Canton falls,
One by one the lights are going out.

When I'm not here I want to sleep,
I want to die. The child comes when I sleep
And says to me in his new bones: Here's blood.
And it's blood, it's blood . . . If this head had a tongue
For kisses or a hand for breasts or any
Except for death, it was an empty head.

I thought that I could never cry again; I'm crying now.
When I lost you I lost more than you,
I said my tongue was false and my head death,
I said—what does it matter what I said?
I said the truth: no love can last
That locks our lives up in a separate womb.

That cries to any blood: not mine, not mine.
Love says to it all night: O my own blood!
To be good for one instant in this universe
Means—how do I know what it means?
The boy dies and Canton falls; here while I sleep
The lights come on, the lights go out.

[1940?]

THE TREES IN SPRING

We looked at the hawthorn with the helpless joy
That Noah wept with, when the trembling dove,
Letting the leaf fall, gave its witless sigh.
After his thousand anxious looks, and all the tears

He poured to the wild water, past his matchless beard—
That tender sound, and sight, were more to him
Than all the lowing of his beasts, the noisier kin
That through that rainy voyage vexed his old ears.

The blessed hawthorns! Yet who blesses them?
Whom can we call to bless them? They are blessings.

[1940]

THE HAPPY CAT

The cat's asleep; I whisper *kitten*
Till he stirs a little and begins to purr—
He doesn't wake. Today out on the limb
(The limb he thinks he can't climb down from)
He mewed until I heard him in the house.
I climbed up to get him down: he mewed.
What he says and what he sees are limited.
My own response is even more constricted.
I think, "It's lucky; what you have is too."
What do you have except—well, me?
I joke about it but it's not a joke:
The house and I are all he remembers.
Next month how will he guess that it is winter
And not just entropy, the universe
Plunging at last into its cold decline?
I cannot think of him without a pang.
Poor rumpled thing, why don't you see
That you have no more, really, than a man?
Men aren't happy: why are you?

[1941]

Today is almost over,
Tomorrow what will you do?
I'll weep all day in a bucket
And send my tears to you.

Yesterday was tears.
Tomorrow what will you do?
I'll cut my throat with a razor
And send my blood to you.

Yesterday was blood.
Tomorrow what will you do?
What else can I do but die?
I leave my life to you.

Poor ghost, you left me guilt.
Tomorrow, what shall I do?
What you can do is done.
I come no more to you.

[1941?]

PROLOGUE TO WILEY ON
NOVEMBER 17, 1941

Welcome, deep WILEY! from the sylvan dells
Of Denton, Texas. Lo, the tower's bells
Have banged out eight o'clock—it is the cue!
Come, Muse, and with thy sacred rage imbue
Our former fellow DR. AUTREY WILEY.
Fellow, I say: for here MISS WILEY shyly
Read, wrote, snored, and scurried—got a Ph.D.—
And left for England (back in '33)
A Fellow of some wise Society.
For many a sleepy summer WILEY read
The verse of many an author long since dead

Who wrote rare epilogues to earn his bread—
Yea, prologues too. She read, and sneezed, and swore
Till suddenly—there were no more!
"I'm done! I'm done!" she cried, and whistled thrice;
And wrote a book—definitive, precise;
The great von Krinklekronkle cried: "It's nice."
Said von und zu Berwaden, "Verily,
This wretched woman's an authority."
The jealous Germans flew to London town,
And burned the firm of ALLEN and UNWIN down;
MISS WILEY'S pages, lost in the debris,
Are now a part of modern history . . .
Th' unmatched incendiaries quite forgot
That if her work is done, MISS WILEY'S not;
And here she sits, undubitably intact,
To tell you many a quaint and curious fact.
Let's clap, and stamp, and yell like cats and dogs
To greet great WILEY and her epilogues.

[1941]

The rabbit hurries to the brim of its wood
In three lolloping jumps, and I stop sorry
And personal and tired, in the firm new spring
Of the wood and the farmer and the regular beauties
I can't understand and badly love.

And my new shoes and my new shirt
(My spring, in their way) are a poor success
With me or anyone else; and I climb
For years and years to the farmer's house
Where nobody knows me; the farmer's son

And a sow and a horse and the farmer's wife
All stand in the yard and stare at me.
Look as long as you like. I'm going by,
You won't see me again. And you can forget
That you ever saw me; if you ever saw me.

But the boy doesn't know about that and waves,
And the pig grunts at me. My wife said to me,
"I'm real and you're real": meaning, only a story
Has joy as simple, and the plaster heads
All good with their love in each steady feature.

Here no one meets; and love is the drug
That races for its instant through the brightening limbs
Of the flashing stranger who falls unnamed
And unknown from the desperate arms—the heart
That is real and beating in the pan of blood.

[1942?]

TO BE DEAD

"Woman," men say of him, and women, "Man."
The corpse says nothing, he is stripped away,
Lies like a disused word, the letters of an aunt
Dead too; *dead, dead,* say—all lips say
At once; once; and then are sealed, we lie no more
Among the notions of a man's unliking tongue,
Are what's not thought of, or not much, the bulb
The boy smashes when it gives no longer light.

[1942]

THE FAREWELL SYMPHONY

A few miles ago, a year, a year,
  They were all playing.
It is all there in my head. . . .
  But something is beating

Louder than the few left, the notes
  Slow in the plunging night;
The men tiptoe into the darkness,
  The notes puff out, and the light

Is hushed till my stiff throat locks
  And one note, one light—it is one—
Lasts: then song, light, listener
  Tremble, are gone.

[1947?]

THE TIMES WORSEN

If sixteen shadows flapping on the line
All sleek with bluing—a Last Morning's wash—
Whistle, "Now that was thoughty, Mrs. Bean,"
I tell myself, I try: *A dream, a dream.*
But my plaid spectacles are matt as gouache;
When, Sundays, I have finished all the funnies,
I have not finished all the funnies. Men
Walk in all day (to try me) without knocking—
My jurors: these just, vulgar, friendly shades.
The cutting-garden of my grandmama,
My great-great-great-grandfather's padded calves
(Greeted, at cock-crow, with the soft small smile
Of Lilith, his first morganatic wife)
Are only a tale from E. T. W. Hoffmann.
When Art goes, what remains is Life.

The World of the Future does not work by halves:
Life is that "Wine like Mother used to make—
So rich you can almost cut it with a knife."

[1947?]

The lot is vacant still
Except for a five-story brick apartment.
The red clay, red creek are under concrete.
On a clothespin of the clothesline of 4–C
A butterfly settles naturally
A yard from my hand. Too far for leaning—
And why should I lean?
                        Years ago, yards below,
Barefoot, wide-eyed, I stretched on tiptoe
To reach through the limbs of the weeds to the leaf
Where once the butterfly, gold-dusted, peacock-eyed,
Hovered—too far for stretching,
And yet I stretched. I stretched for everything.

In those days crickets looked me in the eyes,
My goat's stare grazed my hair.
The world was a different size,
A different age: there were giants, those days.
Snow lay on the ledges of their foreheads,
They boomed above me in a different tongue.
The beasts and I played at their feet,
Sharing or bearing the weather of their faces.

[1947?]

THERE WAS GLASS AND THERE ARE STARS

Whether one walks around the hill, or over,
One comes at last to the town.
In the town there are many days, and a day
When the days themselves are over.
One stands in the station, and the train
Is late. Still, there is a train.

I have put your bags in the compartment.
The faces, there in the darkness,
Wake emptily, or are full of sleep.
Here in the light of loss
Our hands are wired in pain
And their dragged touch runs off into space.
Say what you have said, and I will say
What I have said.
     Nothing is over.
If, when the days are over;
If, when your eyes are drawn
At last, past seas and cities, from my eyes;
If, as I turn from the darkness
Of the rails to the empty light
Of the station, and feel on my lips
After the echo of a failing pressure, space;
If, as we whisper
Again, apart, what we have whispered
Together—and we and the words and the world
Are emptied into a dream—
Remember that all these, that even these
Are a dream from which we wake;
These last but not forever;
Remember that after pain, that after loss
There is only love.

[1948]

"Do such, wait so," you said; I waited. Did you wait?
"Be good, don't cry." I waited. Did you cry?
"Till then, goodbye." And then. And after then? "Goodbye."
To die; to live; to die. And then to die.

"Away is not; was is not; now is—is now."
You said—"Said's not say." Not now? "Not now."
I die then. "Die then." —And love is so?
"So . . . *Was* ends *is not, then's yes now's no.*"

[194–]

CITY, CITY!

Turn out the light, turn over, shut your eyes.
There is still no darkness: the light comes in from the signs.

Wrap your arms and your pillow round your head.
There is still no silence: the sounds come in from the street.

So for smell, so for taste, so for touch—and sleep
Is soiled all over with you . . . Still, dream: long ago the leaf

Swung to the dragonfly, the wings of the great sky
Touched you, like fur, in their gold dust: so that you were

And were not? So that you are
And are not? When, now, in yearning,

In loathing, you stretch your arms out past this
City, city!—to the world where there is nothing

There is always something; and past that something
Something else: and all these somethings add to nothing.

[1950]

THE ROMANCE OF SCIENCE

The man remembers from the tales the rocket
Of the old scientist and his friend, a boy:
They named it and it rode them to the moon.
There they named craters, ranges, and an ore,
And were diverted by their cook, a stowaway.
What had they nicknamed him? The man forgets.
But remembers the slow-voiced, sober-sided man,
The useless boy, and their fun-loving cook. . . .
And nothing happened to the Head, the Heart,
And their poor humble Body, on the moon.

The man shifts in his crater, thinks: "And then?"
The man smiles wryly, and the story ends:
The harmless officious lunatics blaze home
From Space; their ship shines like a dream
Among the simpler rockets of the sane.
Sell! cry the nations; and they name their price.

[1950?]

THE BIRTH OF VENUS

The thunderbolt strikes the ocean.
A furious wave
Tosses her from the depths to the shore.
She stands there knee-deep in water,
Netted in dripping seaweed, plastered with slime.
Returning to their wet home,
Tiny crabs run down her body,
Star-fish and sea-urchins fall from her head and shoulders.
Raising her arms, she rubs her sandy eyes—
Eyes that see, still, the forests of coral,
Sea-anemones, electric fish,
Creatures of supple forms, of tender hues:

The killers of the abyss
Disguised as flowers of paradise.

The thunderbolt strikes the fishing-village
Huddled between red cliffs,
Its few huts tumble into the sea:
She has nothing to fear now—the heavens have annihilated
The witnesses of her shameful birth.
A cloud rains down, its hard streams
Wash the slime from her body.
In the light of the setting sun
Her body is incandescent with rainbows
Of mother-of-pearl. Having rained itself out,
The cloud throws over her a transparent veil.
Breathing cautiously
The unaccustomedly pungent air of the land,
Smiling to herself, she walks from the beach
To the nearest tavern where, with some passing
Merchant, even tonight, she will begin her merry, dirty,
Brimming-with-incalculable-triumphs
Life on earth.

[1952]

DREAMS

It is already late, my sister.
Out from the door the sea is snoring,
He dreams all night of thee.
The moon looks over the hill like a leopard
And rubs his silver fur at thy feet.
The dachshund whines in his sleep.

It is already late, my sister.
Out from the cliffs the seals are sleeping,
They dream all night of thee.

The white stove burns with a hissing purr,
The darkness puts to its lips its finger.
The children spell in their sleep.

It is already late, my sister.
Up over the roof the stars are turning,
The world dreams of thee.
Close thy lids, sewn together with lashes
Of starlight, tight around me—
I sleep all night in thy sleep.

[1952]

THE SCHOOL OF SUMMER

Out somewhere in the middle of the crickets
By voices, anybody's voice; out in the air
Set to my face like anybody's flesh,
Something is running down the night like sweat
—Out there, somewhere, a piano plays
Like what-spoils-everything, that a vein stands for by beating.

The life around me goes on like uneasiness
Unable to bear itself, that locks into the ease
Of being, uneasiness, and life no longer
But only specialties. What is your specialty?
If you will look, at evening, at the license-plate
Hung at each neck, beneath the headlights, like a locket,
You will see a letter prefixed to the sum.
The letter indicates the specialty.
If you will come back from the living to the dead,
To these dead here, and still not die, but speak—but speak—
You will be spectrographed, denied, explained,
Have held out to your lips a marrowy finger
To suck on all your death—but finish floating
In a jar in the Department of Miraculism's

New cork-floored, air-raid-sheltered laboratories.
"An Embryo," the card beneath will say.
For the living *are* the dead: an early stage,
Childish, but still promising a death. The dead
Who understand all, understand all things
About the living but this last absurdity,
That they should wish to live.

                      Life is—why, life:
It is what all our evils have in common.
To trade a thousand ills for one, to feel
No ill but death, and to feel it no ill—
Is this not happiness? Or if not happiness,
Still, satisfaction? Or if not satisfaction, death?

[1952]

PERFECT LOVE CASTETH OUT
EVERYTHING

We lie like the gods,
Forgetting everything,
Ending in our own being.
Men's joys are justified; joys great enough
Are beyond justification.

[1954]

FAIRY SONG

Collected at Levanto (La Spezia), Italia

Warmed over pine-cones
The water washed me;
My mother fed me
A fried squash-flower;

The black priest blessed me
Upon his Vespa.

As I passed by the barber's
They were cutting the hair
Of a boy who, waving,
Sat on a horse-headed chair.

Ah, come away, come away
To the Bar, my beloved—
There, clothed in the jeans
Of a ranch of the West,
We'll dance to the clear strains
Of The Little Complex.

[1959]

FADED

(*Rainer Maria Rilke*)

She carries her handkerchief, her gloves,
As lightly as if she had died.
The odor of her dressing-table
Smothers the scent she loves—

The scent she knew herself by, once.
But nowadays she never asks
Who she is (: a distant relation)
And goes worriedly about her tasks,

Fretting over the poor anxious room
She must care for and set in order
—Because the very same young girl
May be, after all, still living there.

[1952]

Randall Jarrell / The Complete Poems

A LADY ON A BALCONY

(Rainer Maria Rilke)

Clothed with the wind, light in the light,
Suddenly she appears, as though snatched up
And put down here; and the room is as though
It had been cut out to fill the door

Behind her—darkly, the way a cameo
Lets through its rim a shimmering light.
And one thinks: there was no evening
Before she came, and above the railing

Held her hands away from herself a little
To be for a while altogether apart—
Just as, over the housetops, the heaven
Reaches up, to move away from the earth.

[1952]

A VARIATION ON "TO SAY
TO GO TO SLEEP"

(adapted from Rainer Maria Rilke)

If I could I would sing you to sleep.
I would give you my hand to keep
In yours till you fell asleep,
And take it away then, slowly.
I would sit by you and be.

In the world the dark would be deep.
I would watch. And at last I would sleep.

But if rain should star the stream
Of your sleep, I would whisper: "See,

You are asleep"; and, slowly,
Your breath would change in your dream
Till, ages and ages deep
In the dark, you would say to me:
"I love you."
                    I love you,
But I am here always. Sleep now. Sleep.

[1952]

THE UNICORN

(adapted from Rainer Maria Rilke)

This is the animal that never existed.
None of them ever knew one; but just the same
They loved the way it moved, the way it stood
Looking at them, in pure tranquillity.

Of course there wasn't any. But because they loved it
One became an animal. They always left a space.
And in the space they had hollowed for it, lightly
It would lift its head, and hardly need

To exist. They nourished it, not with grain
But only, always, with the possibility
It might be. And this gave so much strength to it

That out of its forehead grew a horn. One horn.
Up to a virgin, silverily, it came
And there within her, there within her glass, it was.

[1960]

THE WIDOW'S SONG

(*Rainer Maria Rilke*)

In the beginning life was good to me.
It humored me, it encouraged me.
It does that to all the young—
But how could I know that then?
I didn't know what life was.
All at once it was just year after year,
Not good any more, not new any more, not wonderful any more,
Torn right in two.

That wasn't his fault, it wasn't mine.
We both had nothing but patience,
But death had none.
I saw him coming—oh, so cheap, so vile—
And I watched him while he took and took:
It wasn't any of it mine at all.

Then what was mine—my own, mine?
Wasn't even my misery
Only lent me by fate?
Fate wants back not just the joy,
It wants back the torture and the screaming,
And it buys the wreck second-hand.

Fate was there and got for a song
Every expression of my face,
Even the way I walked.
Every day there was a sellout,
And when I was sold out, it quit
And left me standing there open.

[1960]

THE READER

(*Rainer Maria Rilke*)

I had read a long time. All afternoon
The rain had lain rustling at the window.
I no longer heard the wind outside:
My book was hard.
Through the leaves I saw it like a look
Darkened with meditation; and the time
Dammed itself around my reading.
All at once something shone above the pages,
And instead of the words' uneasy mazes
There was: evening, evening . . . on them everywhere.
I still do not look out, but the long lines
Break, and the words come loose from their strings
And roll away wherever they please.
And then I realize: above the packed
And glittering gardens is the far-off sky.
The sun has come out again . . . And now it is night
As far as one can see: the summer night.
What was separate gathers in little groups
And men go, darkened, their long ways,
And strangely far away, as if it meant more,
One hears the little that still happens.

And now when I lift my eyes from the book
Everything will be great, and nothing strange.
Out there is what I live in here,
And here and there it is all endless
Except that I weave myself into it
More even, out there where my look is shaped
To things, and the grave simplicity of masses—
Out there the earth goes out beyond itself.
It seems to be surrounding the whole sky:
The first star is like the last of the houses.

[1964]

THE EVENING STAR

(Rainer Maria Rilke)

One star in the dark pass of the houses,
Shines as if it were a sign
Set there to point the way to—
But more beautiful, somehow, than what it points to,
So that no one has ever gone on beyond
Except those who could not see it, and went on
To what it pointed to, and could not see that either.
The star far off separates yet how could I see it
If there were not inside me the same star?
We wish on the star because the star itself is a wish,
An unwilling halting place, so far and no farther.
Everything is its own sigh at being what it is
And no more, an unanswered yearning
Toward what will be, or was once perhaps,
Or might be, might have been, or . . .

And so soon after the sun goes, and night comes,
The star has set.

[1964]

THE LOVE FOR ONE ORANGE

Prokofiev's sick prince can't laugh.
The big baby sits there and cries
Oh-h! Oh-h! The crying satisfies
The big babies in the audience, who laugh.

But a few of them look perplexed.
The *Oh-h! Oh-h!* reminds them of—
Of the fool in *Boris Godunov*
Crying *Gore, gore, Rusi*—weep, weep, Russians—

To the same tune. They have laughed at one,
Cried at the other; but the one's the other.
The prince and the fool cry *Mother! Mother!*
And the big babies in the audience all cry.

[1964]

(*A SEDUCTIVE PIECE OF BUSINESS*)

When at the end of *Don Pasquale*
The bride's brother surreptitiously
Fingers the bridecake, and then licks his finger,
All the brothers and the bridecakes
In the darkened playhouse laugh with joy,
As though a stolen bridecake *were* the sweetest.

[1964]

THE SIGN

Having eaten their mackerel, drunk their milk,
They lie like two skeins of embroidery silk
Asleep in the glider. The child repeats, "It's *such* a pity!"
And paints on a piece of beaverboard, FREE KITTY.

[1964]

THE WILD BIRDS

In the clear atmosphere
Of our wishes, of our interests, the advertisers
Of the commodities of their and our
Existence express their clear interests, their clear
Wishes, clearly, year after year.
What they say, as they say,

Is in our interest, in theirs.
Explaining the inscrutable, denying the unbearable,
Bespeaking for us, in life, in death, a clear
Salvation,
In their saying all is transparent
Except our interests, except theirs;
And these are there, there clearly, darkly there, are there
Regardless.
                Regardless of what?
Regardless of life, regardless of death,
Regardless.

But these others—who we are not sure—
Who say to us—but what we are not clear—
From the atmosphere, dream-cleared, dream-darkened,
In which they live their dark lives, die their light
Deaths, in darkness or in light, obscurely
As, mirrored in them, we who dream them are obscure:
Those who call death death, life life,
The unendurable what we endure:
Those who beat all night at our bars, and drop at morning
Into our tame, stained beaks, the poison berry—
O dark companions,
You bring us the truth of love: the caged bird loves its bars.

[1950?–1964]

MAN IN MAJESTY

He looks. Looks. Looks in rapture,
Pure rapture, in pure—
                Looks at what? What matter?
His spirit has gone out into his sight
And the rest, when the light has set, is darkness:
Darkness older than the light, starred with the darknesses
Of wish-stars, stars unseen

Since the first heaven opened over all. Ah, wishing-well
Where the roots of all things go down into water!

He looks into the swan's-down of a statue,
And the swan's-S'd, unseeing alabaster,
Lit with his look's light, flames to him in pure
Seduction. See, how his dark eye lights up with his statue,
Whose small mouth, sweet mouth, sweet forever,
Is shut forever. *I close about myself in bliss,*
But what is bliss? To be is to be beautiful,
The statue says, shut-mouthed, stone-nippled, silent.
What do I wish? To wake, is sounded
In the last notes under hearing, by the beating
Of the alabaster's heart—still heart, black heart.
Touch me and I will wake,
Say the stone lips to the stone ears of the sculptor.

He looks at them in ecstasy—bemused, bemused—
And parts his lips to suck in the supernal
Aether: the maker, man, in majesty,
Touches the stone with his hand, to make it stone.

—The stone of another statue.
See how the second statue's growing small,
Rounding, the mouth is, now, a swell
And the milky, nippled breast a ball.
The animal in whom, an egg, he lay ensphered,
Becomes an egg, the egg becomes a sphere:
The statue of a statue of a statue.
Long ago the stone wished, and was flesh.
The flesh wishes itself back, wishes the wish
Unwished.

To look is to make; what I have made I see.
What I have made I love; or love, almost, would love
Except that—

He says each day, to each new statue, *Stay,*
And his hand goes out to it: to make a statue.

[1958-1964]

WOMEN ON A BUS

These sacks of flesh piled in a pile,
Dressed in a dress—this fat grandmother
Makes me think: "*You* were a girl?"
The thin older woman, her mother,
Folds in her lap the legs of a chicken
And looks out with the face of an old man.
You were a woman?
          Old women and old men,
Approaching each other in life's pilgrimage,
In their neutral corner, their third sex,
Huddle like misers over their bag of life
And look with peasant cunning, peasant suspicion,
At every passer-by, who may be Death.

May I die, not on the day
When it no longer matters that I'm a woman,
But on the day that it no longer matters
That I am human: on that day
When they put into me more than they get out of me.
So I say, in human vanity: have they ever
Got out of me more than they put into me?
May I die on the day the world ends.

[1964]

What was longed for and, once, certain
Now is only an uncertain longing for
—For itself; an encore.

Play me again to show that I was played,
Really played once.
                    Was I really?
And must it come to this?
What else is there for it to come to?
She goes dyed to her death; and her old skin, crone's skin
Is crowned with a child's hair. So the maple
That on the spring's first day was red,
Pure red, is red as purely
The day it comes down through the air to die.
So music, that before it was at all was silence,
After it has been is silence.
All pieces share their end,
Their end is silence.

[1964]

A PRAYER AT MORNING

Cold, slow, silent, but returning, after so many hours.
The sight of something outside me, the day is breaking.
May salt, this one day, be sharp upon my tongue;
May I sleep, this one night, without waking.

[1952–1963]

BAMBERG

You'd be surprised how much, at
The Last Judgment,
The powers of concentration
Of the blest and damned
Are improved, so that
Both smile exactly alike
At remembering so well
All they meant to remember
To tell God.

[1965]

Let's love each other for what we are
And for what we happen to become,
Not for what we can make of ourselves.

No one makes anything of anyone but God.

[1965]

The old orchard in the middle of the forest
Through which, six years ago, I walked in misery,
My beggars'-lice-streaked trousers wet with the dew of dawn,
Is a road now, and some houses, and two apple trees,
And I am no longer miserable.

[1965]

WHAT'S THE RIDDLE . . .

"What's the riddle that they ask you
When you're young and you say, 'I don't know,'
But that later on you will know—
The riddle that they ask you
When you're old and you say, 'I don't know,'
And that's the answer?"

"I don't know."

[1965]

Index of Titles

Index of First Lines

INDEX OF FIRST LINES

INDEX OF FIRST LINES

Turn out the light, turn over, shut your eyes, 475
Twice you have been around the world, 316
Two little girls, one fair, one dark, 301

Under the orchid, blooming as it bloomed, 182
Under the separated leaves of shade, 351
Up in the sky the star is waiting, 379

Very bitter were the sorrows, 447

Warmed over pine-cones, 479
We are all children to the past, 78
We lie like the gods, 479
We looked at the hawthorn with the helpless joy, 467
We went there on the train. *They had big barges that they towed,* 193
Welcome, deep WILEY! from the sylvan dells, 469
"Well, I have had a happy life," said Hazlitt, 116
What a girl called "the dailiness of life," 300
What does the storm say? What the trees wish, 369
"What dreams you must have had last night," 464
What was longed for and, once, certain, 489
"What's the riddle that they ask you, 491
When Achilles fought and fell, 425
When at the end of *Don Pasquale*, 486
When I looked at the tree the bough was still shaking, 464
When I was a girl in Los Angeles we'd go gleaning, 343
When I was four my father went to Scotland, 195
When I was home last Christmas, 28
When I was twelve we'd visit my aunt's friend, 288
When I woke up this morning, 361
When the planes come in all night, and the lights reach, wavering, 398
When the runner's whistle lights the last miles of darkness, 397
When the swans turned my sister into a swan, 54
When the train whistles, it wants to say, 386
When they killed my mother it made me nervous, 189
When you and I were all, 375
When you first introduced me to your nurse, 294